MONEY IN STAMPS

MONEY IN STAMPS

JAMES A. MACKAY

JOHNSON
—
LONDON

First Published 1967

H. L. Lindquist Publications, Inc.
Exclusive Representatives in the United States

SBN 85307 000 8

SET IN 11/12 POINT BASKERVILLE AND PRINTED AND MADE IN GREAT
BRITAIN BY MORRISON AND GIBB LTD., LONDON AND EDINBURGH,
FOR JOHNSON PUBLICATIONS LTD., 11/14 STANHOPE MEWS WEST,
LONDON, S.W.7

CONTENTS

LIST OF ILLUSTRATIONS

PLATE I [*facing p.* 16

TWELVE 'PENNY BLACKS', GRADED ACCORDING TO THEIR CONDITION, IRRESPECTIVE OF THEIR PLATE NUMBER.

(1) a fine unused copy with good margins and fresh appearance; (2–3) good margins, lightly postmarked. (4, 6) margins close on one side, moderate postmarking. (5) good margins, but vertically creased. (7–8) margin cut close on one or more sides. (9) margins cut into and slight tear at top. (10) cut into, but moderately postmarked. (11–12) poor specimens, heavily postmarked and cut into. Nos. 1, 2, 3, 4 and 6 are the only ones which should be admissible in a good collection; the rest could only be regarded as 'space fillers'.

PLATE II [*facing p.* 32

RARE, BUT NOT VERY VALUABLE: STAMPS ISSUED BY THE ROYAL NAVY AT LONG ISLAND (MAKRONISI, GULF OF SMYRNA), MAY 1916.

Numbers printed, with *Gibbons* valuation in parentheses: (1)–25 (£40), (2)–25 (£38), (3)–20 (£45), (4)–60 (£7), (5)–72 (£8), (6)–144 (£7), (7)–72 (£8). These stamps are only listed by *Gibbons Part I Catalogue*.

PLATE III [*facing p.* 48

BRITISH COMMONWEALTH RARITIES.

(1) Kenya £75, 1925 (£8,500), (2) Johore $500, 1926 (£2,750, $6,000), (3) Kenya £100, 1925 (£10,000), (4) Straits Settlements $500, 1915 (£2,500, $4,500), (5) Sierra Leone £5, 1921 (£300, $425), (6) Ceylon 1,000RS., 1925 (£3,500, $3,000), (8) Malta 10s., 1919 (£200, $375), (7, 9–11) examples from the long commemorative sets of 1923–34.

PLATE IV [*facing p.* 64

ELIZABETHAN RARITIES.

(1–3) three of the four stamps released by St. Helena in 1961 for the Tristan Relief fund; only 434 sets exist (£800), (4) Papua 1s. 7d., 1958 (£6, $7), (5) Norfolk Island 2s. 8d., 1960 (£7 10s., $1.75). Stamps tipped in 1967: (6) Gibraltar, Our Lady of Europa, (7) Rhodesia, Churchill 5s., (8) Malta, Catholic Doctors' Congress.

PLATE V [*facing p.* 80

UNITED STATES RARITIES.

(1) $1, 1903 (£25, $80), (2) $2, 1918 (£28, $90), (3) $5, 1923 (£8, $25), (4) $1, 1915 (£22, $125), (5) 24c., 1923 (£7, $22.50), (6) Norse-American 5c., 1925 (65s., $9), (7) Pilgrim Fathers 5c., 1920 (60s., $11.50), (8) Graf Zeppelin $2.60, 1930 (£80, $285), (9) Huguenot 5c., 1924 (65s., $9.75), (10) Parcel Post $1 (£15, $52.50), (11) Century of Progress 50c., 1933 (£8, $25).

PLATE VI [*facing p.* 86

FOREIGN RARITIES.

(1) Iceland, Balbo flight, 1933 (£110, $375), (2) Mexico, 20p. airmail, 1934 (£100, $375), (3) Sweden, 8ö., 1918 (£90, $300), (4) San Marino 2l., 1903 (£165, $900), (5) Turkey, 500k., 1923 (£50, $135), (6) Russia Sports,

1935 (£10, $40), (7) Spain, Montserrat 4p., 1931 (£50, $150), (8) Thailand, Red Cross 20b., 1918 (£30, $90).

PLATE VII   [*facing p.* 112
FOREIGN RARITIES.

(1) Austria, Dollfuss, 1936 (£150, $500), (2) Japan 10s., 1916 (£35, $125), (3) Saar, Charity 10fr., 1928 (£85, $350), (4) Belgium, Red Cross 10fr., 1918 (£55, $200), (5) France, 50fr. airmail, 1936 (£48, $175), (6) Egypt, Port Fuad 50p., 1926 (£150, $275), (7) France, Orphans 5fr., 1917 (£100, $375), (8) Italy, Philatelic Congress 40c., 1922 (£50, $250), (9) Germany, Chicago flight 1m., 1933 (£60, $225), (10) Bulgaria, Balkan Games 50l., 1933 (£30, $125).

PLATE VIII   [*facing p.* 128
POST-WAR RARITIES.

(1) Luxembourg, Europa 2fr., 1956 (£12, $50), (2) Netherlands, airmail 25g., 1951 (£12, $60), (3) United Nations, Human Rights 3c., 1954 (£5, $18.50), (4) Saar, Stamp Day, 1950 (£9, $37.50), (5) Vatican, airmail 500l., 1948 (£135, $550), (6) West Germany 90pf., 1952 (£20, $90), (7) West Berlin, Goethe 20pf., 1949 (£14, $75), (8) West Berlin 1m., 1949 (£20, $100), (9) San Marino, airmail 1,000l., 1951 (£90, $400), (10) Switzerland, Peace 5fr., 1945 (£25, $70).

PLATE IX   [*facing p.* 144
POST-WAR RARITIES.

(1) South Korea, Olympic Games 5w., 1948 (£11, $37.50), (2) Spain, Canary Islands Visit 25p., 1950 (£33, $135), (3) Liberia, UNICEF, 1954 (£18, $45), (4) Israel, 1,000m., 1948 (£32, $175), (5) Ireland, Europa 1s. 3d., 1960 (27s. 6d., $7). This is an example of a stamp which dropped in catalogue price by 50% in the past year!

PLATE X   [*facing p.* 160
'UNDESIRABLE' STAMPS OF YESTERYEAR.

(1–2) New South Wales, Diamond Jubilee charity stamps, 1897, (3) San Marino, Regency, 1894, (4) Greece, Olympic Games, 1896, (5–7) Diamond Jubilee Commemoratives from Mauritius, Leeward Islands and Canada, 1897, (8–9) United States commemoratives for the Columbian Exposition (1893) and the Trans-Mississippi Exposition (1898).

PLATE XI   [*facing p.* 176
OMNIBUS ISSUES.

(1) French colonies, Colonial Exhibition (1931), (2) British colonies, Silver Jubilee (1935), (3) French colonies, Revolution sesquicentennial (1939), (4–7) British colonies, Victory (1946), Freedom from Hunger (1963), International Telecommunications Union (1965) and Red Cross (1963).

PLATE XII   [*facing p.* 192
LONG SETS AND 'HARDY ANNUALS'.

(1–2) Netherlands, Child Welfare and Summer stamps, (3) Austria, Costumes, (4) France, Art, (5) Spain Provincial Arms, (6, 8) Switzerland, 'Pro Juventute' and 'Pro Patria' stamps, (7) New Zealand, Health, (9, 11) West Germany, Youth and Welfare stamps, (10) France, Arms.

Prices given are according to the *Gibbons* and *Scott* catalogues (1967 Editions).

PREFACE

TODAY, philately or stamp collecting is a science and a serious pursuit of millions. More leisure time and better wages and salaries have put the hobby within the reach of countless people who, a generation ago, would have had neither time nor money to take up stamp collecting on a large scale. At the same time, stamps tend to be better in design and more frequent in issue than they were even a decade ago. Consequently stamp collecting is at present undergoing a boom as more and more people are turning to it.

Philately occupies an exceptional position in the world of hobbies in that, if undertaken shrewdly, it offers a financial return on the original outlay as well as giving endless enjoyment and recreation. Most collectors, who take the hobby seriously, have to buy much of their material, and although true philatelists often affect to scorn interest in the financial aspects of philately, secretly everyone derives not a little pride of possession from his collection by assessing its monetary value.

This book is designed to help the budding collector to spend his money wisely in the formation of his collection, to give the tips and point out the pitfalls. But while the object of this book is primarily to demonstrate that stamps can be a good investment, it is fervently hoped that, from collecting and studying stamps, a real love of the hobby for its own sake will develop.

I am indebted to my friends in the philatelic trade for their advice in compiling this book, but especially I wish to thank Mirko Bojanowicz, Cyril Harmer and Robson Lowe. I am also grateful to Harry Lindquist for keeping me right on many points with special reference to philately in the United States.

Finally, I would like to record my gratitude to Mrs. Gillian Gillot who had the unenviable task of sorting out the manuscript and producing the typed version.

JAMES A. MACKAY.

AMERSHAM, BUCKS.
May 1967.

To

MY WIFE

CHAPTER I

THE WORLD CUP 'WINNERS' STAMP

I BEGAN writing this book on 18th August 1966—a day which will long be remembered in philatelic circles in the United Kingdom. This was the day that a 4d. stamp went on sale to commemorate England's victory in the World Cup Football Championship. The decision to issue this stamp was taken at very short notice and the printers, Harrison & Sons of High Wycombe, had to fit it in with their existing commitments. To avoid holding up the production of other special issues in the United Kingdom programme (Technology Stamps on 19th September, Battle of Hastings Commemoratives on 14th October and Christmas Stamps on 1st December) it was found necessary to restrict the print to 100,000 sheets (12 million stamps). These were distributed only to post offices in England and by the date of issue every post office in that country had a supply, if only, in many cases, a nominal one.

The postal authorities optimistically estimated that 12 million stamps would last for several days and, by way of explanation after the event, a G.P.O. spokesman said, 'In fact, the print of 12 million was considerably more than the print of many of the special issue stamps in recent years.' If this was so, what happened to cause the un-British stampede to get the new stamp? In the first place, while it is true to say that more World Cup 'Winners' Stamps were issued than many other recent commemoratives, this applies only to stamps of other (and less used) denominations. The average print for a 4d. stamp, pre-paying the inland letter rate, is 120 millions—*ten times* that of the 'Winners' Commemorative. Secondly, the estimate that the stamp would last for several days is sadly out of line with the

acknowledged fact that approximately 40 million 4d. stamps
are used every day in the United Kingdom. Even allowing for
the alternative fourpennies available—the regional issues and
other commemoratives—12 million stamps could scarcely have
lasted a day.

Moreover, the Post Office itself forecast, a few days beforehand, that the stamp would be in short supply and an official
Press notice, released two days prior to the stamp going on sale,
stated that supplies to many post offices would be restricted.
The national Press seized on this and gave it maximum publicity, thereby stimulating an unprecedented demand from
collectors and speculators.

Several hundred people massed outside Trafalgar Square
Branch Post Office during the evening of 17th August, awaiting
the witching hour of midnight when the 'Winners' Stamps
went on sale at the all-night counter. Some attempt at rationing
was apparently made, but nevertheless the stamps were sold
out by 12.25 a.m. and the protests of the vast crowd of dis-
appointed collectors grew into a near-riot, which the newspapers were to report as the Battle of Trafalgar Square. Plate-
glass windows were smashed, people fainted, others were rushed
to hospital, while thousands of pounds worth of 4d. stamps
changed hands in under half an hour. No post office in Britain
had ever done such lightning business before.

The story was repeated, in less sensational terms, at countless
post offices up and down England when they opened for business
at 9 a.m. Queues began forming anything up to an hour previous
to opening time and many passers-by, who paused to enquire
the reason, promptly joined in, in the hope of making a quick
profit. An increasing amount of publicity in the newspapers
and on radio and television in the previous two years had
magnified the investment potential of stamp-collecting and
here, apparently, was ready proof that money was to be made
for the asking. Genuine collectors, who would normally have
been content with a block of four, a pair or a few copies for
first-day covers, caught the investment fever and bought one or
two sheets, swallowing any qualms by reasoning that, when all
was said and done, the stamps could always be used for postage

if the expected rise in value did not materialise. Office workers, labourers, housewives, all joined in the panic to buy the stamps.

In my own case I happened to pass a post office at eight-forty and was taken aback to see that a sizeable queue was already forming. By nine o'clock some 200 to 250 people had gathered in an orderly fashion, patiently waiting for the doors to open. My original intention was to buy a couple of dozen, just sufficient to acquire that portion of the sheet showing the cylinder numbers and the 'traffic lights' (colour dabs applied by the printer as check in multicolour photogravure), and leave a few over for mailing on first-day covers to various philatelic friends all over the world. Everyone, however, seemed to be buying two sheets at least and no rationing was in force, so when it came to my turn I promptly bought two sheets also— an outlay of £4. By the time I had walked over to the writing desk, folded the sheets and put them away safely in my case, the counter clerks were already putting up 'Sold Out' placards on the grilles. The time was exactly 9.10 a.m.

The pattern was the same all over the London area; in the provinces the supply lasted till the afternoon and a Post Office spokesman has recorded (in *The Stamp Magazine*, October 1966) that, in some cases 'people were still buying the stamps at least two days later', but I have not been able to locate any district where the stamps were available on 19th August. As the event commemorated was a purely English affair the stamps were, naturally, not put on sale outside England. Of course, collectors north of the Border were upset at, as they felt, being unfairly discriminated against and as a sop to them a supply of World Cup 'Winners' went on sale at the General Post Office in Edinburgh on 22nd August, though, as before, the stock was very quickly exhausted. The reason that a concession was made was that every year, during the Edinburgh Festival, the General Post Office runs a special philatelic counter, selling stamps not normally available in Scotland (i.e. the regional issues) and a stock of World Cup 'Winners' was requisitioned in the normal way. It does seem strange, however, that the release in Scotland was delayed for several days.

The intervention of the non-philatelic public in the stampede for the stamps caught many philatelists and stamp dealers napping. Although the latter could have availed themselves of the Post Office's concession to them to purchase bulk orders a few days prior to issue in order to prepare their first-day covers, many of the smaller dealers were relying on getting their usual supplies from their local post office and consequently were unable to obtain sufficient to service all their souvenir envelopes. If there ever was a day for *selling* the stamp this was it. A dealer whom I happened to visit at lunch-time that day asked anxiously if I had any 'Winners' Stamps to spare and in a moment I had parted with my uncut sheet for £12—a remarkably quick profit of 500%. The dealer concerned was able to service another 120 covers which, when postmarked with the special 'First Day' cancellation, would find ready buyers the following day at anything up to 10s. each, providing my dealer friend with a nice profit in turn.

By midday the big stamp dealers in the Strand either had 'Sorry—Sold Out' notices in their windows or were doing a roaring trade at prices around 3s. each. The evening newspapers, which appeared on the news-stands in the early afternoon, were confidently predicting that by the end of the week this 4d. stamp would be changing hands at 15s. to £1. As it happens, the stamps did not attain such meteoric heights though the retail price hovered about 5s. for some time before inevitably sagging to half that figure. Stamp dealers, once the 'first-day' rush subsided, were able to buy satisfactory quantities of the stamps at about £7 to £9 a sheet from speculators who decided shrewdly that a quick small profit was better than the hypothetical possibilities of a bigger one in the long term. During the weeks following 18th August a sizeable proportion of the stocks held in non-philatelic hands came into dealers' possession and, as the supply increased to meet the, by now, not so considerable demand, the price dropped to a more reasonable level (still a handsome premium over face value).

Nevertheless, a common feature of the Personal columns of the evening and Sunday newspapers for several months after the date of issue were hopeful advertisements of which the following are typical:

WORLD CUP WINNERS: a few stamps available—
what offers?

WINNERS Sheet: Only £40.

It is true that a sheet *did* fetch £57 in an auction, but when it is remembered that the proceeds went to the fund for the dependants of the three policemen murdered in London, it will be realised that this was a special case.

In my capacity as Curator of the philatelic collections at the British Museum I meet many people every week who wish either to have stamps valued or to sell their stamps to the Museum. Since August 1966 I have been visited by many of those who purchased sheets of the 'Winners' stamps, fondly hoping that the Museum will buy their treasures. Many of them, unfortunately, have failed to look after their investment properly, for condition (as fresh as they were when they left the printers) is all-important in stamps, whether they be the 'classics' or the latest issue. I have witnessed housewives actually producing sheets, crumpled, creased and badly folded, from the mysterious recesses of their handbags, where they had lain uneasy bedfellows with lipstick, face powder and so forth.

Normally, it can be estimated that in a 4d. commemorative issue printed in an edition of 120 million about a tenth will survive in unused condition, eventually to end up in stamp collections. Of the remainder, a large number will inevitably be destroyed because people throw away used envelopes and wrappers. Many more will be irremediably damaged on parcels and packets or too heavily postmarked to be of use to a collector. Just how many will survive in collectable used condition, that is to say, with all the perforations intact, with fresh colour preserved and in a lightly postmarked state, is difficult to conjecture, but possibly fewer than those in mint condition. The true rarity of the World Cup 'Winners' Stamps may be seen when it is realised that a very large proportion of the 12 million issued are in unused condition, while such as were used at all were almost invariably on first-day cover. Consequently the number of fine, *commercially*, used specimens must be very small. Admittedly one could always pass a few through the posts in order to get them postmarked, if it should turn out that used copies were preferable to unused, but one is always taking the risk of getting a badly postmarked, or otherwise mutilated stamp.

That the World Cup 'Winners' Stamp is a good investment there is no denying. The design, a spirited action shot by David Gentleman, is attractive; the theme of Sport is popular and the fact that it is linked to the dramatic final of the 1966 World Cup Championship will ensure that this popularity is maintained; and the print of 12 million, though seemingly astronomical, will hardly suffice for the myriads of collectors all over the world who want to have it in their album. It is fair to suppose that about 7, or at the most 8, million stamps are now in collectable mint condition—not by any means enough for the 20 million collectors who want it. Possibly as many as 3 million were used on first-day covers, and perhaps another million or so were used commercially by those who did not realise in time the folly of paying postage with such a good item. Obviously in the long run this is a stamp which will increase moderately in value and even now it is not too late to buy some (even at dealers' rates) as a long-term investment, but I doubt if it will ever be in the 'pounds' class unless fantastic inflation overturns the economy of Britain.

PLATE I

(1) a fine unused copy with good margins and fresh appearance; (2-3) good margins, lightly postmarked. (4, 6) margins close on one side, moderate postmarking. (5) good margins, but vertically creased. (7-8) margin cut close on one or more sides. (9) margins cut into and slight tear at top. (10) cut into, but moderately postmarked. (11-12) poor specimens, heavily postmarked and cut into. Nos. 1, 2, 3, 4 and 6 are the only ones which should be admissible in a good collection; the rest could only be regarded as 'space fillers'.

CHAPTER II

WHAT MAKES A STAMP VALUABLE?

IN THE preceding chapter I have told the story of one stamp which was issued in a blaze of publicity and, in spite of being tipped to the skies and undoubtedly the subject of much speculation, has a bright future. The factors affecting the investment potential of this stamp have been outlined and basically the same seven criteria can be applied to every stamp in an attempt to assess its future prospects. These factors are design, method of production, numbers issued, theme, country of issue, the prevailing political and economic situation, and condition.

This is, of course, a gross over-simplification, subject to many ahs, buts and ifs. Nevertheless these points have some bearing on every stamp, good, bad or indifferent in varying degrees and each one should be examined in turn.

DESIGN

Generally speaking, the maxim 'a thing of beauty is a joy for ever' applies to stamps as to anything else which has any pretensions to being an art-form. For this reason a great deal of time, trouble and money is expended nowadays by postal administrations in selecting competent artists and designs which are aesthetically appealing, even for strictly utilitarian stamps —even for Postage Due labels in some cases. The British General Post Office, which for far more than a century regarded the postage stamp as merely an indication of prepayment, has awakened to the philatelic sales of its merchandise and in recent years has devoted an increasing amount of thought to improving the quality of designs. A highly eminent panel of art critics, industrial design experts and philatelists form the Postmaster-General's Stamp Advisory Committee and their task is to examine designs and select those suitable for production as stamps.

As a rule six artists are commissioned to submit designs to each prospective commemorative issue; three are 'established' artists who have already been successful in previous cases, while three are artists who have not had their designs accepted before. Some of the designs which are ultimately rejected actually get as far as being printed as stamps (technically these are known to philatelists as 'essays') and out of a score or more pieces of art work perhaps two designs will emerge to form the basis of finished stamps. Even the more prosaic definitive issues are getting this hypercritical appraisal. In 1964 the then Postmaster-General, Mr. Anthony Wedgwood Benn, established a Fellowship in Miniscule Design at the London School of Art. Mr. Andrew Restall was appointed to this Fellowship to explore the possibilities of improving the design of the stamps in everyday use, and the results are now being seen in the new definitive series being released during 1967.

This care in the selection of designs is by no means confined to the United Kingdom. In the United States the Post Office Department makes use of its Citizens' Stamp Advisory Committee, which consists of a distinguished historian, a representative of the fine arts, two representatives from the field of commercial art and six outstanding philatelic authorities. Liaison between the Department and the Committee is maintained by a Special Assistant to the Postmaster-General. The Committee examines requests, meeting the established criteria for commemorative stamps, and selects subjects of general interest with the most appropriate and appealing themes for recommendation to the Post Office Department.* Other countries have similar committees and some, such as Czechoslovakia and Canada, take design standards so seriously that nation-wide popularity polls are conducted every year as an incentive not only to artists to produce better work, but to the

* *Postage Stamps of the United States, 1847–1961.* (Post Office Department Publication, Washington, 1961.)

public to take a greater interest in and appreciation of the stamps on their mail.

The most valuable, most sought after stamps in the world, however, are the Primitives of a hundred years ago. (This term is used to denote those stamps which were designed and printed by local artists and printers in many of the remoter parts of the world, and in contrast to the beautifully engraved and produced stamps which emanated from such countries as the United Kingdom and the United States.) These ugly scraps of paper have a fascination all their own and the normal criteria of aesthetics cannot be applied to them. It is nevertheless true to say that, for the modern issues which are freely available today and are likely to appreciate in value tomorrow, good design is essential. It is significant that British stamps have only become popular in the past two or three years since the quality of design has improved. It is axiomatic that stamps are most popular in their country of origin but in the past Britain was the exception to this rule. It is a staggering fact that the majority of collectors in the United Kingdom preferred the brightly coloured 'pictorials' emanating from the Commonwealth countries and largely neglected the home products. Now all this has changed. Not only have the established philatelists found their interest awakened in the British stamps but countless thousands of new collectors have been recruited to the hobby by taking note of the prettier stamps on their mail.

METHOD OF PRODUCTION

All manner of production methods have been used to print postage stamps—from photography to typewriting and woodcuts. Ignoring the odd methods used in times of emergency there are four major techniques used nowadays—photogravure, intaglio or recess-printing, offset-lithography and typography or letterpress. The last-mentioned has lost ground to photogravure and offset-lithography in the past twenty-five years as the economic method of stamp production, but although they are technically capable of producing stamps in up to nine or ten colours they lack the indefinable appeal of stamps printed by intaglio, the process by which the world's first stamps—the

Penny Black and Twopence Blue of 1840—were produced. Recess-printing, in the United Kingdom, is nowadays confined to the higher denominations, from 2s. 6d. to £1. The demand for the lower values is so great that the cheaper photogravure method has to be used for them.

In the United States, however, every postage-stamp since they first appeared in 1847 has been recess-printed, yet many of them are produced by the thousand million. Admittedly intaglio has its limitations—it does not produce the photographic likeness which can be achieved by photogravure, but is this to be expected from an art form such as the postage-stamp? The Giori presses used by the U.S. Bureau of Engraving and Printing can print up to four colours simultaneously and the finished article, such as the annual Art stamps since 1962, are far more satisfying aesthetically than anything printed by photogravure or offset-lithography.

France and Czechoslovakia are another two countries which are outstanding in their application of the intaglio process to stamp production. With regard to the latter, stamps have long been treated as artistic creations *per se*, apart from their utilitarian purpose. From the first issues of 1918, which were designed by the famous painter Alfons Mucha, to the emissions of the present day produced by such outstanding artists as Max Svabinsky and Karel Svolinsky, Czech stamps have been miniature works of art, beautifully designed and delicately engraved. Among the countries of the Iron Curtain group Czechoslovakia stands alone in the universal popularity of its stamps, a popularity earned by the superior skill and craftsmanship which has gone into their making.

Under the heading of production methods, one other technique deserves mention—metal foil embossing. As a means of printing stamps it is expensive and rather impractical. Theoretically the end product simulates the appearance of a coin or metal sculptured in high relief, but in actual practice the quality of the original sculpture, on which the dies are based, leaves much to be desired. This is a method of printing which *could* bring to stamp printing something of the beauty and the three-dimensional quality of the medallist's art, but there is a great deal of room for improvement and at the present time stamps embossed on metal foil tend to be despised and ridiculed by philatelists (especially those of the orthodox 'printed, perforated in sheets and no nonsense' school). They have been variously nicknamed as beer-mats or bottle-tops.

The first series of stamps to employ this embossing technique (which, incidentally, has been the preserve of one firm alone, the Walsall Lithographic Company Ltd.) emanated from Tonga in 1963, and consisted of a set of thirteen stamps commemorating the gold coinage of that country which had been put into circulation a short time previously. The stamps were produced in three sizes, ranging from 40 mm. to 80 mm. in diameter. Each reproduced either the reverse of the quarter, half or one Koula coins (a Koula—the Polynesian word for gold—being equivalent to £20 in Australian currency). The 'coins' were surrounded by a coloured band bearing the inscription and denomination and the stamps, being circular in shape, were die-stamped singly. This in itself was sufficient novelty to ensure their immediate popularity. Not since the ½ anna red of Scinde (1852) and an issue of Russian Zemstvo (local) stamps from Vessiegonsk in 1871 had stamps been circular in shape and printed singly. The Tonga 'coin' stamps were available at 30s. when they first appeared on the London market, but rapidly rose to £5 and for a short time went even higher before settling down at around this figure. Supplies were somehow delayed in getting to the United States and collectors and dealers had to obtain sets through London; consequently the U.S. starting prices were substantially higher than those in Britain.

Collectors had been wary of Tonga since the previous year when a number of stamps were suddenly released with an overprint commemorating the Centenary of Emancipation and it was found that certain denominations were in woefully short supply. From the very beginning, therefore, the 'Tonga Beer-mats', as they were quickly nicknamed, were regarded with suspicion as a gimmick reducing the science of philately to its Victorian ancestor of scrap-collecting. Several of the biggest London dealers conferred about whether to trade in these stamps or not. In the end they decided to give it a trial and

were agreeably surprised to find that the much-maligned issues
(which were thoroughly slated by the philatelic press) sold like
hot cakes.

Undoubtedly the sheer novelty of the stamps contributed in
large measure to their popularity and it is significant that
though there have been subsequent metal-foil, circular issues
not only from Tonga but from the Persian Gulf sheikhdoms,
Burundi, Bhutan and Sierra Leone, none has had the impact,
or so far shown the investment potential, of that first set. The
novelty has worn off, but I would reiterate that, if the quality
of the engraving were improved, metal-foil embossed stamps
would establish themselves as a distinct art-form mid-way
between engraved ephemera (prints, stamps and bank-notes)
and pure numismatics (particularly commemorative medals).
At the moment, however, their many disadvantages (size,
awkward shape and delicate embossing which necessitates
special care in handling) outweigh their novelty, which is
waning, and their aesthetic value, which has not yet been
established.

On similar lines to (and from the same printers as) the coin-
shaped stamps are the so-called free-form, self-adhesive stamps
which have so far been confined to one country alone—Sierra
Leone. They made their debut in 1964 with a long series of
airmail and ordinary postage stamps to commemorate Sierra
Leone's participation in the New York World's Fair. The basic
design of the stamps was the map of the country and the shape
conformed to the outline of Sierra Leone's national boundaries.
Though the stamps were die-stamped singly they were issued
to the public attached in groups of thirty to sheets of backing
paper. The backs of the stamps themselves were coated with
a special gum which did not require to be moistened; they
were merely peeled from their backing paper and affixed to
the envelope.

Hailed, in the 125th year of the adhesive postage stamp, as
a major landmark in stamp development, it has to be admitted
that the 'sticky-backs' had hygienic advantages over their
orthodox contemporaries, but the high cost of production pre-
cludes them from ever being used on a large scale. The Sierra

Leone postal authorities found a way round this, however, by selling advertising space on the backing sheets of the next issue of self-adhesive stamps. This was a series publicising the industries of the country, particularly diamond-mining. The stamps were even shaped like a diamond and, taking commercialism into its extreme, were inscribed with the name of a prominent New York jeweller who also took 'full-page' advertisements on the backing paper. In this way, Sierra Leone financed the production of these unusual stamps, collectors were eager to purchase the latest gimmick in stamp design and production and, presumably Mr. Harry Winston's world-wide sales went up.

NUMBERS ISSUED

Although exquisite design and perfection in production are important in assessing a stamp's future prospects, undoubtedly the chief factor to watch is the number issued. Here the age-old law of supply and demand has to be taken into consideration. If Britain issued a commemorative stamp in an edition smaller than 1 million it would automatically be a sound investment, since there are at least 2 million collectors in the United Kingdom alone, and a vast number abroad who collect British stamps. On the other hand 1 million copies of a commemorative stamp from Libya or Iceland are probably more than enough to supply all likely collectors of these countries.

Many countries automatically publish the print order of their commemorative stamps, in advance of the date of issue. This figure is not always the same as the number actually sold and in some cases large quantities of stamps have to be destroyed after their period of validity ceases. Both the United States and Britain habitually announce the figures of stamps printed, before they go on sale. In 1964 it was announced that the 2s. 6d. Shakespeare Commemorative would be released in an edition of 3,500,000, a figure based on the normal monthly requirements for that denomination (used almost entirely on parcels or prepaying the double airmail rate). Immediately, shrewd collectors and dealers realised that this would be a good stamp to buy for investment; a sheet of forty at £5 would bring a handsome dividend in a reasonably short time. Consequently,

on the day of issue, the half-crown stamp speedily vanished
from the post offices. Having misjudged the demand for this
stamp the General Post Office endeavoured to put the matter
right by ordering a second printing from Bradbury, Wilkinson
& Co. Ltd. Another 800,000 stamps were run off, making a
grand total of 4,300,000. At the time of the reprinting there
was a tremendous howl of protest from the philatelic trade,
which felt that the General Post Office had broken faith with
philatelists.

When the dust of battle had cleared it was found that (a)
only some 3,664,920 stamps had actually been sold, the balance
being subsequently destroyed, and (b) the second and third
printings required to produce the additional 800,000 stamps
did not exactly match the first in colour. Consequently, instead
of adding to the total for the stamp, the G.P.O. created two
other distinct varieties both of which are quite distinct from
the original shade of deep purple-brown and worth a substantial
premium. The question of the colours in which this Shakespeare
stamp can be found is a vexed one and unfortunately neither
of the two leading British catalogues helps matters. The
Elizabethan Catalogue lists the basic stamp as 'deep purple-brown'
but merely adds a footnote: 'A later printing of the 2s. 6d. was
in a deeper shade which is not listed as intermediate shades
are known'.

The *Commonwealth Catalogue*, however, lists the basic stamp as
violet-grey in colour and lists one variant as violet-black. I do
not wish to confuse the matter further but my own personal
views incline to the *Elizabethan* description, with *two* variants
—a deep blackish-brown, devoid of the reddish tinge which
gives warmth to the normal stamp, and an almost pure black
stamp which in my opinion deserves catalogue status on the
same level as the 2½d. Silver Jubilee Stamp in Prussian blue
instead of blue. It is almost certain that the 'black Shakespeare'
stamps were in fact colour proofs which were inadvertently
perforated and put into circulation as normal stamps.

The 1967 *Elizabethan Catalogue* prices the Shakespeare 2s. 6d.
stamp at 15s., while the contemporary edition of the *Commonwealth* lists it at 10s. and the second printing at 16s. 6d.—a

pretty hefty premium which the former catalogue chooses to ignore. Both neglect the 'black' stamp which has changed hands at around £50, such is its great scarcity. *Scott*, on the other hand, merely lists the stamp as 'dark gray' and prices it at only $1.

The mere figures of stamps issued are not sufficient, especially in the case of British commemorative stamps in recent years. Since the National Productivity Year series in 1962 all photogravure commemoratives, except the De Montfort 2s. 6d. and the World Cup 'Winners' Stamps, have also been issued in the London, Southampton, Liverpool and Glasgow areas with phosphor lines across their face. These lines (which are, more strictly speaking, fluorescent rather than phosphorescent) facilitate the handling and sorting of mail in the electronic equipment used in these areas and, since they can be easily detected with the naked eye, they are listed separately in the stamp catalogues and the General Post Office publishes separate lists of these stamps sold.

Thus, in the Shakespeare series, the following figures show sales of the 1s. 3d. and 1s. 6d. denominations, both phosphor and non-phosphor.

	Non-phosphor	Phosphor	Total
1s. 3d.	7,067,200	727,800	7,795,000
1s. 6d.	6,910,120	657,120	7,567,240

It will be seen immediately that the phosphor varieties of these two stamps are scarcer than any other stamp of the series, including the much sought after 2s. 6d. (except, perhaps, the second printing of it). The phosphor varieties in each case are ten times rarer than the normal stamps yet the *Commonwealth* prices for the 1s. 3d. are 3s. 6d. for the non-phosphor and 4s. 6d. for phosphor, while the prices for the 1s. 6d. are 4s. 6d. and 5s. respectively. The reason that the greater scarcity of the phosphor stamps is not reflected in their comparative pricings is that, as yet, there is not a great deal of demand for them. Sooner or later (and usually later) collectors are going to wake up to the fact that the phosphor varieties are desirable property and then the hunt will be up.

Making a recent tour of the stamp shops in London's Strand area, the Mecca of the stamp world, I found, on going through their stocks of modern Great Britain, a dearth of phosphor stamps, particularly in fine used condition. When electronic handling of mail becomes commonplace and *all* stamps are phosphor-lined, collectors will want the pioneer issues and it is then that their value will be appreciated. Collecting both phosphor and non-phosphor states of every commemorative stamp can be expensive, especially if one takes them in corner blocks and on cover, but in the long run it will pay handsome dividends.

Shortly after the release of the much-publicised World Cup 'Winners' Stamp the 1967 edition of *Stanley Gibbons Catalogue, Part I (British Commonwealth)* was published and, while the prices of most British stamps had shown a substantial increase over those of 1966, one set of stamps remained stagnant. This was a pair of stamps issued in May 1948 to commemorate the third anniversary of the Liberation of the Channel Islands. Almost twenty years after their issue these stamps had shown only a nominal advance over their face value of 3½d. and yet only 5½ million sets were printed—less than half the number of the World Cup 'Winners' Stamp. While British commemoratives in general had soared in value in the last two years this set was still priced at 10d. and, indeed, it was possible to purchase large quantities at a discount off face value until fairly recently.

Initially the set was restricted in sale to the Channel Islands and the eight largest post offices in the United Kingdom. This had the effect of stimulating an inordinate amount of interest in it at the time and many people, collectors and non-collectors alike, flocked to buy them in sheets as a 'sound investment'. The fact that *Gibbons Catalogue*, the arbiter of the fashions in British collecting habits, did not list them under the main heading but relegated them to the section covering the local (wartime) emissions of the Channel Islands, damned them utterly and after topical interest in them subsided they were almost completely neglected. Furthermore, their choice of subject was hardly edifying and not one likely to sustain collectors' interest—carting seaweed for manure!

With the boom in all British stamps, but especially com-memoratives, it is nevertheless amazing that this pair should have remained so long in the doldrums. When the new edition of the catalogue showed that their price had not moved up, many great minds apparently thought alike and in no time at all the Liberation Commemoratives were being eagerly bought up.

The fact remains that for years dealers and philatelists, having purchased large quantities of the stamps below face value from disillusioned speculators, were accustomed to frank their correspondence with them. This was true, to a lesser extent, of many other British commemoratives and the short-lived definitive series of King Edward VIII, so much so that one well-known dealer boasts that for years this practice gave him a 20% discount off his mailing expenses. It will never be known how many of those 5½ million stamps were used for postage in this way, but suddenly, in the autumn of 1966, it was realised that this despised set was not so common as it had been and it rapidly changed hands at three or four times its catalogue price.* A complete sheet of each value (i.e. 120 sets) appeared at a Robson Lowe auction in March 1967 estimated at £15, but in fact realised £14 10s. Undoubtedly it will go higher still, for the many new collectors of British stamps will require the set to be complete, though it will never possess the universal appeal of the 'Winners' Stamp.

An even more spectacular 'sleeper' which awoke dramatically in 1966 was the £1 stamp issued in 1929 to commemorate the Ninth Postal Union Congress. Four low values, in denomina-tions from ½d. to 2½d., were issued to mark the event, but collectors severely criticised the Post Office for tacking a stamp of such high value on to the series. Few philatelists could afford to buy the stamp at the time (it was in the midst of economic recession), far less invest in sheets of it. Although the stamp, designed by Harold Nelson and featuring St. George and the Dragon, is regarded as one of the most beautiful examples of line engraving as applied to the postage stamp, it was unpopular

---

* *Gibbons Specialised Stamp Catalogue, Gt. Britain, Vol. 2*, published since this was written, prices this pair at 5s., mint or used!

for a very long time. For several years it remained on sale at the London Chief Office but, even so, only 61,000 stamps were sold. The majority were bought for postal use, franking registered or insured packages, and surprisingly few got into philatelic hands. Most collections lacked this stamp, though it could easily be purchased in unmounted mint condition for less than its catalogue price of £5.

Gradually it moved up, from £6 to £12. In the 1966 edition of *Gibbons Catalogue* it was priced at £13 mint and £11 used. Suddenly the boom in British commemoratives, initiated by the flood of new issues in recent years, began to affect the earlier stamps, helped in no small degree by the appearance on the market about that time of a special album, published by Gibbons, to house all the British commemorative stamps. The price doubled overnight then rose to £35 before doubling once again. The 1967 edition shows it at £75, and it now seems to have levelled out—for the time being, at any rate. It is more likely to go up again. Compare it with other high value stamps of the same period and you will see that further expansion is inevitable:

	1967 price	
	Gibbons	Scott
Falkland Islands: Centenary, 1933, £1	£125	$200
Sierra Leone: Abolition of Slavery, 1933, £1	£90	$200

In the category of the great rarities the numbers of stamps in existence has some bearing on their value, but this factor on its own is not as important as it might seem. When one is considering items which are unique, or exist only in small handfuls, the popularity of the issuing country is more important. Normally, where a stamp is unique and the likelihood of it coming on the market is remote, the stamp catalogues list it but do not price it, so that one has no real indication of the value or the price it would fetch were it to appear in an auction.

The best example of this is the unique 1 cent 'black on magenta' of British Guiana, 1856, reputed to be the world's

most valuable stamp. A recent hand-book on stamp collecting*
states that it is worth £200,000 today. This remarkable state-
ment rests solely on the fact that the owner insured the stamp
for that sum when it was lent to Stanley Gibbons Ltd. for their
Catalogue Centenary Exhibition at the Festival Hall, London,
in February 1965. This is an arbitrary sum and it is obvious
that, when an object is unique and in great demand, the
owner may set any figure on it that he chooses. If, on the other
hand, this stamp were ever put up for auction again, it is
extremely doubtful whether even two wealthy collectors would
so far lose their heads as to run the bidding so high.

This stamp was found by a Guianese schoolboy in 1873 and
sold by him to a local philatelist shortly afterwards for 6s. In
rapid succession it changed hands and ended up in the collection
of Count Ferrary, who is reputed to have paid £150 for it.
During Ferrary's long possession of it the stamp became almost
legendary in philatelic circles and when it was sold in 1923 it
fetched the record sum of 300,000 francs, which, with 18%
sales tax, was equivalent to £7,343 at the rates of exchange
current at that time. It was purchased by the American textile
millionaire, Arthur Hind, and after his death his widow put it
up for auction at Harmer's in London, but it failed to reach
its reserve price of £7,500. Some years later it was sold privately
for a sum alleged to have been in the region of $40,000 and
it is now in the hands of a prominent American collector who
prefers to remain anonymous.

It is not by any means the only 'unique' stamp in existence
but it is the one which has attracted the most ballyhoo in the
past hundred years. It is interesting to note that, from the same
country, has come an item even more unique. The use of the
comparative is correct since only *half* of this item exists. It is,
in fact, a bisected 4 cents stamp of the 1866 issue. Bisected
stamps, by which denominations of half the total value could
be created, are rare but not unknown from British Guiana in
this early period. This stamp normally exists perforated but a
few examples, possibly one sheet only, have been recorded

* *Stamp Collecting*, by Stanley Phillips: 1966 Edition revised by James M. C.
Watson.

imperforate. The combination of non-perforation and bisection was theoretically possible, but no example had ever been recorded, until a cover was found in 1965 bearing a bisected, imperforate 4c., neatly tied by the Demerara postmark of 16th April 1868. It came into the hands of a stamp dealer in Surrey, who, realising its rarity, submitted it to the Royal Philatelic Society's Expert Committee and they duly pronounced it to be authentic. This item has never come on the market but has changed hands at around $7,000. It is a more attractive looking item than the 1 cent of 1856 (whose surface is badly rubbed and whose corners are clipped) and it would require little prophetic genius to forecast a bright future for this bisect.

Robert Graves wrote an amusing novel about a fictitious stamp, the Antigua Penny Puce, and described its meteoric rise in value, culminating in the high drama of the spirited bidding by a Chinese war-lord and an Indian prince at an auction. In real life there are many 'unique' stamps, but few achieve the fame of the British Guiana 1 cent or the Swedish 3 skilling error of colour (whose present whereabouts are not known). There is an unsubstantiated story that Thomas Tapling (whose magnificent collection is on permanent display at the British Museum) exchanged an unique pair of the ½ anna stamp from the Indian state of Poonch for an unused Mauritius 'Post Office' 2d. Though the Poonch stamps are unique, whereas there are four unused copies and nine used copies of the Mauritius 2d., Tapling had the better bargain. Admittedly, two of the four unused 'Twopennies' will never come on the market again (the second copy reposes in the Royal Collection at Buckingham Palace); but while an unused 'Post Office' 2d. fetched £13,500 at auction in 1965, the Poonch ½ anna pair only made £320 at a Robson Lowe auction in January 1967.

COUNTRY OF ORIGIN

The unused 'Post Office' 2d. is catalogued by *Gibbons* at £14,000 and by *Scott* at $42,500; yet another stamp, of which only three copies exist in used condition, is the Somaliland Protectorate 1 rupee of 1904 overprinted for official use—listed at a mere £35 in *Gibbons* and $35 in *Scott*.

Only twenty sets of the overprinted Turkish fiscal stamps used in 1916 at Long Island in Asia Minor exist, but a set may be had for about £120 (when they appear, once in a blue moon, in the auction room), yet other stamps a hundred times commoner fetch four figures. Numbers issued are important, but not enough; if only two people in the whole world were to collect Long Island stamps then two sets, let alone twenty, would suffice. It follows therefore that whether the numbers of stamps in existence are sufficient to meet the demand or not depends very largely on the popularity of the country of origin.

It has been stated previously that stamps attain their greatest popularity in their own country, but much depends on what percentage of the population are stamp collectors. Many countries have as yet little indigenous philatelic activity—these include the underdeveloped countries, especially those in regions of great temperature and humidity, conditions which militate against stamp collecting. Much depends also on the degree of literacy of the people, their living standards and income and the amount of free time available for hobbies.

The most popular countries from a philatelic viewpoint are the European States, especially West Germany, Switzerland, Italy (including the Vatican and San Marino), France and the United Kingdom, the last-named coming up fast on the outside lane. Outside Europe, the stamps of the United States, and the older Commonwealth countries such as Canada, Australia and New Zealand, are among the most popular. At the bottom of the popularity poll are the 'dead' countries which have ceased to exist politically and which therefore have no continuous issue of new stamps to awaken and maintain interest. There is little current interest in the stamps of Manchuria or Montenegro, for example, and yet it would be wrong to assume that all dead countries are not worth bothering about.

Where the territory of the dead country is now part of a state with flourishing philatelic interest the obsolete issues retain their popularity. Few groups contain more of the highly prized blue chips of philately than the old Italian kingdoms and principalities or the states which amalgamated a century ago to join the German Empire. In the same way the stamps of

Hawaii and the Confederate States have a large following in the U.S., while the issues of Newfoundland and Nova Scotia are perennially in demand in Canada.

Certain countries blot their copybooks from time to time and their stamps go into eclipse. Liberia was for many years under a cloud, on account of its practice at one time of cancelling stamps to order—that is to say they were 'postmarked' in complete sheets to prevent postal use and then sold at a heavy discount to stamp dealers. Such stamps, with their gum intact, have obviously not performed the legitimate function for which they were produced and therefore they are despised and condemned by collectors. This remark applies also to the stamps of the British North Borneo Company, which were often treated in this way at the Company's headquarters in London and thus were never near the country itself. Nowadays many of the Iron Curtain countries practice cancelling to order and their popularity consequently suffers.

Italy earned a certain amount of opprobrium recently when the Ministry of Posts decided to sell by auction large quantities of obsolete issues. Many of them were comparatively scarce and priced quite highly in the stamp catalogues. The Ministry's decision created a great deal of uncertainty in the philatelic world and affected the market for the stamps already in circulation. When a sale was attempted in 1960 it was a complete fiasco, since collectors and dealers unanimously boycotted it. For several years *Gibbons Catalogue* marked these stamps with a star as a warning. After years of protest and considerable pressure from philatelic circles the Italian authorities finally decided that the best thing to do with these stamps would be to destroy them. They were duly consigned to the flames in December 1966. Collectors and dealers heaved a sigh of relief and in a remarkably short time confidence in Italian stamps was restored.

Politics play a part in philatelic popularity too. The stamps of the Soviet Union, low in face-value, colourful and, on the whole, well-printed, are not popular anywhere—except behind the Iron Curtain where their heavy political overtones are tolerated if not appreciated.

PLATE II

RARE, BUT NOT VERY VALUABLE: STAMPS ISSUED BY THE ROYAL
NAVY AT LONG ISLAND (MAKRONISI, GULF OF SMYRNA), MAY 1916.

Numbers printed, with *Gibbons* valuation in parentheses: (1)–25 (£40), (2)–25
(£38), (3)–20 (£45), (4)–60 (£7), (5)–72 (£8), (6)–144 (£7), (7)–72 (£8). These
stamps are only listed by *Gibbons Part I Catalogue.*

The political and economic stability of a country is reflected in its stamps and there is thus little market for the issues of Ghana and the Congo. Germany's inflation provisionals of 1923, when postal rates changed daily and eventually fifty thousand millions of marks would hardly pay the postage on a letter, are still common in complete sheets and most schoolboy collections can be guaranteed to contain a fine showing of them. Yet, even here, there are unconsidered rarities which astute specialists can snap up at bargain prices.

There is no country, past or present, whose stamps are too unpopular or esoteric to preclude interest being shown in them somewhere or by someone. Afghanistan is regarded as one of the world's obscurest countries, with the dullest of stamps; yet the late Major Hopkins of Bath had formed an outstanding collection of Afghan stamps that had won many international awards for him, including the rarest distinction of all, election to the Roll of Distinguished Philatelists. But purely from an investment point of view the country of origin is of great importance, since universal demand, as well as a strong indigenous market, are the prerequisites of the stamp's future prospects.

CONDITION

All other things being equal, it is a stamp's condition which determines its value, and yet this is probably the most difficult factor to assess. Nevertheless, it is much more straightforward than in coins and medals, for example; and the terms used to describe a stamp's condition have not become debased as they have in numismatics. The terms most commonly used to describe a stamp are as follows:

1. *Unmounted mint.* This denotes a stamp which is in that state of unsullied perfection in which (theoretically) it was sold over the post office counter. It has not been affixed to an album page in any way, so that its gum is impeccable.

2. *Mounted mint.* As above, but very lightly hinged, or bearing exceptionally minute traces of a previous stamp mount.

3. *Unused, part o.g.* This indicates a stamp which has been heavily mounted in an album, either by hinges or by means

of a portion of its gum, but still retains some semblance of original gum (hence the abbreviation).

4. *Unused, without gum.* An unpostmarked specimen which has none the less been stuck down at some time and, on being soaked off the album page, has had its gum washed off. Many of the very early stamps circulating on the market or in collections today lack the gum for this reason.

5. *Fine used.* A stamp with the lightest possible postmark and otherwise intact.

Categories 1, 2 and 5 are the ideal standards to aim at. The top prices will always be paid for the finest material and anything second-rate will suffer accordingly. There are several criteria which should add up to the ideal stamp. In mint stamps a great deal of emphasis is laid just now on the state of the gum —altogether too much emphasis. Many of the early classics, including most of the very valuable stamps, are now without gum. The chief reason for this is that, prior to the 1880's, when stamp mounts or hinges became fashionable, stamps were invariably 'stuck down' in albums. Used stamps were well and truly affixed by gum, paste or even glue, while the mucilage on unused stamps provided a convenient means of holding them in place. When the old-style collectors wished to change the arrangement of their treasures they soaked or steamed them off.

Stamp hinges came into use very gradually and even after they were invented many collectors habitually used stamp-edging and other unsuitable forms of gummed paper which rendered subsequent remounting difficult without destroying part of the gum. Consequently many stamps, even of the middle period and later, have not preserved much of their gum. The modern hinges, manufactured of superfine transparent paper, double gummed to ensure ready peelability, leave little trace on an unused stamp and for all practical purposes are ideal, so long as they are not too generously licked.

Nevertheless, since the Second World War, there has developed a fad for the condition known as unmounted mint. How this began is obscure, but in the United States and in Europe the obsession with gum condition has greatly increased the basic cost of collecting. There are now on the market a variety of transparent 'pochettes' and strips into which stamps may be inserted and held securely in place without affixing anything to their backs.

On the Continent the fashion is for stamps to be housed in so-called hingeless albums or stock books whose pages are covered in narrow transparent strips into which the specimens can be tucked. Some collectors will not buy stamps which have been mounted and dealers, sensing this, charge more for stamps in virgin condition.

This insistence on as much of the original gum as possible has two inherent dangers. In the first place it has given rise to a profitable industry in the regumming of specimens which have lost it and it is advisable, therefore, to treat classics with full gum cautiously and not purchase them without a certificate guaranteed by an expert. Secondly, it is a proven fact that the gum can be detrimental to certain stamps. Some of the earlies were printed on paper of poor quality with thick gum, which, over the years, has hardened and cracked. These gum fissures eventually warp and split the paper and a stamp cracked in this way is no better than a torn one—the ultimate in philatelic mutilation.

It is the practice in many museum collections to wash the gum off old stamps, especially those on thin, brittle paper. Admittedly, the gum serves no real academic purpose and the museum authorities are never likely to be worried by the financial consideration. But it would take a revolution in philatelic thinking to get collectors to remove the gum from the early stamps; who will make the first move?

Turning to the front of a stamp, one must consider the perforations and the positioning. If a stamp is perforated, then all the 'teeth' should be intact and not missing, clipped or pulled in any way. The perforations should not bite into the design of the stamp, although some issues are particularly difficult to find well-centred. Either the stamps were printed too close together to permit the perforating blades to pass between them, or when perforation was still at the experimental stage the blades were imperfectly aligned in relation to the stamps.

Because sheets of stamps were cut by guillotines into panes before distribution to post offices, many stamps in Canada and the United States in particular are found with a straight edge on one or sometimes two adjoining sides. Generally speaking these are regarded as second-class specimens, but they are of interest to specialists who try to reconstruct the imperforate positions in groups of nine stamps, each having one or more straight edges in a different combination.

In the same way stamps from slot machines or booklets sometimes have their perforations clipped, owing to the faulty alignment of the guillotines separating them into strips or booklet panes as the case may be. These are inferior stamps, worth less than perfectly perforated ones and not to be confused with the truly imperforate stamp of which one reads occasionally and which fetches high prices in auctions. Unfortunately, all too often people buy a stamp booklet, find a straight edge, and immediately rush to the conclusion that they have an imperforate variety. The same effect can be achieved with a pair of scissors and true imperforation only exists when there are no holes between two adjoining stamps.

When stamps *are* imperforate the criterion to be applied is clear margins all round. The imperforate stamps of the last century had to be separated by scissors or a knife, or were torn apart with the fingers. In the ideal state they should have generous margins on all sides and not be cut or torn into the design at any point. In auction catalogue descriptions imperforate stamps are sometimes qualified as being 'touched' or 'close' on one or more sides, indicating that the margin is barely present at that point.

The surface of a stamp should be freshly coloured and without blemishes. Foxing or rust-stains, occasionally encountered on older stamps whose paper contains iron impurities, can be removed by the careful use of a little chloramine-T in a weak solution brushed on carefully and rinsed well afterwards in cold water. This should only be done in cases of recess-printed, lithographed or typographed specimens, but *never* on chalk-surfaced examples of the latter or on modern photogravure stamps. The appearance of the early line-engraved stamps can often be improved by careful brushing with a solution of hydrogen peroxide to remove the sulphuretting caused by the polluted atmosphere.

Stamps printed on surfaced paper, particularly those manufactured by De La Rue with their famous single and double fugitive inks, have to be treated with great care. Unused examples with full, fresh colours are worth a premium since so many of these stamps (of the period 1880-1930) have had their surfaces rubbed or the colours faded. Yet this is a group of British Commonwealth issues which are rapidly going up in value as their popularity increases.

Apart from having good gum, the back of a stamp should not be damaged, thinned or torn in any way. Imperforate stamps with designs in an unusual shape (circular, octagonal, etc.) should ideally be cut square and are worth a handsome premium in this state. So many copies of the 4 annas 'indigo and red' of India, 1854, were trimmed by native traders (who were anxious to keep the weight of their letters down) that cut square copies are twenty times as scarce. Another reason for classics such as the Ceylon 'Pence' and the British embossed 6d., 10d. and 1s. being cut to shape is that many of the early collectors trimmed them neatly to fit the printed spaces in their stamp albums. Gum creases and paper folds also detract from the appearance of stamps and affect their value.

In purchasing rare stamps, particularly the early classics, careful attention should be paid to the stamp catalogue listings. Not only are the prices accurate indications of what one can expect to pay, but the copious footnotes which are often to be found there should be studied. Catalogues are not only dealers' price-lists, but valuable reference works which serve to guide the cautious collector. There are so many ways of repairing or faking a stamp and transforming it into what is apparently a desirable piece that expensive items should not be purchased except from a reputable dealer and preferably also with the guarantee of an acknowledged expert. More will be said on the subject of guarantees in a later chapter.

* * * * *

So much for the various factors affecting a stamp's desirability; it remains for something to be said on the subject of the different periods of stamp collecting: and also about errors and varieties. Stamps can be divided roughly into three periods—classics, middle issues and moderns. Each has a following of its own and, while the same criteria can be applied to them all, the emphasis on the various factors differs considerably from one to the other. Thus the standards of condition which have to be accepted for the classics of the mid-nineteenth century would not be tolerated for the modern issues; conversely the modern stamps of present-day Mauritius lack the drawing power of the locally-printed Primitives of the 1840s.

Classic stamps may be defined as the pioneer stamps of a country, sometimes printed by hand under crude conditions, invariably rare and exceedingly difficult to find in fine condition. Their rarity and simplicity—almost naïveté—of design and production make them particularly appealing to the connoisseur. The term is often loosely applied to high value middle and modern issues and generally speaking any stamp in the price bracket above £50 or £100 is often, though incorrectly, regarded as a 'classic'. Conversely, however, any stamp from the period 1840 to 1860 can be termed a classic; these stamps are the *incunabula* of philately.

The middle period begins roughly in the 1860s, when the craftsmanship and artistry inherent in the earliest issues began to be sacrificed for utilitarianism and expediency and mass-production methods broke the monopoly of line-engraving. The De La Rue surface-printed stamps, which made their debut in 1855 with the 4d. stamp of Great Britain, and had their heyday in the monotonous keyplate designs of the colonies, typify the middle period which may be said to have endured until the early thirties. This was a period of monotonous stamp designs everywhere with few exceptions; and for a long time these stamps were in the doldrums. It is only now that interest in the middle period is reviving and the colonial stamps of the Edwardian and early Georgian eras are beginning to rocket in value. This has not reached its peak by any means, as the steady upward trends in auction realisations indicate.

The modern period begins with the greater use of pictorialism instead of portraiture and heraldry, the adoption of two or more colours instead of monochrome and the introduction of photogravure on a large scale. Add to this the greater frequency of commemorative issues and one can understand the interest shown in stamps from about 1932 onwards. Many collectors in Britain concentrate on the stamps issued since the accession of King George VI in 1936 only. In even more recent times there is a great vogue, particularly in the U.S.A. and on the continent of Europe, for the stamps of a country only since it achieved independence. Thus the former French colonies in Africa, the erstwhile mandated territories and ex-British possessions have begun to be popular.

In thit context it used to be a safe bet that any new country was worth collecting. One only has to look at the catalogue listing for such post-war countries as Israel (1948), the Ryukyu Islands (1948) and West Berlin (1948) to realise the good fortune of those who were shrewd enough to collect them from the very beginning. The following summary of the prices for the first set in each case illustrates this forcibly:

	1950		1967	
	(S.G.)	(Scott)	(S.G.)	(Scott)
Berlin	8s. 8d.	$1.50	£22 11s.	$116.25
Israel	£2 16s. 4d.	$14.83	£64 1s.	$325.00
Ryukyu Islands	4s. 3d.	60c.	£4 11s.	$85.50

Even allowing for devaluation and the passage of time, this represents a very attractive rate of appreciation. Not all new countries, however, have lived up to their early promise and much depends on the integrity of the issuing authorities and the country's career after independence. The Gold Coast achieved independence in 1957 as Ghana and there was an immediate rush to purchase its first stamps, particularly the three denominations of the Black Star Line set of December 1957. This set, with a face value of 6s. 5½d. was easily obtainable, while current, at 7s; but it rapidly rose to £3 on becoming

obsolete. It was heavily tipped and even more heavily over-
bought by speculators. The bottom fell out of the market for
Black Star Stamps in 1961–2 when a great deal of speculative
stock was suddenly unloaded, coinciding with the universal dissatisfaction with the way in which Ghanaian stamps were being
handled and a general lack of confidence in the economic
soundness of the country itself. At the time of writing, Ghana
is virtually bankrupt and her stamps discredited. Fashions in
philately change, however, and Ghana's stamps may become
popular again, but at present it would be very difficult to
recommend them as a good investment.

ERRORS

One of the peculiarities of philately is that so much attention
and monetary importance should be lavished on errors and
imperfections. This is the chief argument against the pretensions
of philately to be a branch of art. Paintings, jewellery and
antiques suffer considerably in value if their workmanship is
faulty, but quite the reverse is the case with stamps. This
tendency is also beginning to spread insidiously to numismatics,
though fortunately the majority of collectors sensibly refuse to
pay ridiculous prices for mis-strikes and brockages.

It is difficult to determine at what stage in the infancy of
philately undue attention came to be focused on errors in
stamps, but by the end of the nineteenth century their desirability had certainly become established and the Tapling Collection, bequeathed to the British Museum in 1891, is replete
with them. Perhaps the most dramatic and consequently the
most valuable, are the errors of colour—stamps printed in the
wrong colour, due to the inadvertent substitution of a cliché
of one denomination in a forme of another denomination, or
the accidental printing of a plate with the ink reserved for
another. The Cape of Good Hope 'Woodblock' errors fall into
the first category and the Spain 2 reales 'blue instead of red'
of 1851 comes in the second. The 'Woodblock' errors are now
worth £1,400 to £2,000 used, while the 2 reales blue catalogues
at £7,500.

Stamps printed at two or more operations give rise to freaks with inverted centres or overprints. This is caused by the accidental reverse of a sheet on which part of the design has been printed, as it is being passed through the press for the second stage of the printing.

The best known examples of this are the 4 annas 'indigo and red' of India (1854), the U.S. 15, 24 and 30 cents of 1869 and the 24 cents 'biplane' of 1918, and, in more recent times, the Canada 5 cents St. Lawrence Seaway issue of 1959. All of these are immense rarities which command high prices, yet they began in the normal, humble way by being sold over the post office counter at face value.

Stamps with inverted overprint are also regarded very highly by collectors, but here a word of warning is advisable. The high prices which errors of printing fetch have often tempted the forger to turn out a few more. While it is difficult to forge or fake an inverted centre it is a relatively simple matter to forge an overprint, whether as a normal or as inverted or double aberrations. Many experts are chary about giving guarantees to stamps where the overprint makes the item valuable.

Missing colours are a favourite form of error, to which modern photogravure stamps seem to be particularly prone. A fold or crease in the reel of paper as it goes through the multicolour presses, the presence of extraneous matter such as a scrap of paper or just the omission of one or more stages in the printing process, can result in a colour being partially or wholly omitted.

This can give rise to some spectacular varieties, such as the British 4d. Churchill Commemoratives with the Queen's portrait missing. Only two examples, from different sources, have been discovered and they have recently changed hands for almost £900 each. A sheet of stamps issued in 1962 by the Canal Zone to mark the inauguration of the Thatcher's Ferry Bridge was subsequently found with the silver metallic ink missing, resulting in the omission of the bridge itself from the design. This stamp is now worth several hundreds of dollars. When the omission of a colour is not so significant, as in the Battle of Hastings 4d. stamps printed in nine colours, the price which such items fetch is appreciably less, since these errors are not so impressive to the beholder.

Quite often, although all the colours are present, their registration is poor and, depending on the degree of the colour shift caused, so is the variation in value of such curiosities. Unless the shift is particularly marked these 'errors' should not be considered. In the Churchill omnibus series a sheet of ½c. stamps of Antigua was discovered showing the gold colour laterally displaced by about half an inch. This meant that on thirty stamps the position of the country name and the denomination were reversed, ten stamps (from the left-hand vertical row) had the denomination entirely omitted and, conversely, the value inscriptions had jumped out on to the right-hand marginal paper. These errors caused by an outstanding colour shift fetched very high prices and will continue to go up. A similar shift on the 1 rupee stamp issued by Dubai in 1964 in memory of President Kennedy resulted in the reversal of the position of the two medallions, one containing the President's portrait and the other showing the emblem of the United States.

In the main, however, colour shifts of a millimetre or two have curiosity value only and are not worth the fancy prices which dealers ask for them. Though some dealers will ask outrageous sums for shifts which they have discovered in their own supplies, they are invariably most reluctant to purchase similar varieties when offered to them by collectors or the general public who happen to purchase them in the normal way at their post office.

Flaws occasionally occur in printing stamps and where these are constant on one position in the sheet they are usually worth a premium. In the 1966 British 3d. Christmas Stamp (number 2 in row 6, on sheets printed from cylinders 1A3B1C1D1E no dot) the initial T of 'T. Shemza' is missing from the imprint. As this only occurs on one stamp out of the 160 positions for the two panes of stamps it is obviously that much rarer than the normal, but as millions of 3d. Christmas Stamps were sold it is not a scarce variety and is unlikely to go much higher (for some years at any rate) than the £1 which is its current market value.

In photogravure printing minor flaws can be caused by specks of grit adhering to the cylinder, creating a coloured or albino spot on the stamp. Some of these flaws are constan during an entire printing of a cylinder—such as the 'colon' variety in the British 1937 Coronation Stamp, or the 'butterfly' flaw on early samples of the British 1½d. stamp of 1952–4. Others, however, are quite ephemeral and although some of them are quite spectacular they have little permanent philatelic interest or value. The study of such minutiae is largely pointless and the 'fly-speck philately' which was fashionable ten or fifteen years ago seems to have passed its peak of popularity, mainly because its adherents have become disillusioned at the racket whereby dealers specialising in such material tend to sell it in large 'positional' blocks.

Another type of error is imperforation, where the stamps are normally issued in perforated condition. Stamps may be found imperforate either horizontally or vertically or completely devoid of perforation. In all cases it is not sufficient to have a single copy—a pair showing no perforation *between* them is the minimum required to establish that the perforations have not merely been trimmed off with scissors.

Considering the exceptionally high degree of care taken at the stamp printers it is surprising that imperforate stamps should get on the market, but they do occasionally. The most sensational case of this in the United Kingdom in recent years concerned an entire sheet of 2d. stamps which was discovered by a counter clerk in the head post office at Dartford in Kent. The usual procedure if freaks of this nature are found is to report the matter to the postmaster, but the young lady in this case bought the sheet herself and subsequently disposed of it to a dealer who shortly afterwards marketed the stamps at £50 each. In view of the irregularity surrounding the so-called 'Dartford Twopenny', *Gibbons Catalogue* refuses to list it, though it is referred to in a footnote; but the *Commonwealth* and *Woodstock Catalogues* both list it, priced respectively at £110 (for a pair) and £110 (for a block of four!).

The likeliest sources of part-perforated or imperforate stamps are stamp booklets. The collating of the uncut sheets which form the booklets is one of the few jobs still done by hand and the printers would not be human if occasional slips did not occur. Nevertheless it says much for the system of checks and controls that, out of countless millions of booklets produced each year, only one or two will be found with an error of perforation.

I always buy stamps in books, not only because this is the most convenient form in which to carry them around, but in a spirit of eternal optimism that sooner or later I am going to be the lucky one who finds an imperforate pane. They occasionally turn up, and find a ready sale for hundreds of pounds. For some inexplicable reason the newspapers always highlight a discovery of this sort and publicise the large sum fetched at auction. This unfortunately gives rise to a very common fallacy among non-philatelists that single stamps with straight edges are imperforate. This is merely the result of faulty trimming and nothing more. Before stamps may be considered as truly imperforate they must be in a pair, or a block of four, with no holes between adjoining stamps.

I have mentioned earlier in this chapter that faulty trimming of stamps in slot machines results in clipped perforations also. This should not be confused with stamps of certain countries which are produced in coils for automatic vending machines and which are genuinely imperforate on either horizontal or vertical sides. This is true of the United States and Canada and these stamps are collectable items, catalogued separately and usually worth more than their contemporaries printed in sheet form. Ireland experimented with coil-stamps imperforate vertically. The 2d. stamp of 1922–35 perforated on all four sides is catalogued at 6d. mint and 3d. used, whereas imperforate vertically it rates £90 mint and £35 used. Sweden is a country the majority of whose stamps, since 1920, have been produced in booklet or coil form and are imperforate on one or more sides.

Errors of watermark have always been found in those stamps which bear this security device in their paper. These are not so popular with collectors since they are not so obvious as imperforation or misplaced colours, but on the other hand they offer more scope to the knowledgeable philatelist who can spot, among otherwise cheap stamps, a major rarity worth a great deal of money. Some of the best known (and most highly priced) watermark errors are the Great Britain 3d., 6d., 9d. and 1s. of 1865–7 with the Emblems watermark. In the normal stamp the watermark consists of four tiny floral emblems, a shamrock for Ireland, a thistle for Scotland and two roses for England and Wales. A few stamps, however, show an incorrect watermark consisting of three roses and a shamrock, and these are nowadays worth up to several hundred pounds to the lucky finder. The normal 6d. catalogues at 35s. in used condition and is not an uncommon stamp, so there is always a chance that you may be fortunate in turning up the error worth £65.

In more recent times quite a furore was created when it was discovered that a defective bit in the dandy-roll, on which the paper used for Crown Agents' stamps were printed, had been replaced by a crown and monogram device of an obsolete type. Stamps containing the error may be worth anything up to £150.

Apart from substitution errors, watermarks may occasionally be found upside down in relation to the design of the stamp. In the old days when stamps were often hand-printed and the sheets were likely to be fed into the press either way up, inversion of the watermark was not uncommon. The catalogues seldom list these earlier varieties, though to a specialist they are of interest and therefore command a premium. Modern stamps issued in booklets are originally printed in large sheets, usually of 284 subjects, grouped in panes of six or four, and these panes are printed upside down in relation to each other. Thus 50% of booklet stamps in the United Kingdom have their watermarks inverted. *Gibbons* ignores these variations, but both the *Commonwealth* and *Woodstock* catalogues list them.

In a different category altogether are the modern stamps with inverted watermark where this has happened by accident. They first came into prominence in 1964 when a few examples of the Shakespeare Commemoratives of Antigua, Dominica, Gambia and Bahamas were found to have inverted watermarks. There being a boom at that time in Shakespeare stamps, the inverted watermark errors found ready buyers at prices ranging from £5 to £30. Simultaneously a few of the British 1s. 3d. and 2s. 6d. Shakespeares were also found in this condition and they likewise fetched £30 to £50. Bowing to popular demand Stanley Gibbons decided to list these watermark errors in their *Elizabethan Catalogue* and subsequent cases have dutifully been recorded. The *Commonwealth Catalogue* had listed this type of error previously.

The listing of these errors stimulated new interest and it is hardly surprising therefore that inverted watermark varieties have begun to turn up regularly every time Britain has a new commemorative series. Late in 1962, while supplies of paper were being gummed and coated for use in the production of the National Productivity Year series, edge cracks were found in the paper and it was feared that these would cause actual breaks during the gumming process. The paper was therefore trimmed, which necessitated re-winding, prior to gumming. This resulted in the reels being wound in the reverse direction to normal and thus the stamps came to be printed with the watermark inverted. This was the case with the 2½d. and the 3d. denominations, though the 1s. 3d. had the watermark in the normal position. Subsequently, the Freedom from Hunger and Paris Postal Conference Centenary Stamps were also printed on inverted watermarks and are not recorded with upright watermarks. People tend to forget that this apparent error was normal for these stamps and it is a well-substantiated fact that one London dealer actually purchased for a very large sum an entire sheet of Freedom from Hunger 2½d. Stamps, fondly believing that he had secured a major rarit!y

Whether the present boom in watermark errors will be maintained remains to be seen. They are difficult to spot or demonstrate to one's fellow-philatelists (without a watermark detector) and stamp collectors are notoriously fickle about anything not immediately obvious.

Indeed, summing up the investment potential of errors, they are not so good as the normal stamps in the long run. Unless you are fortunate enough to find the error for yourself you must expect to buy dear. When it comes to selling them a few years later one finds that the profit made on the transaction is a slim one—for the demand is at its greatest for errors when they are topical and in the news. Too many of today's errors are of ephemeral interest and even those which succeed in getting into the catalogues have a nasty habit of remaining stationary for many years.

Normal stamps, bought on the open market at new issue rates (see Chapter IV) show a better percentage increase than most of the errors. 'Philatelia', the market columnist of *Philatelic Magazine*, writing on 20th January 1967 stated: '. . . and everybody is rushing after the bright new errors of Queen Elizabeth II. Here you can spend some really big money. What about misplaced graphite lines?* Look at the 1957 G.B. 2d. (S.G. 564) with "Line at left". What did it rate in *Gibbons* 1961? What does it rate today? £75. What about the normal graphite-lined 2½d. of the same set (S.G. 565)? Then—6d.; today—1s. 6d. That's 200% profit using the Catalogue as a standard.'

It is easy to be wise after the event, but the same conclusions could be drawn from a comparison of other relatively minor errors with 'good' normals in the same series. Apart from the really spectacular items such as the genuine imperforates and inverted centres, errors are not such sure-fire material as might appear at first. Admittedly the dealers do a roaring trade in them, acting as they do as the middleman between the lucky finder and the eager buyer who just *has* to have the unusual in his collection, to give it the edge over that of the other fellow.

---

* Vertical lines printed on the back of low value British stamps in 1957. These graphite lines were used in connection with automatic letter-sorting equipment introduced at Southampton and were subsequently replaced by the phosphor bands overprinted on the stamps in use in those areas where automatic equipment is now employed.

CHAPTER III

WHAT TO COLLECT

THE PHILATELIST who has grown up with the hobby usually started off as a schoolboy with a general whole-world collection, comprising stamps culled from family correspondence and the business mail of fathers, uncles and neighbours, mixed packets sold in stationers and multiple stores being the only outside source of material. Gradually, as the collection grows, the philatelist tends to concentrate on the stamps of one country or a group of countries, disposing of the remainder to provide the cash needed to build up the selected portion. This is a gradual process, evolving over many years in some cases, and all the time the collector is learning more and more about less and less—the true test of the expert!

In recent years, however, many people have come to the hobby in maturity and, unlike their juvenile counterparts, waste little time in getting down to the serious business of collecting the stamps of a limited field rather than roaming aimlessly over the entire range. Gone are the days of Tapling, Ferrary and Manus who were able to put together reasonably complete collections of the stamps of the world. With the dispersal of the fabulous accumulations of the millionaires, Caspary and Burrus, at auction (the former netted over $2,750,000 in 1958 while the latter has realised over £2,000,000), the last of the great general collections have disappeared.

At whatever level one collects and regardless of the money available for stamp purchases, it is universally acknowledged that the secret of successful collecting lies nowadays in concentration on a specific group, or country or period of issue of one country, or even on one particular series. One of the most

48

PLATE III

BRITISH COMMONWEALTH RARITIES.

(1) Kenya £75, 1925 (£8,500), (2) Johore $500, 1926 (£2,750, $6,000), (3) Kenya £100, 1925 (£10,000), (4) Straits Settlements $500, 1915 (£2,500, $4,500), (5) Sierra Leone £5, 1921 (£300, $425), (6) Ceylon 1,000Rs., 1925 (£3,500, $3,000), (8) Malta 10s., 1919 (£200, $375), (7, 9–11) examples from the long commemorative sets of 1923–34.

valuable collections in Britain today consists of a study of *one stamp*, the 10 kopecks issue of Poland, 1860, formed by M. A. Bojanowicz. Mr. Bojanowicz has made a thorough study of this stamp, the various shades of the different printings, the postmarks found on it, the flaws and varieties and the reconstruction of the sheet lay-out. This stamp is not common, but neither is it unduly scarce since a fair proportion of the 3 million produced have survived. Nevertheless it is currently priced in *Gibbons* at £60 and in *Scott* at $150. On sheer numbers alone Mr. Bojanowicz's collection is worth a great deal, since it contains over 2,000 of these stamps, but many of them command a considerable premium because of some flaw or rare postmark or because they are still attached to the entire cover. Although it might appear that the absorption of so many specimens of one stamp into a single collection may have forced up the retail market price, this is not so since there are still a very large number of 'Poland Number One' (as it is popularly known) in circulation and Mr. Bojanowicz need not fear that the market would be depressed were he to sell his collection—such is the great demand for this stamp, not only in America but, to an increasing extent, in Poland itself and even Russia.

One need not take specialisation to this extreme, but it is still advisable to concentrate on a limited field. Only by getting to know everything possible about his pet subject can the philatelist succeed. Knowledge enables the expert to profit at the expense of the not as well-informed and obviously, unless they themselves handle only one class of material, dealers can never hope to know as much as the specialist-collector. It is sometimes said jocularly that dealers make a profit out of *collectors* to recoup their losses from *philatelists*. I do not wish to get involved in the age-old argument concerning the point at which a collector graduates into a philatelist, but this maxim illustrates one of the chief differences between the two categories.

What one eventually decides to concentrate on depends to a very large extent on the source of supply. If the collector has unlimited funds at his disposal this need not concern him, but there is not the same zest and enjoyment to be had out of 'cheque-book philately' as in acquiring stamps at minimum cost and selling at a good profit. There are several methods of getting stamps; these methods and their various merits are discussed in this and the following chapter.

DIRECT CONTACT

Obviously the closer one can get to the original source of supply the more economical collecting becomes. If one could eliminate all the middlemen—agents, dealers and auctioneers— the ideal situation would be reached. Thus direct contact is an attractive method. The reason why stamps are at their most popular in the country of origin is because collectors can get their new issues at least at face value merely by walking into the nearest post office and buying them over the counter. Fine commercially used specimens can be picked up from day-to-day correspondence, and there then is the nucleus of the collection. Older stamps may come to light through 'finds' of old accumulations and files of correspondence in lawyers' offices, etc. In this way, for example, the salvage drives of the Second World War liberated far more good material than was destroyed by enemy action.

Sometimes, however, one finds that one cannot get certain stamps in the local post office. In the United Kingdom one may live in an area where phosphor-lined stamps are used and therefore the non-phosphor variety is unobtainable, or *vice versa*. Perhaps the collector requires the various regional stamps (used in Scotland, Wales, Northern Ireland, the Channel Islands and the Isle of Man) or Postage Due labels or experimental booklets in order to complete the collection. These can all be obtained from the Philatelic Bureau, G.P.O., Edinburgh 1. Details of the service and an order form are included in each issue of the G.P.O.'s *Philatelic Bulletin* which is published monthly.

In the United States similar facilities are operated by the Philatelic Section of the Post Office Department, Washington, D.C., 20260; these are useful for obtaining cylinders of sheets not obtainable at local offices, such items as the $1\frac{1}{4}$ cent stamp in uncancelled condition, coils, booklets, stationery and an extensive repertoire of commemorative issues no longer on general sale.

Many countries operate a Philatelic Bureau on these lines, servicing first-day covers and supply stamps at face value plus a small handling charge. The position has improved greatly in the past thirty years,* from the time when the primary object of a post office was to handle mail and stamps were meant solely for the prepayment of postage. Philatelists were regarded by the authorities as a nuisance and philatelic sales revenue was ignored. Nowadays it is universally realised that the income from sales to collectors can be a considerable asset.

One used to pour scorn on the handful of countries which derived no little part of the national revenue from philatelic sales, but even the British Post Office is wide awake now to the possibilities. An enquiry to the Ministry of Posts in the country concerned will elicit the necessary information about philatelic sales. Most postal administrations are only too glad to furnish details of their philatelic services, together with brochures, order forms and advice on how to make the necessary remittances. I only know of one postal administration at the present time which apparently will not entertain philatelic orders and that is the Post Office in Manama, a dependency of the Arab sheikhdom of Ajman (which itself is surprisingly up to date on the best ways of 'raising the wind' philatelically). The reasons for Manama's extraordinary reluctance are, for the moment, obscure; no doubt in the fullness of time we will learn the motive behind it.

A growing number of postal administrations operate philatelic counters at the larger post offices, thus enabling collectors to get what they want without hindering other customers intent only on receiving their old-age pensions or family allowances. Philatelic counter clerks are usually well versed in the requirements of collectors and show a patience and good humour which is all too frequently absent at ordinary post office grilles. The European countries, particularly Germany, East and West, have developed the philatelic counter system to a high degree. In the United Kingdom it is, as yet, confined to the London

---

* See 'The Post Office and its Relation to the Philatelist', by Ernest F. Hugen, in the Philatelic Congress of Great Britain *Year Book*, 1937, for details of the services then operated throughout the world.

Chief Office in St. Martin's-le-Grand and, of course, at the Philatelic Bureau itself.

As well as dealing directly with the Philatelic Bureau of one's chosen country, one can acquire stamps by exchange with a fellow-collector resident in the country. Contact with a philatelist who is actually on the spot can be extremely rewarding, for through him one can get hold of used stamps, first-day covers, special postmarks and other out of the way items which are not as a rule available through the postal authorities. As payment is usually arranged in kind, the costs are trimmed even further since one is relieved of the bother of money orders, international reply coupons and a lot of red tape and form-filling.

There are a number of ways of contacting collectors in the country of one's choice. That extremely useful book, the *Stamp Collector's Annual* (Harris Publications, London), unfortunately now ceased publication, printed a directory of the main philatelic societies all over the world and the names and addresses of their secretaries. A letter to one of them asking for a correspondent interested in exchanging stamps invariably has the desired result. If the country concerned boasts a philatelic magazine, a letter to the editor will also have the effect of producing a great number of replies—usually far more than one can cope with.

Business connections with extensive trade and commercial intercourse with overseas countries can be a lucrative source of used stamps acquired at minimal effort or cost. This is not quite so good as a philatelist contact abroad, since the tendency is to get loads of stamps of a few denominations (quite often the very high values, prepaying airmail postage and registration) but seldom the others which are intended mainly for internal postal rates. If this source is combined with a contact in the country, however, the result can be mutually rewarding, since the other fellow can usually lay his hands on plenty of the ordinary material, but lacks the denominations used on mail going out of the country.

There is a tremendous demand by stamp dealers for high-grade office accumulations from banks and trading concerns

and many an office-boy has been known to supplement his
wages very handsomely by popping round to the nearest stamp
shop regularly with the latest salvage from the firm's waste-
paper basket.

EXCHANGE PACKETS

Contact with other collectors, not only abroad but in one's
own country, can be a very lucrative means of acquiring stamps.
Most towns of any size have their own philatelic society or
stamp club and details of their meetings are frequently reported
in the philatelic press. The British Philatelic Association's handbook lists all the affiliated societies in the United Kingdom,
together with such useful details as subscription rates and the
name and address of the club secretary in each case. Swapping
surplus material with fellow club-members is a useful way of
building up a collection.

Most philatelic societies operate an Exchange Packet scheme.
If you have duplicate stamps which you wish to convert into
cash you mount them in club booklets (usually octavo-sized
booklets of eight or twelve pages), put the price and, if possible,
the catalogue number above each one, insert your name and
the total value of the contents on the cover, and send the
material along to the Exchange Packet Secretary of the club.
He adds your booklets to a box which may contain as many
as thirty and then sends it on its rounds. Each club has one or
more circuits, with perhaps twenty members on each, gradually
working up to the top of the list. Provided your stamps are not
common rubbish that everyone has already or does not want
and your prices are not too high, you should be able to shift
a fair quantity of your surplus stamps in this way. I know of
several part-time dealers whose sole trade is conducted through
the medium of Exchange Packets. There always seems to be
a dearth of good packet material and Packet Secretaries welcome the booklets of the 'semi-professionals' with open arms.
I know of a schoolmaster and his son who have a flourishing
sideline in supplying various clubs with booklets and they
reckon that they have over £5,000 worth of stamps in circulation at any one time.

Selling stamps in this way, apart from a small commission deducted by the Packet Secretary, the proceeds are all yours. Conversely, it is a cheaper way of buying stamps, as a rule, than purchasing them from a dealer. If you belong to a specialist society or study circle, where all the members have common interests, you stand a much better chance of finding the out-of-the-way material.

Apart from the Exchange Packets organised by clubs there are several similar schemes run on a full-time professional basis. One of the biggest and best-known of these is the Robson Lowe subsidiary, Associated Exchange Clubs, whose office is located in Bournemouth. Although buying membership is restricted to the United Kingdom, clients abroad may submit their duplicate or surplus items and have them individually priced.

Exchange clubs of this kind circulate thousands of pounds worth of stamps to their members every month thus enabling them to select the items they want in the comfort and leisure of their own homes.

The rules of these clubs and the more humble stamp club Exchange Packet are simple. At regular intervals the collector receives a box containing a number of booklets, a list of the contents, a list of the names and addresses of the members on the circuit and a supply of forms. Before proceeding any further the inventory should be checked against the booklets to ensure that they have all been forwarded. Before you actually remove any stamps from the books go through them carefully, checking that where stamps have previously been removed there are signatures of the members who have taken them. Should any blank space be unsigned you must report the fact to the Packet Secretary immediately. When you remove the stamps you want, sign your name *legibly* in the spaces and enter the relevant details in the appropriate columns on the cover of the booklet. These are invariably:

No. of Stamps taken	Total Value	Member's Name

The same details have to be given on one of the forms supplied with the packet. Here the number of each booklet, the quantity of stamps and their value have to be filled in, with the total number and value. Cheques or postal orders for the total amount are forwarded with this form to the Packet Secretary, together with a certificate of posting, then the packet is sent on to the next member on the list.

Members are usually expected to keep the packets for two days only before passing them on. Where the Exchange Packet is run by a philatelic society whose members all live in the same locality it is usually possible to pass on the packet by hand— in which case the signature of the recipient on the account form serves instead of a certificate of posting. If there are thirty members on a circuit it can be seen that, with unavoidable delays in the post, anything up to four months can elapse between the first and the last members handling it. This means a delay at least as long for the member whose material is being circulated before he receives that welcome cheque in payment. This is the major drawback of the system, but like everything else, it often pays more to sell slowly. If you have to raise the cash in a hurry, dealers will oblige (providing the material is what they want) but the net gain will be substantially less.

MIXTURES

Considering the enormous quantities of stamps used on mail every day in the United States, Britain and the major countries of Western Europe, a surprisingly small percentage ever manage to be preserved in collections. If you have a lot of correspondence, but most of it originates in your own or some other country, there comes a time pretty soon when you have salvaged all the specimens you or anyone else could possibly want. Thereafter the bulk of stamps goes straight into the waste-paper basket; it just is not worth your time or trouble to tear them off. Or so you think.

It may seem surprising, but there is seldom, if ever, enough of a good thing in the philatelic world. There are many dealers all over the globe who do big business by importing and exporting wholesale accumulations and mixtures sold by weight. In Britain there are dealers who will pay 5s. for a pound weight of common stamps clipped off mail. The piles have to be

reasonably small, but not so small that the postmarks (particularly hand-stamps) are cut into. With the great upsurge in
the past two years in the use of commemorative stamps the
quality and variety of the average pound of British stamps has
gone up—and so has the price offered. If you get into the
regular habit of clipping the stamps off mail almost as soon as
you open the envelope and put them in a drawer or box set
aside for the purpose, it is surprising how quickly a pound
mounts up.

Other dealers will pay quite good sums for stamps which
have been removed from their backing paper, sorted and graded
into countries, issues and denominations. These stamps can
then be sold at so much per hundred. These stamps find their
way eventually into the 'juvenile packets' which are made up
by the thousand for sale in department stores and stationers'
shops.

Even large accumulations of stamps haphazardly put together
can bring in a surprising amount of money. One lifelong
collector of my acquaintance was an inveterate hoarder of
used stamps which he clipped from his firm's correspondence,
but he never troubled to dispose of them. After his death at
the age of eighty no less than fourteen suitcases and eight large
sacks were found to be crammed full. This huge accumulation
fetched several hundred pounds when it was sent to auction.
Another case which springs to mind concerns the late Mr.
W. G. Peterkin who managed to accumulate 15 million German
Inflation provisional stamps which were sold in 1949 at
Harmer's in New York, where they fetched $2,300, possibly
the biggest 'junk lot' in philatelic history.

What happens to large accumulations of this sort? Many
collectors, with hope springing eternally of turning up a rarity
among the other fellow's unconsidered trifles, pay quite large
sums at auction for these mixtures. And although this may seem
surprising, I have never known anyone to be dissatisfied with
these lots. It depends very much on the philatelic knowledge
of the purchaser just how much he profits from his bargain.
Friends of mine have unearthed some very choice stamps in
'junk lots'. One collector discovered three used examples of the

scarce Indian Red 3c. of Canada (priced by *Gibbons* at £8 and by *Scott* at $3) in a small accumulation of Canada 'Small Cents'—not to mention many useful paper, perforation and postmark varieties which amply repaid his initial outlay of £2.

It used to be quite a common practice for newspapers, clubs, etc., to organise stamp-collecting competitions in aid of charity, the prize winners being those who could accumulate the largest quantity of material. The stamps would then be disposed of to the stamp trade and the resulting sum raised for the good cause sponsored by the promoters. From time to time charity accumulations of this type are still offered at so much the pound weight and surprisingly good they are too—providing a rich source of material for the specialist and the postmark enthusiast.

Some dealers specialise in handling wholesale accumulations and junk lots. Perhaps the best-known is Anthony Annetts of Sandford St. Martin, near Oxford, whose intriguing advertisements appear regularly in the British philatelic magazines. Many of his customers come back time and again, proof that they are satisfied with the quality of his 'mixtures', as they are termed in the trade.

Obviously the value of a mixture to the hopeful collector lies in the degree to which it is unsorted. You frequently find this sadly-overworked adjective in dealers' descriptions of junk lots and mixtures, but you can seldom, if ever, guarantee that yours are the first eyes to scrutinise it for the gems. Just as the old-time confidence tricksters in the goldfields 'salted' the odd nugget or two to give the impression of latent riches in the soil, some stamp dealers have been known to attract sales by planting a few better stamps in otherwise mediocre accumulations.

Such is the cynicism with which many collectors of long standing now greet these advertisements, both good and bad, that dealers have had to devise other methods of making their offers more tempting. The following quotation from an advertisement which appears regularly in British periodicals proves that you just cannot lose!

'When you order your Mixture (including much fine material of all periods both on and off paper) simply remove the stamps

cancelled condition. These bags are ideal for the postmark collector and the advanced philatelist who requires large quantities of certain stamps for research purposes. There has been an unfortunate tendency in recent years, however, for postal authorities to grade this material and keep the top quality for home consumption, letting the inferior stuff go for export. I have had no personal complaint on this score though others claim this to be the case. The last lot of kiloware which I sampled emanated from Iceland and yielded not only a good variety of recent commemorative issues, but also a large number of different postmarks from all over the island, few of these being seen in normal circumstances.

The biggest bonanza in post-war kiloware was undoubtedly the bags released in the early 1950s by the German Bundespost and containing the 1948 Buildings series. This turned out to be an exceptionally rich series for varieties of printing, colour and perforation and volumes have already been written on the subject (with, no doubt, many more to come). The vast majority of the studies carried out on the Buildings issues would not have been possible but for these kiloware bags. About 1955 I acquired the remainder of one of these bags after a German philatelist had taken out what he wanted. Not only did I get endless fun out of it, but I was able eventually to sell my research collection based on it for a very good figure. Kiloware bags of the Buildings series are things of the past, regrettably; if any came to light today, they would be likened to gold dust in the price they would fetch.

CHAPTER IV

DEALERS AND AUCTIONEERS

PHILATELIC BUREAUX

PHILATELIC BUREAUX are very useful if you intend spending a lot of money with them and buy stamps by the sheet or in large multiples. If, on the other hand, you only want a straight set of singles and the occasional first-day cover, the handling charges plus the form-filling make this method of acquisition rather expensive and tedious. This is where the stamp dealers play an important part. The larger ones deal directly with the Philatelic Bureaux or have a reciprocal arrangement with many dealers overseas; many of the lesser dealers get their supplies from the big wholesale importers, paying a smaller percentage for this, but helping the large dealers to increase their turnover—and it is turnover which is the significant factor in stamp dealing. A few Philatelic Bureaux will not fulfil orders below a certain quantity and thus, of necessity, the collector can only get his requirements via a stamp dealer.

The bulk of stamp dealing nowadays lies in new issues and nearly every dealer operates a New Issue service for his customers. The value of this is twofold; it ensures for the dealer a steady clientele enabling him to trade with greater freedom and confidence and conversely the New Issue customer can rest assured that in 99 cases out of 100 his dealer will not fail to come up with even the most *recherché* items. The value of subscribing to such a service has been amply demonstrated in the past few years when many British colonial territories suddenly began to change the watermark on their definitive issues and, as these were unheralded and in some cases had a very short life, the only way in which one could be sure of getting everything was to be on the books of a reliable dealer.

Collectors have been known to profit considerably by such a service. In 1961, when southern Africa adopted decimal currency, the three High Commission territories of Basutoland (now Lesotho), Bechuanaland (now Botswana) and Swaziland surcharged their sterling stamps in South African cents and rands. Two collectors of my acquaintance received in their New Issue packets the Bechuanaland 10s. surcharged 1 rand with the first type of overprint. At New Issue rates this cost them 11s. 6d. each, but within a few weeks it was realised that several types of surcharge existed and that the Bechuanaland 1r. on 10s., type I, was the scarcest of them all. As the dust of the initial dealing in the decimal surcharges settled, the prices hardened and this particular stamp rose rapidly. Now it is catalogued at £110 mint and £75 used by *Gibbons* and at $275 mint or used by *Scott*.

When a collector joins a New Issue service he agrees to take all the stamps within a certain group, e.g. every stamp of the British Commonwealth up to the shilling or equivalent denomination, or right up to the highest face-value, or only the stamps of the West Indies, but in blocks of four from every printing, and so on. The dealer can then order supplies from his wholesaler or the Philatelic Bureaux accordingly. The collector pays the face-value of the stamps plus a percentage. This used to be only 10%, but gradually it crept up to 12½% and is now fairly standard at 15%. I personally fail to see why an increase in the percentage is necessary since even the most modest collector has to spend a great deal more nowadays in order to keep up with the spate of new issues and dealers freely admit that the volume of trade (and consequently their turnover) is larger than ever.

On the other hand the collector benefits greatly from a good New Issue service, since his dealer is morally bound to supply him at 'face plus fifteen per cent' even when it is obvious to the dealer that a particular stamp is particularly good property. Thus collectors were able to get Gibraltar's 'Our Lady of Europa' 2s. stamp for 2s. 6d. at most, even though non-subscribers had to pay 10s. ($1.50) as the starting price, and even more if they delayed a week. Dealers cannot be collectors, or more precisely, hoarders. In this particular case the dealers' orders placed with the Crown Agents were slashed by as much as 75%, leaving them precious little after their New Issue subscribers were catered for. The moral here is definitely 'get in with a good New Issue service and don't be left out in the cold'.

Sometimes, one would never realise it, stamp dealers also handle older material. Nowadays with so many lucrative new issues to contend with, many dealers tend to neglect the 'antiquarian' side of the business—and to them anything issued earlier than two years ago is an antique, and usually out of stock unless it comes from a particularly popular country. Outside of New Issue trading most dealers prefer to specialise in a particular area or group of older issues. Nevertheless it is frustrating to find just how often one is unable to purchase obsolete stamps to fill the gaps in one's collection. There are thousands of stamps priced at pennies which one could spend ages in trying to track down. Sometimes the only way to acquire them is to buy intact collections and carry on from there.

While all dealers nowadays tend to restrict their interests in obsolete issues to a few countries only, there are a number of dealers who might be termed as specialists in the true philatelic sense. A perusal of the advertisement columns of the stamp magazines or an examination of the trade directories published by the Philatelic Traders' Society or the American Stamp Dealers Association will reveal the specialists and their particular fields. For random example, the Westminster Stamp Co. of London deals only in the stamps of the United States and Associated terrirories; Lava of New York only handles aerogrammes and air letter sheets; Angus Parker of London is the leading British dealer for proofs, specimens and postal history items; and Francis J. Field of Sutton Coldfield, England, is Europe's top aerophilatelic dealer.

Other dealers, while not so well known either because they do not have a shop on Nassau Street or the Strand or because they do not advertise extensively in the popular periodicals, have built up a lucrative business in catering to the wealthier collector. This select group of dealers do not merely buy and sell stamps but are often more in the nature of philatelic counsellors and have a genuine interest in building up a collection for a client. The wealthy collectors who make use of their services are often scorned by their less fortunate brethren as 'cheque-book philatelists', using their money not only to buy stamps but also to acquire the very considerable know-how of the specialist dealer. Many of the Gold Medal collections in existence today owe their existence to these professionals who seldom get the recognition which is their due. Not for them the coveted letters F.R.P.S.L. after their names, for the Royal Philatelic Society continues to bar from membership, let alone Fellowship, philatelists 'who engage in trade', and only rarely does one achieve the supreme accolade of being invited to sign the Roll of Distinguished Philatelists. In Europe and in America the professional philatelist is recognised and respected; but the not so subtle distinction between 'gentlemen' and 'players' is still maintained in Britain.

The dealer in this category acts rather in the capacity of a philatelic broker or consultant, often working on a commission basis, purchasing choice material on behalf of clients at auctions. As the great majority of better-class items never appear in dealers' stock-books but pass briefly through an auction room, flitting as it were from one collection to another, the collector has to be on his toes all the time or else the opportunity of acquiring a fine piece will be lost for another ten or twenty years. It is well worth the specialist-dealer's fee to leave this matter in his hands. It is his task to comb patiently through the auction catalogues, to examine likely lots with care, to place bids with his agents in New York, London, Paris, Basle, Hamburg or the other leading auction centres, or to bid at auction himself on his client's behalf. Several of these dealers not only purchase stamps for their customers but advise them on arrangement and mounting in albums and will even undertake to have the collections professionally written up by an expert calligrapher, since presentation, as well as rarity, scores the points in international exhibitions.

If and when the time comes to sell the collection, the

PLATE IV

ELIZABETHAN RARITIES.

(1–3) three of the four stamps released by St. Helena in 1961 for the Tristan Relief fund; only 434 sets exist (£800), (4) Papua 1s. 7d., 1958 (£6, $7), (5) Norfolk Island 2s. 8d., 1960 (£7 10s., $1.75). Stamps tipped in 1967: (6) Gibraltar, Our Lady of Europa, (7) Rhodesia, Churchill 5s., (8) Malta, Catholic Doctors' Congress.

specialist-dealer will advise on the most advantageous method or place of disposal. He will also carry out valuations for insurance and probate and give advice generally on the legal and tax problems which sometimes beset the philatelist in the surtax bracket.

The stock-in-trade of all dealers, general and specialist alike, is usually priced according to the catalogue in use in that particular country. Thus *Scott* numbering and pricing prevails in the United States and Canada, while *Gibbons* is the standard in the United Kingdom. Frequently one can buy stamps at a discount off the catalogue price, if a dealer has less overheads than Gibbons or has made a particularly advantageous purchase and feels like passing on some of the bargain to his customers. One should be wary, however, if the discount is on the large side. Stamp dealers are not philanthropists and there is invariably a very sound reason for offering stamps well below catalogue listing. Careful examination usually reveals that the stamp is thinned, slightly torn or repaired and the effect of even the most minor damage is to reduce its real value to about a third in most cases. Where a stamp is exceptionally rare in perfect condition the drop in value may be appreciably smaller, but as a general rule a 66% cut is about average. It is more than a dealer's reputation is worth to pass off inferior material as top quality (and therefore commanding top prices).

But nowadays even the second rate is becoming much more acceptable as the demand for classics and the better stamps of other periods grows. In a Harmer's auction in January 1967 an example of the Newfoundland 'Martinsyde' airmail stamp (catalogued by *Gibbons* at £3,500), used on cover, but having a slight tear on the top edge, was estimated to fetch £2,000 but in fact went for £3,000—not far short of the full catalogue figure. Not so long ago perfect specimens of the Martinsyde stamp could be purchased for £2,500, so there has obviously been an enormous jump in the 'blue-chips' of philately. At one time damaged stamps would never have been given album space by philatelists, let alone recommended as a good investment. Standards seem to be changing, however, and I know of several collectors who have quietly been buying up 'seconds' of rare and valuable stamps which are becoming increasingly desirable as the next best thing when perfect specimens are unobtainable. It could therefore be postulated that this is a form of shrewd investment. But, a word of caution, you have to know your stamps well and particularly the relationship of condition to value in each case.

AUCTIONS

The most important source of material these days is the philatelic auction. At one time stamp sales were conducted by the established fine arts auctioneers such as Sothebys, Christies and Puttick & Simpson; nowadays only the last-named hold regular stamp auctions and these are very much subsidiary to the main business of selling books, pictures, antiques and *objets d'art*. The first exclusively philatelic sale was held as long ago as 1865 in Paris when the entire stock of the deceased dealer, J. W. Elb, was auctioned for the modest total of 800 francs. Nowadays London is the centre of the stamp auction business, with sales by the Big Three (Harmers, Stanley Gibbons and Robson Lowe) topping the £1,000,000 mark annually. Harmer's of London are in association with H. R. Harmer Inc. of 6 West 48th Street, New York, one of the leading auction houses in the United States. Other leading American firms include J. & H. Stolow Inc., Robert Siegel, Irwin Heiman Inc., Max Pool, Stampazine, Hugh C. Barr and Vahan Mozian Inc., all of New York: likewise Robert Lippert of Detroit and Earl Apfelbaum of Philadelphia. The leading auctioneer in Canada is J. N. Sissons of Toronto.

In Europe there are Corinphila, Zurich, and Edgar Mohrmann, Hamburg.

H. R. Harmer Ltd. of London have a subsidiary company in Sydney, Australia, which specialises in the stamps of Australia and the Pacific area, catering to a vigorous home market as is borne out by the £24,500 turnover in 1963–4 (the latest sales figures available at the time of writing).

Robson Lowe Ltd. also operates a branch in Australia, in Melbourne. This firm has made its mark, lately, however, by its extraordinary penetration of the European market. While

British politicians have been dithering over the prospects of joining the Common Market, Robson Lowe has taken the initiative and formed a close working partnership with Jacques Robineau of Paris, Urs Peter Kaufmann of Basle and J. L. Van Dieten of Holland, known as the Uncommon Marketeers. Buying and selling stamps is truly a cosmopolitan business and by forming these European links Robson Lowe and his partners are giving their clients a far better service than ever before.

Thus the fabulous collections of the late Maurice Burrus have been auctioned through Robson Lowe and his Continental associates over the three-year period 1962–4. Most of the Burrus sales were held in London, but the Swiss section were disposed of by Kaufmann in Basle while, more recently, the French section, which had been purchased intact by General Robert Gill, was handled by auctions held by Robineau in Paris and Kaufmann in Basle respectively. In this way the maximum publicity, and consequently selling-power, has been achieved by breaking up the Burrus material in those countries which would naturally attract the most attention and at the same time afford the greatest convenience to the greatest number of bidders. In the same way, the Louise Hoffman Airmail Collection was handled by Harmer's New York and London houses, depending on the popularity of the material in America and Europe respectively.

Apart from the great international auctioneers, there are many smaller ones (at least a score of them in Britain alone) whose aggregate turnover is quite large and who handle a reasonable quantity of first-class material and individual rarities, though perhaps not the greatest gems. Auctions these days can be general or one-country, of postal history or aerophilately, or even entirely of dealers' stocks and wholesale material. The study of postal history (or 'pre-philately' as it is sometimes loosely termed) was largely pioneered in the United Kingdom and this is where most of the postal history sales still take place, with Robson Lowe organising ten or twelve auctions a year exclusively devoted to it.

Buying stamps at auction is not the formidable or complicated operation which many collectors believe. Broadly speaking

there are two methods: either by bidding in person in the sale-
room or by placing a fixed bid by post. It may take several
months for material to come from the vendor and be put up
for auction. In the interim the auctioneer has to split it up into
suitable lots, estimate values, describe it, compile the sales
catalogue, arrange the necessary publicity and finally hold the
auction. Auction catalogues are published several weeks prior
to the sale and circulated to subscribers, giving them sufficient
time to view the lots which interest them beforehand. In most
cases lots can be sent by post to a prospective bidder for viewing
—anything from forty-eight hours to a week is usually allowed
for this—subject to the customer paying postage and insurance
in both directions. Viewing arrangements are also made during
the week or fortnight prior to the sale, and sometimes immediately prior to the sale itself, at the auction rooms. Nowadays the auction catalogues of the bigger firms are beautifully
and lavishly illustrated and the descriptions so very meticulous
and detailed that there is seldom the same necessity there once
was to view the actual material in advance.

Many of these auction catalogues deserve to be regarded
not merely as lists of material for sale but as valuable reference
works. This is particularly true of the bound volumes of
catalogues relating to the sales of the great collections of
Ferrary, Hind, Caspary and Burrus, or the specialised collections of such philatelists as Hennan (Haiti) or Orme (Malta),
which often contain useful notes and information on out-of-the-
way items which seldom appear in the standard reference
works.

An annual subscription to the catalogues of the leading
auctioneers is a reasonable outlay, if one has the time to study
them all carefully and therefore not overlook material of
particular interest. Since many clients do not have the time
to do this, big auctioneers operate a 'Busy Buyers' service which
provides specific catalogues only, or excerpts from them dealing
with individual countries and special studies, and the additional
fee charged is certainly worth it to the philatelist with limited
leisure time at his disposal.

Buying at philatelic auctions is much the same as at any

other kind of auction, though, in view of the rather peculiar nature of the merchandise, there are several points to observe, particularly as regards the technical nomenclature employed. Prospective bidders should read the pamphlet entitled: *Philatelic Auctioneers' Standard Terms and Conditions of Sale*, a copy of which can be obtained from any of the leading auctioneers. Auction catalogues invariably reprint a synopsis of these conditions which cover such matters as the regulating of bidding advances, resale of lots, bidding by agents on behalf of clients, liabilities of the purchaser and vendor, terms of payment and 'extensions'.

The last named requires special scrutiny, and consequently the Conditions of Sale relating to them are reprinted here in full:

'The purchaser to be at liberty to reject the lot by giving written notice within seven days (or, in the case of overseas buyers, within a reasonable time of the date of the sale) if he proves that the lot is not genuine or is incorrectly described and returns the lot within thirty days of the sale (or within such longer period as the Auctioneer may in his discretion allow). The onus of proving the lot to be not genuine or wrongly described lies with the purchaser; proof of the inability of an Expert Committee to express a definite opinion will not discharge this onus.

'If a purchaser wishes to obtain an expert opinion on any lot (not being a mixed lot or a collection containing undescribed stamps), the Auctioneer may, if so requested in writing within seven days of the date of the sale (or in the case of overseas buyers within seven days of receipt of the lot), extend the period within which the lot may be rejected to not later than two months from the date of the sale. Where such extensions are requested the purchaser shall give notice in writing to the Auctioneer who will submit the lot to a mutually acceptable expert body. Extensions necessitating more than two months delay from the date of sale will, unless the circumstances are exceptional, only be granted if the permission of the vendor for a longer extension has been obtained by the Auctioneer prior to the sale. The Auctioneer may require the lot to be paid for pending the receipt of the expert opinion, the cost of which is the liability of the buyer. If an extension is required on an item which already possesses a certificate dated within ten years of this sale, written notice must be given at least two weeks prior to the auction in order that the owner's permission for further expertisation may be obtained.'

Undoubtedly bidding in person is the best way to buy at auction—providing you fix your maximum bid in your own mind and not be swayed by stiff competition into going wildly beyond it. Some surprising prices have been fetched in auctions where two collectors, both bent on securing the same lot at any price, have lost their heads and bid well over the reasonable value of the lot. Auction catalogues usually have an estimated or catalogue (e.g., *Gibbons* or *Scott*) value entered opposite each lot. These estimates are surprisingly accurate and serve as a useful guide to the would-be purchaser. Of course, it sometimes happens that the auctioneer's estimate is well below the actual realisation (particularly for lots from popular countries) and new values are continually being set, but in the main it is a good rule never to go more than 10% beyond the estimate, unless you are (a) very wealthy, (b) very determined, or (c) certain that the auctioneer, in your opinion, has not appreciated the true value of the lot, but another bidder in the room has.

Bidding by post is often an uncertain business, though many collectors invariably bid in this way and never visit the auction room. Every auction catalogue contains a Bid Form specially printed for that particular sale. Space is provided for the signature, name and address, total purchase limit of the bidder and details of special instructions regarding posting if required. The back of the form has printed columns for the insertion of the lot number, the country or other brief description and the maximum sum bid in each case.

Theoretically if your maximum bid for a lot is, say £25, and the highest bid at the auction is £21, then you secure the lot for the *next highest* bid, i.e. £22. If the auction is reliable (and the main ones are) this works out; but all too often one finds in postal bidding that one secures a lot at one's maximum figure. The converse is also true, but there is nothing that can be done about it. One can just as often find that a lot has been knocked down to a bid which is just one stage higher than one's maximum. I myself have attended an auction and been bidding against no one in the room, but eventually secured a lot when the postal bidder's maximum had obviously been reached. Auctioneers usually publish a list of prices realised following each sale and either send them on to interested clients or insert them in the next sale catalogue, so you can always check on the price fetched by any lot and compare it with your bid.

The bidding in an auction is regulated by the auctioneer and, if there is no reserve price, it is left to his discretion to determine the starting price and the rate of the advances in the bidding.

If you cannot attend a sale in person, but do not wish to take a chance on a postal bid, you can commission an agent on your behalf. Many of the dealers who regularly attend the auctions will bid for you and charge a small fee for so doing.

Whether you bid by post or through an agent it is extremely unwise to give the instruction to 'buy at best' or give an unlimited bid, even should the auctioneer or agent agree to do so. This places too much responsibility on them and, if they were to continue bidding on your behalf and eventually secure a lot regardless of the cost, you might be highly dissatisfied, not to say outraged, at the price you had to pay.

In recent years a kind of stamp auction has developed which is entirely dependent on postal bids. One firm which specialises in this 'postal only' form of auction is Rigby Postal Auctions Ltd. of Bournemouth (specialising in postal history material). Auction catalogues are despatched to clients in the normal way but all bidding is done by post. Another form of postal auction, which is increasingly popular in Britain and the United States, is conducted by a firm which takes a large advertising 'spread' in one or more of the large-circulation magazines. Each item has an estimated value and bidding is solicited by post before a certain date. The best-known exponents of this form of auction are Edmund Eastick (New Milton, England), Edward

F. Deschl (Wayne, N.J.), J. Ethier (Ontario, Canada), Nor-Cal Stamp Company (Eureka, Cal.), Charles Russ, Cross Stamp Co., Hobbs Stamp Co. and the Metropole Co. (New York), Lambert Gerber (Tamaqua, Pa.), George Drasin (Philadelphia) and Elmer Long (Harrisburg, Pa.).

Lots in these postal auctions tend to be smaller and more selective than in the big auctions attended by bidders. Often lots consist of one set or even a single stamp, and this is quite a good way for the medium collector who wishes to fill odd gaps rather than purchase large accumulations.

Other auctioneers, who hold the non-postal variety of auction, occasionally publish the full details of lots in a forth-coming sale in large advertisements in the philatelic press: Midland Stamp Auctions of Rugby, England, have advertised as many as 500 lots for an auction in a three-page spread in *The Stamp Magazine*. The cost of advertising in this way must be enormous but a much wider public can be reached. These 'advertisement' auction catalogues can seldom be illustrated, which is quite a drawback, but the auctioneers usually publish a proper auction catalogue as well, containing photographs of the better items.

Perhaps the most unusual philatelic auction ever held was that organised in 1966 by Robson Lowe on board a ship in mid-Atlantic. On 16th May, on board the *Queen Mary*, which was carrying among her passengers a large contingent of European philatelists bound for the Sixth International Philatelic Exhibition in New York (SIPEX), 332 lots of exceedingly choice stamps were put under the hammer. With the co-operation not only of the Cunard Steamship Company, but of the British General Post Office and International Marine Radio, radio communication during the first ninety minutes of the sale was maintained with bidders in New York, London, Milan, Paris and Basle. None of the lots (many of which were of single stamps) was estimated at less than £100, while no less than sixty lots were estimated at over £1,000 and the outstanding item in the sale was a 'fantastic' mint block of 21 of the 90 cents blue of the United States, 1860. Estimated at £12,000 it in fact realised £20,000. Unfortunately radio contact between the *Queen Mary* and the land-based auction rooms was only intermittent so that the bidding was rather sporadic and not as spirited as had been anticipated. Nevertheless, it marked an interesting experiment in international auctioneering, being the first to be linked by radio telephone with five different cities and an ocean liner, just over 2,000 miles away from Europe and just over a thousand away from America. The auction catalogue was in itself quite a memento of the occasion, almost every lot being illustrated in full natural colour.

The importance of good auction catalogues as permanent reference works cannot be over-emphasised. The better quality stamps, the 'classics', are given lavish descriptions and are often illustrated, sometimes in full colour. A library of past auction catalogues would contain all the information required by the connoisseur and discerning philatelist and it is this information and deep knowledge of the classics which pays handsome dividends in the long run.

That this fact is realised by eminent collectors and dealers alike was borne out by the publication by Grapheion Editions Internationales of a handsome volume entitled *Philatelique 1965* which contained within its 382 pages a superb distillation of the classics which had come up at auction during the previous year. More than 4,000 items were selected from no less than 115 auctions held by 27 of the leading auctioneers in Europe and America for listing, together with the prices realised in each case. The publishers hoped that *Philatelique* would serve as a practical basis for the valuation of classic stamps which, because they seldom passed through the hands of stamp dealers, could not be accurately priced in the standard stamp catalogues. The intention was that a new edition should be published each year, but regrettably no subsequent issue of *Philatelique* has yet appeared.

PRIVATE TREATY

Sometimes auctioneers have collections of stamps for sale which, by virtue of the specialised nature of their contents, are offered intact. Instead of splitting them up into lots for disposal and dispersal at auction these collections are sold by 'Private

Treaty' to a collector who can appreciate the property and can hope to build on it. Robson Lowe himself has set out the advantages of buying a collection by this method in his 'Private Treaty' brochure of September 1964:

'At a certain age one becomes aware of the value of time and while the years may not have limited my collecting ambitions, I am fully conscious that, even if I live another twenty years, this cannot suffice to complete the studies that I want to make. The thrill of compiling a collection is not replaceable, but if you can find a study which has taken someone else thirty years to amass, the work can be carried on to a much greater degree of completion than could have been achieved if you had started at the beginning.

'In every collection there are items that can readily be replaced. Regardless of value, it is only a matter of writing a cheque. In nearly all the collections that are described in this brochure there are some pieces which are unique or to all intents irreplaceable. Half my blood is Scottish and when I want something for my collection I value it, add 25% or 50% for the pleasure of owning it, and then leave that as my bid at the auction. Alas, more often than not, some hot-blooded Latin (who is used to paying more for his pleasures) or a Lancashire Lad (who is so rich that he does not care) outbids me. When I buy a collection intact, all the irreplace-ables are mine from the start.

'The lazy collector, who loves to look and drool over his treasures (no dripping pipes please) is saved the bother of mounting and writing-up and he can even win a Gold Medal at some exhibitions because he has been rich enough to buy another man's work.'

CHAPTER V

KNOWLEDGE PAYS OFF

I HAVE already mentioned the old saying that stamp dealers make money out of *stamp collectors* to recoup their losses at the hands of *philatelists*. There is no doubt at all that the true philatelist is the man (or woman) who makes his hobby pay, profiting by his superior knowledge of his subject, and enabling him to spot the rare and the unusual among the otherwise mundane and mediocre. Stamp dealers are seldom omniscient and many a specialist has been known to pick up unconsidered gems, while browsing through the stock-books. Knowledge is usually born of long experience, and years of handling stamps and the instinct (which does not grow overnight) for nosing out a good item.

Much depends on knowing what are the precise factors which distinguish the rarity from its common brothers. Perhaps it is a matter of perforation, or shade or watermark. Sometimes the design of a stamp is subject to slight alteration—the die may be re-engraved for a subsequent printing and this can mean a vast difference in the value. British stamps are particularly prone to this sort of thing. The basic design remains in use for many years but subtle changes in colour, engraving, paper and perforation are inevitable for technical and production reasons. The British Post Office has not only been ultra-conservative in the past but perfectionist too and these qualities have often been reflected in its stamps.

One of the commonest stamps encountered is the 'Penny Lilac' which was in use from 1881 till 1902—a life of more than twenty years. Countless millions of these stamps were used to prepay the letter rate in Britain and even now you can buy them by the sackful. Not for nothing, however, has this unprepossessing stamp been dubbed 'the poor man's Penny Black', because of the varieties which are worth good money. But it takes knowledge to spot the good ones. A comparison of the listings in the three *Gibbons Catalogues* indicates that there is more in this stamp than appears at first glance.

If you use the *Simplified Whole World Stamp Catalogue* you will find it listed simply as:

1881

54. 40. 1d. lilac 1 0   0 3

That is to say, the year of issue, the stamp's number, its type number, denomination and colour, and its price (in shillings and pence) unused and used respectively.

Turning to the catalogue used by the medium collector, the 'Red' *Gibbons, Part One, British Commonwealth*, you will find:

1881. Wmk. Imperial Crown T.**49.**
(a) *14 dots in each corner, Die I (12 July).*

170.	57.	1d. lilac ..	..	..	..	45 0	8 6
171.	„	1d. pale lilac	..	..	..	35 0	7 6

(b) *16 dots in each corner, Die II (12 December)*

172.	57.	1d. lilac ..	..	..	..	0 8	0 3
172a.	„	1d. bluish lilac	..	..	..	£8	50 0
b.		blued paper	..	..	..	£50	
173.	57.	1d. deep purple	..	..	..	1 0	0 4
a.		Printed both sides	..	..	..	£40	
b.		Frame broken at bottom	..	..	£35	£40
c.		Printed on gummed side	..	..	£32	
d.		Imperf. three sides (pair) ..	..	..	£85	†
e.		Printed both sides but impression on back inverted ..	..	..	£65	†
f.		No watermark	..	..	..	£12	

Thus we find that two dies of this stamp exist. The 'fourteen dots' had a very short life—only five months—before the 'sixteen dot' type (supposedly an improvement in the design) was issued. It takes some practice to be able to spot the difference at a glance without having to count the dots in each corner, but it is worth it if you can pick up a stamp worth 35s. for pennies.

Note that differences in shade can make differences in value;

but could *you* recognise the scarce bluish lilac colour among a a sackful of lilacs and deep purples? The 'no watermark' variety is also worth a handsome premium—so it pays to study the back as well as the front of each stamp. The 'broken frame' variety also repays the diligent searcher who knows what to look for, though this catalogue does not illustrate this flaw, and many a hopeful collector has exercised his imagination too vigorously and discovered a 'swan' which turned out in the end to be a 'goose'.

If we turn to *Gibbons Specialised Stamp Catalogue, Great Britain Vol. I: Queen Victoria* we find that almost two pages are devoted to this stamp. Apart from copious notes, which no advanced collector can afford to ignore, details are given of such things as proofs, imprimaturs, colour trials and specimens which need not concern us at this juncture. But, under the heading:

1881 (DEC. 12) 1d. LILAC, TYPE K6 DIE II (16 DOTS): there are listed four distinct shades:

(1) Lilac	..	..	..	..	..	o 8	o 2
(2) Bluish lilac ..	..	..	..	..	£8	50 0
(3) Deep purple	..	..	..	..	o 8	o 2
(4) Mauve	..	..	..	..	..	o 8	o 2

and no less than twelve varieties:

(a) On blued 'safety' paper	..	..	..	£50	
(b) On laid paper	..	..	..	..	
(c) No watermark	..	..	..	..	£12	
(d) Inverted watermark	..	..	..	10 0	5 0
(e) Imperf. (pair) mauve	..	..	..	£6	
(f) Imperf. 3 sides (pair)	..	..	..	£85	† *
(g) Printed on gummed side ..	..	..	£32	†
(h) Printed both sides ..	..	..	..	£40	†
(i) Printed both sides, back print inverted ..	£65	†
(j) Frame broken at bottom (Row 1, No. 2,					
sheet Control S. upper pane) ..	..	£35	£40
(k) Frame break, right side broken ..	..	—	£25
(l) 'Pears Soap' advertised on back in orange,				
blue or mauve ..	..	..	*From*	£50

---

* Gibbons indicate by † those stamps which exist, but for which they do not quote a price.

Thus, not only are we told the exact location of the 'broken frame' variety, listed in the 'Red' *Gibbons* as S.G. 173b, but another 'frame break' is listed in addition. The error showing the printing on both sides is now further divided into the upright and inverted printed varieties. Laid paper and inverted watermarks are indicated as further points to look out for.

But still we are not very sure what to look for, with regard to the elusive 'frame break' varieties. Where the catalogues leave off, the specialised handbooks take over and, in this case, there is an excellent monograph* to refer to. Not only are the prominent flaws mentioned in *Gibbons* illustrated by means of clear diagrams, but a whole host of other varieties are enumerated and depicted, to make the study of the Penny Lilac all the easier. This handbook lists no less than 548 varieties and, as a great deal of research has yet to be done, the total number of collectable varieties may well be much larger. And all this from one very common stamp which can still be bought cheaply by weight!

HANDBOOKS

The essential tools, therefore, which no collector should be without are the stamp catalogues relevant to his subject. These handy reference works are also the market guides and, because of their supreme importance, they are treated more fully in Chapter VII. In the example given above a brief reference was also made to specialised handbooks and these also, where they exist, are indispensable to the shrewd philatelist. Many years of experience by many philatelists go into the compilation of a handbook such as the one alluded to and it would be false economy for any collector not to invest in it. Yet it is an astonishing fact that there are still a few people around who would rather squander the cost of a good monograph on a selection of stamps which have no hope of showing a good return for the money.

Specialised philatelic handbooks are seldom commercial propositions, so their publication is usually borne by a philatelic

---

* *A Specialised Study of the 1881 One Penny Lilac, Part I—Frame Damage*, by R. A. G. Lee.

society or by the author himself—if he is wealthy and dedicated enough to pay for the privilege of sharing his knowledge so that others may profit by it. The Royal Philatelic Society of London, the American Philatelic Society, the Collectors' Club of New York and the French Academie de Philatelie are only four of the leading institutions which have published valuable series of monographs to aid the specialist. Germany has given the philatelic world the Kohl *Briefmarken Handbucher*, authoritative studies covering many countries and facets of philately.

In the past twenty years there has been a remarkable growth in the number of study 'circles' and specialist philatelic societies and many of these have published the pooled knowledge of their members in the shape of a monograph.

Of particular value to the student of British Commonwealth stamps is *The Robson Lowe Encyclopedia* whose publication is still in progress. *Volume I*, first published in 1949, but subsequently revised and enlarged in 1952, covers the stamps and postal history of the British Empire in Europe, i.e. the United Kingdom, Malta, Gibraltar and Cyprus, former colonial territories such as the Ionian Islands and Heligoland, and, for the sake of convenience, the Irish Republic which became an independent sovereign state outside the Commonwealth in 1949. *Volume II*, published in 1951, deals with the British Commonwealth in and around the continent of Africa, *Volume III* (1954) covers Asia and *Volume IV* (1962) Australasia. *Volume V*, which should be in print by the time this book is published, is devoted to the stamps and postal history of the British Commonwealth territories in the West Indies, Central and South America (including the British postal agencies which operated in many countries in that continent prior to about 1880). *Volume VI* will cover British North America—Canada, Newfoundland and the other provinces which today make up the Dominion of the North—and presumably the 'pre-philately' of the ex-colonies in North America which became the United States.

The Robson Lowe Encyclopedia contains a great amount of useful background information, such as postal rates and numbers of stamps issued, and deals with many of the by-ways ('specimen' overprints, local stamps and postmarks) not dealt with in the stamp catalogues. This encyclopedia also makes an intelligent attempt at appraising and assessing the value of items which are not easy to put a price on: covers with unusual postal markings or combinations of these markings with adhesive stamps. The main drawback to these volumes is that their pricings are so soon out of date. All but *Volume IV* are out of print anyway, and they fetch large sums when they come up in literature auctions, but they give at least a comparative guide to values. New information is continually turning up and supplements to the *Encyclopedia* appear regularly in *The Philatelist* published monthly by Robson Lowe.

There is no other encyclopaedia comparable to this for other parts of the world, though recently Mabeosz, the state publishing organisation in Hungary, has begun the mammoth task of compiling a six-volume encyclopedia on the postal history and philately of Hungary. Many of the 'one country' catalogues, referred to in Chapter VII, verge on the encyclopedia in the amount of additional information given.

PERIODICALS

To acquire the knowledge by which to profit from philately it is absolutely necessary to keep abreast of current developments and newly published research. These are disseminated by means of the various magazines and journals, both general and specialist, which cater to the hobby.

In the United Kingdom there are five main magazines in the general category. Of these *Stamp Collecting* is a weekly, the only philately periodical of its kind independently published. Its strong points are its up-to-the-minute news items and shrewd comment on current trends. Although at one time it contained a high proportion of original articles, in recent years it has come to rely more and more on features reprinted from other sources to fill its pages. One recent number contained six articles, only one of which had not appeared somewhere else first. The *Philatelic Magazine*, published fortnightly, is also strong on its news reportage and often contains articles of specialist interest as well as more general features. This magazine is

PLATE V
United States Rarities.

(1) $1, 1903 (£25, $80), (2) $2, 1918 (£28, $90), (3) $5, 1923 (£8, $25), (4) $1, 1915 (£22, $125), (5) 24c., 1923 (£7, $22.50), (6) Norse-American 5c., 1925 (65s., $9), (7) Pilgrim Fathers 5c., 1920 (60s., $11.50), (8) Graf Zeppelin $2.60, 1930 (£80, $285), (9) Huguenot 5c., 1924 (65s., $9.75), (10) Parcel Post $1 (£15, $52.50), (11) Century of Progress 50c., 1933 (£8, $25).

published by Harris Publications Ltd., who are the leading booksellers in Britain for all manner of philatelic books, accessories and stamp albums.

Of the three leading monthlies, *The Stamp Magazine* is one of the Link House group of hobbyist periodicals (its editor, Arthur Blair, also produces the companion monthly *Coins and Medals*). The original articles published in it are backed by several regular features, including a regular column by Britain's veteran philatelic journalists, the brothers L. N. and M. Williams, dealing with out-of-the-usual material and a useful column by Kay Horowicz on hints for beginners. A hallmark of all the Link House periodicals is their extensive advertisements and *The Stamp Magazine* is no exception. Every issue contains the advertisements of hundreds of dealers, large and small, from all over the world and a careful examination of them will reveal not only the market trends but where the bargains are to be had.

Gibbons Stamp Monthly, being the house journal of the Stanley Gibbons group, contains no advertising outside the company. Nevertheless it has the largest readership of any British magazine. It is noted above all else for its supplements to the stamp catalogues by which they are kept reasonably up to date on new issues. At one time changes in the prices quoted for older issues were also notified in *G.S.M.* in full, but in 1966 it was decided merely to give a note on the market trends, indicating in a general way the movement of prices in particular sections. This was naturally not as helpful as the former system and often the first indication that a collector had that prices had gone up was when he went into Gibbons' shop to purchase it. Because of the widespread dissatisfaction at the new system Gibbons decided at the beginning of 1967 to revert to the previous practice of listing price alterations in full. Under the progressive editorship of Russell Bennett *Gibbons Stamp Monthly* has changed in content and layout over the past four or five years. An eye-catching cover reproducing stamps in full colour has helped to attract new readers, many of whom owe their introduction to it by seeing it on a railway bookstall or in a stationer's shop, while the contents are exceptionally well illustrated and often include first-class research studies of permanent value.

The other leading monthly is *The Philatelist* published by Robson Lowe. It too has recently received a face-lift, with its attractive Astralux board covers illustrating stamps in full colour. The contents of this old-established magazine* are more specialised than general, with a strong emphasis on postal history. This firm also publishes a quarterly, the *Philatelic Journal of Great Britain*, which, in continuous publication since 1891, is now the oldest philatelic periodical in the United Kingdom. It is now confined solely to articles and specialised studies dealing exclusively with the United Kingdom.

Several philatelic societies publish their own journals, which are free to members, though non-members can usually buy them. Of these the principal one is the *London Philatelist*, published monthly by the Royal Philatelic Society. It embodies the cream of serious philatelic research and has a world-wide contributorship. Its advertisements are particularly useful, since they tend to be for the better class material of the select band of specialist-dealers. *The Stamp Lover* is the organ of the National Philatelic Society (formerly the Junior Philatelic Society). The standard of scholarship in *The Stamp Lover* is generally lower than that of the *London Philatelist*, but it is still extremely valuable for the philatelic student. In particular, its excellent Index to Current Philatelic Literature is to be commended since it gives an invaluable guide to the student of published work in his own field. The *Postal History Society Bulletin* does for its subject what the *London Philatelist* does for pure philately and contains lengthy articles on various aspects of postal history.

Most of the specialist societies and study circles produce their own newsletters or bulletins. Like their handbooks, which have been referred to earlier in this chapter, their periodicals contain the ultimate in the philatelic knowledge of their subject. The growth of specialist periodicals of this sort since the Second World War has largely impoverished the general magazines. While the general periodicals, because of their mass circulation

---

* It first appeared in 1866 and ran for twelve years. In its present form it was revived by Robson Lowe in 1934.

and advertising revenue, can afford to put good feature articles
and research studies in a good setting, with ample illustration,
all too often they cannot get the material which tends to
appear solely in the specialist magazines.

Printing costs being what they are, only a handful of these
periodicals are type-set and illustrated with good half-tone
blocks. Far too many are duplicated with no illustrations whatsoever. Undoubtedly, however, the content of these journals is
superlative and no one proposing to collect and profit by the
stamps of a particular country or group can afford to ignore
the requisite specialist society or neglect to read its bulletins.
Too many serious collectors are nevertheless unaware of the
existence of these study circles and societies and the information
imparted in their small circulation periodicals is thereby missed.
Obviously a partial solution is for the general philatelic
magazines, whose circulation and advertising revenue ensure
their quality against rising costs of commercial publication, to
reprint more from the specialist periodicals than they do at
present. The advantages are material; the readers of the weekly,
fortnightly or monthly magazines get good quality stamp
articles, and the specialist societies get much needed publicity
which should, inevitably, boost their membership and the
popularity of the countries they study.

It would be impossible to mention all the specialist publica-
tions in the United Kingdom but among the best are the
Bulletin of the British Postmark Society, The *G.B. Journal* (the
Great Britain Philatelic Society), *Thai Times* (the Thailand
Philatelic Society), *Springbok* (the South African Specialists
Society), *Cruzada* (the Spanish Civil War Study Group), *Pacifica*
(the Pacific Islands Study Circle), the *Bulletin* of O.P.A.L. (the
Oriental Philatelic Association of London), the *British Journal
of Russian Philately* (the Russian Philatelic Society of Gt. Britain),
Polar Post (the Polar Postal History Society), and the *Sarawak
Journal* (the Sarawak Study Circle). A comprehensive list of the
specialist societies is published annually in the British Philatelic
Association Yearbook.

In the United States the academic standard of philatelic
periodicals is, if anything, lower than it is in Britain. This is

not an indictment of the level on which the hobby is generally conducted in America. Scanning the pages of the general magazines one finds few specialised articles or any sign of depth in philatelic research. But in America it would be true to say that there is a far larger proportion of *collectors* to *philatelists* than in Britain, which, in turn, lags behind Europe. The emphasis in the general philatelic press of America is laid on background stories, new issue notes and, because Americans tend to have more catholic tastes in their collecting, articles on revenue stamps, pre-cancels, meters, seals and stickers which are seldom to be found in the pages of British or European journals. Such serious research as there is, usually appears in either the *Collectors' Club Philatelist* (published by the Collectors' Club of New York) or *The American Philatelist* (journal of the American Philatelic Society). The leading commercial publications are *Linn's Weekly Stamp News* (published at Sidney, Ohio) and *Western Stamp Collector* (a twice-weekly periodical by Van Dahl Publications of Albany, Oregon). Both of these are printed in newspaper format and, because they carry extensive advertising, are indispensable to the collector who wishes to keep informed on the state of the American market. *Mekeel's Weekly Stamp News* (Portland, Maine) and *Stamps* (produced weekly by Lindquist Publications of New York) are in large magazine format, containing good general articles with plenty of illustrations and occasional specialised studies.

Among the more specialised periodicals pride of place must go to the *Essay-Proof Journal* (the Essay-Proof Society) which caters to collectors interested in the ancillary material produced before the finished stamp. Interest in essays, proofs, colour trials and printers' samples is increasing and this is a field where some pretty spectacular prices have been asked—and paid—in recent years. With the great number of immigrant ethnic groups in the United States it is hardly surprising that each of the European countries has a large following and periodicals such as *Polonus* (Poland) and *Rossica Journal* (Russia) testify to this interest. The American Topical Association, catering to topical, thematic, or subject collectors, produces *Topical Stamp Digest* which reprints the best articles on thematics from other periodicals, and also publishes a series of handbooks dealing with specific topics.

Elsewhere in the American continent the best magazines are the *Canadian Philatelist* (published by the Royal Philatelic Society of Canada), *Chile Filatelico* (published in Santiago and embracing much original research on Latin America generally and Chile, Bolivia and Peru in particular), *Revista Filatelica Brasileira* (published in São Paulo), and *Revista de la Sociedad Filatelica Argentina*.

Europe has the most prolific periodicals of all, with France, Germany and Italy at the top of the list. In France the leading general magazines are *L'Echangiste Universel* and *L'Echo de Timbrologie*, both well produced with plenty of good original material. In Germany the leading magazines are *Der Sammler Dienst* and *Der Sammler Express*—depending on which side of the Wall you live. The former, published in Coburg (Federal Republic) is an octavo-sized journal strong on new issues, whereas the latter (published by VEB Transpress-Verlag of Leipzig and East Berlin) is rather 'political' in its bias and naturally tends to concentrate on the emissions of the Iron Curtain group.

Undoubtedly the best produced periodicals in this field anywhere in the world come from Italy where philately is now very much a rich man's sport as well as the poor man's pastime. The sumptiously glossy *Italia Filatelica* published by Raybaudi is in a class of its own—beautifully, expensively produced for the *cognoscente* of fine stamps. In the popular category *Il Collezionista*, published weekly by Edizione S.C.O.T. of Turin, has a circulation of 70,000 which is rapidly growing outside Italy as well as within. Published by Bolaffi, it contains regular supplements to the Bolaffi catalogue and very extensive market notes, but it is best known perhaps for its illustrations which are on a scale more lavish than any other philatelic periodical. But though the accent is on pictorialism (including full-colour plates of rare or unusual items) it contains some of the best philatelic writing in the world today.

Most of the other European countries have at least one magazine which, containing a wealth of 'home-produced' philatelic research should not be overlooked by the specialist. The best of them include *Mijn Stokpaardje* and *Nederlandse Maandblad* (the Netherlands), *Het Postzegel* (the Flemish portion of Belgium), *Balasse Magazine* (published by Willi Balasse of Brussels), *Le Philateliste Belge* (organ of the Belgian Philatelic Society), *Norsk Filatelistisk Tidskrift* (Norway), *Madrid Filatelico* (Spain), *Berner Briefmarken Zeitung* (*Journal Philatelique de Berne*), the house journal of Zumstein et Cie, and *Schweizer Briefmarken Zeitung* (the journal of the Union of Swiss Philatelic Societies), *Filotelike Hellas* and *Philotelia* (Greece), *Filateliai Szemle* (Hungary), *Svensk Filatelistisk Tidskrift* (Sweden) and *Filatelija* (Yugoslavia), but there are many others which space does not permit to mention.

Outside Europe and America there is not a great deal of indigenous philatelic publishing. Australia and New Zealand are obvious exceptions with many fine periodicals, including the *Australian Stamp Monthly* (Melbourne), *Philately from Australia* (the journal of the Royal Philatelic Society of Victoria) and *Stamp News* (New South Wales), *Pacific Stamp Journal* (Auckland) and the Royal Philatelic Society of New Zealand's *Newsletter* (Wellington).

In Africa the only periodicals worth mentioning are *African Stamps* and *The South African Philatelist*, published monthly in Cape Town and Johannesburg respectively. In Asia, the best magazines emanate from India, particularly the *Philatelic Journal of India* (organ of the Philatelic Society of India, and *India's Stamp Journal* (the house journal of Jal Cooper of Bombay).

The foregoing titles are only a small selection from the vast outpourings of the collectors, the societies and the dealers of the stamp world. Like the specialist-periodicals in Britain and America the great bulk of these magazines from abroad, particularly those in languages other than English, are seldom read by the philatelic general public outside their own countries. There is a great need today for an English-language periodical to act as a clearing-house for the research studies published in other languages and to make this valuable material available to as many philatelists as possible.

PREVIOUSLY PUBLISHED RESEARCH

So much for the current philatelic literature of the world; but there is a great deal of previously published research which has stood the test of time and will still repay the philatelist who has the patience and the diligence to look for it. The first stamp catalogue (by Alfred Potiquet) appeared in 1861, the earliest periodical (*The Monthly Advertiser*) in 1862 and the first philatelic handbook (*De la Falsification des Timbres-poste*) in 1862. Over the ensuing century countless millions of words have covered every conceivable aspect of philately. Here is material which will enable the collector to profit by someone else's knowledge perhaps long forgotten. How can this rich source be tapped? Where can this material be found?

There are several good philatelic libraries in the world, all more or less comprehensive. The best is probably that of the Royal Philatelic Society of London, covering the books, catalogues and periodicals of the whole world, with particular emphasis on those in English. Except in unusual cases, it is necessary to be a member of the Society in order to make use of the Library. On the other hand books may be lent out to members—which is not the case with the other great philatelic library in Britain. The British Museum Library is one of the three largest of its kind in the world and contains a good measure of philatelic books, particularly in English, but it is noticeably weak on modern foreign books and periodicals. The Museum, however, contains the philatelic library of the 26th Earl of Crawford who bequeathed more than 4,000 volumes to the Museum in 1913. This library is unsurpassed in its field anywhere in the world. All the *incunabula* of philately are there: the earliest editions of Potiquet, Gray, Gibbons, Scott, Berger-Levreult and complete files of the earliest (including the most ephemeral) periodicals, indispensable for historical research. A temporary reader's ticket may be obtained from the Director's Office of the Museum at very short notice.

On the continent of Europe the best philatelic library is that maintained by the Staatsbibliothek in Munich. It is particularly strong in modern books and periodicals and also endeavours to file press-clippings on philately. The Association Internationale des Journalistes Philateliques, to which most philatelic authors and journalists throughout the world belong, has urged its members to supply the Munich Library with copies, offprints and clippings of their writings. The best philatelic library in the United States is that belonging to the Collectors' Club. There are also many fine collections of philatelic literature in private hands and there is even a Philatelic Literature Society in America which publishes in its columns useful lists of books for sale.

The *Philatelic Literature Review*, published by this society, often contains bibliographies of countries and subjects, listing all the known articles and separate works, classified into periods and aspects of the subject—a 'must' for the philatelist who aims to profit from the published research of his predecessors. Other bibliographies of a general nature include the *Catalogue of the Crawford Library* (published by the Royal Philatelic Society in 1911), and the notable *Index to Philatelic Literature*, compiled by the late Albert Harris. Cumulative indices have also been published by several periodicals, principally those for *The London Philatelist* and *The Stamp Magazine*.

ARCHIVES AND REFERENCE COLLECTIONS

It is essential for a mastery of stamps, particularly the 'classics', to study good reference collections wherever possible. There are so many pitfalls to trap the unwary—forgeries, reprints, faked postmarks on covers—that comparison with 'controls' is necessary. Collectors in the United Kingdom are particularly fortunate in having two excellent national repositories where material is readily available for study.

The British Museum contains many fine, specialised collections, but the whole-world collection of stamps, 1840–90, bequeathed by Thomas K. Tapling in 1891, is unsurpassed anywhere. Not only are almost all stamps in the first fifty years of their existence on permanent display, but, wherever possible, they are matched by fakes and forgeries so that the collector has a means of direct comparison if he is doubtful about any of his own specimens. The British Museum also holds a large collection of modern stamps received from the Universal Postal

Union, thus acting as a 'control' against which doubtful items, not covered by the Tapling Collection, can be matched. The archives of Thomas De La Rue & Co. Ltd., who have printed stamps for 170 different postal administrations since 1853, are now lodged at the British Museum. Essays, proofs, colour-trials and 'specimen' overprints as well as the finished stamps are housed in 82 large volumes, readily available to the *bona fide* student. Of particular interest to the student of British stamps are the monumental archives of the Board of Inland Revenue, recently transferred to the Museum. Containing proofs and imprimaturs of stamps, both postage and fiscal, from 1712 to modern times, its value to the research worker and the philatelist is incalculable.

Apart from these collections Britain now has its own National Postal Museum, established by the General Post Office in 1966 with the gold-medal collection of Reginald M. Phillips as its nucleus. This collection, worth a quarter of a million pounds, is the finest study of nineteenth-century British stamps ever formed; over a period of forty years Mr. Phillips purchased the best pieces from every major British collection to come on the market. To this the General Post Office has added its own incomparable archives of registration sheets, essays and proofs. Both the Royal Philatelic Society and the National Philatelic Society have their own extensive reference collections.

The United States boasts one of the world's finest philatelic collections, housed in the Division of Philately and Postal History at the Smithsonian Institution in Washington. It combines the archives of the U.S. Bureau of Engraving and Printing with many private donations and bequests, as well as a whole-world collection of mint stamps received from the Universal Postal Union. A second institutional collection is maintained at the Cardinal Spellman Museum in Philadelphia, while the Collectors' Club boasts of a fine reference collection.

The most important collection of British and Commonwealth stamps in private hands is the Royal Collection kept at Buckingham Palace. Well might it be said of philately that it is the 'king of hobbies and hobby of kings', since Carol of Roumania and Farouk of Egypt had, and Prince Rainier of

Monaco still has, large collections; but, overtopping them all, was the valuable assemblage of stamps begun by the late King George V and continued down to the present time by King George VI and Queen Elizabeth. Although originally formed at the personal expense of King George V, it is now mainly added to by presentation of material from the General Post Office, the Crown Agents and Commonwealth postal administrations. The King had a special liking for essays and proofs and it is in this field that it is particularly valuable. In recent years it has been the practice of the Crown Agents to forward to the Palace plate blocks of every printing of every stamp issued in the countries and territories for whom they act. In view of the fact, however, that the Royal Collection is essentially a private one, access to it is extremely restricted. Nevertheless a portion of it was on view in 1965 at the Queen's Gallery, which traced the development of British stamps from 1840 to 1880.

Most European countries have a postal museum, with the emphasis naturally on their own philately and postal history. Nearly all of them have incorporated the archives of other relevant postal administration, thus providing the serious philatelist with ample material to study.

TURNING RUBBISH INTO GOLD

This chapter began by mentioning the possibilities which there are, even with a very cheap stamp—the 'Penny Lilac'—providing you know what to look for. R. A. G. Lee, one of the most eminent philatelists in Britain today—his collection of British stamps won the International Grand Prix in 1965—has made a notable study of this humble stamp and his definitive monograph on the subject will doubtless be the standard reference work on it for many years to come. In the course of his studies he accumulated well over a million copies of the Penny Lilac, but after sorting the gold from the dross he was left with a highly specialised and quite valuable collection which will fetch a good price if and when he comes to sell it. The same story could be repeated with the Victorian 'Jubilee' ½d. stamp of 1887 and the Edwardian ½d. and 1d. stamps of

1902–11 which were produced by no less than *three* printers in turn, a fact which has given rise to a tremendous variety of shades, papers, perforations and plate flaws. The raw material is cheap, but infinite pleasure can be derived from moulding it into a worthwhile collection and the end result should be quite lucrative.

Nor need this activity be a British monopoly. The Charles Lathrop Pack collection of Brazil common stamps is a classic example of what study can do for an inexpensive stamp. This collection won the Grand Award in London some years ago and is now the property of the Collectors' Club in New York. The material was cheap: it was the collector's painstaking efforts that created the excellence.

CHAPTER VI

PHILATELIC AGENCIES

PHILATELIC AGENCIES are something of a mixed blessing; by acting as 'middle men' between the issuing country and the stamp collector they increase the sales, and hence the revenue of the one while facilitating the purchase of stamps by the other. Agencies of this sort are almost as old as the hobby. Broadly speaking, any organisation outside the issuing country which serves to promote its stamps directly comes within this category.

The oldest and most respected of all the philatelic agencies past and present is the Stamp Bureau run by the Crown Agents in London. The Crown Agents' connection with the production of stamps dates back to 1848, in which year they were commissioned by the colonial authorities in Mauritius to furnish them with a stock of stamps of the 'seated Britannia' type. It is odd to recall that, of this first series, two of the stamps were never put to any postal use in the colony and many years afterwards were sold off to stamp dealers for little more than they cost to print and ended up ignominiously with the overprint 'LPE 1890' as souvenirs of the London Philatelic Exhibition of that year.

In spite of this inauspicious beginning, the Crown Agents gradually secured the contract to supply most of the British colonies with stamps—arranging for their designing, printing, distribution and last, but not least, their philatelic marketing. More than 90% of the mint 'colonial' stamps in collections today have never been near the country whose name they bear, having gone straight from the printers to the Stamp Bureau at Millbank in London (shortly moving to Sutton in Surrey).

Undoubtedly the Crown Agents have exerted a restraining influence over the stamps of the territories they act for. New issues have been moderate in frequency and, in most cases, more than enough to go round. No gimmicks such as imperforate varieties, limited denominations or charity stamps with excessive premiums have been resorted to. As a result the name of the Crown Agents is a guarantee in philatelic circles for probity and integrity.

The Philatelic Bureau of the General Post Office has already been mentioned in Chapter IV in connection with the supply of British stamps. Until recently it also acted as the philatelic agency for a number of overseas territories whose postal affairs were supervised by the Overseas Mails Branch of the G.P.O. These consisted of the British Postal Agencies in Ras al Khaima, Abu Dhabi, Muscat, Bahrain and other sheikhdoms round the Persian Gulf. All of them now control their own postal services and consequently their stamps are no longer available at the Bureau. The other 'colonial' powers had or still have philatelic agencies to promote the sale and distribution of stamps of overseas territories. Thus the Agence Philatelique d'Outre-Mer in Paris still handles the philatelic sales of many territories, both past and present members of the French Community, while the Philatelic Service of the Netherlands P.T.T. in The Hague will supply the stamps of Surinam and the Netherlands Antilles, as well as the motherland, to collectors.

Such governmental agencies are usually run on a non-profit basis, supplying stamps to their customers at face value, plus a small handling charge where necessary. They usually take 10% of the sales revenue for such overheads as staff, clerical costs and publicity (the last including press notices, brochures, exhibitions and other promotional projects).

This is only one side of the story, however. Philately was still in its adolescent stage when the commercial possibilities of marketing postage stamps for collectors began to attract shrewd entrepreneurs who were prepared to furnish certain countries with their stamps free or at little cost, in return for the concession to sell them to collectors. The first stamps of the Sultanate of Brunei, on the northern coast of Borneo, were produced under just such an arrangement. Mr. J. Robertson, a personal friend of the Sultan, agreed to provide Brunei with a series of stamps in 1895 at no charge, so long as he was permitted to sell as many as he liked to collectors. Indeed the latter could only obtain mint supplies by purchasing them from Mr. Robertson's brother, Charles, at his office in Bath Street, Glasgow! Because of the rather unusual circumstances surrounding this issue, philatelists and dealers alike were vociferous in their condemnation and none of the contemporary stamp catalogues would list the stamps. There is no doubt whatsoever that the stamps, which depicted a boat at the mouth of the Brunei River, performed a legitimate service, since genuine, postally used examples have been recorded on covers dating up to the end of 1899; but the angry silence of the period at the conduct of the philatelic sales, and the complete boycott of the issue by the stamp catalogues, effectively killed the market for Brunei. It was not until 1934 that evidence came to light which justified these stamps as a legitimate issue and in that year Robson Lowe gave a lead by listing them in his *Regent Stamp Catalogue*, but even now the 1895 series is totally ignored in every other stamp catalogue.

To the north-east of Brunei lies the territory of Sabah which formerly comprised the dominions of the British North Borneo Company. This chartered company issued its own stamps for use in North Borneo from 1883 up till 1899 when it became a British Protectorate. All of the 111 stamps issued in that sixteen-year period were available to collectors at the Company's headquarters in London, but, not content with selling mint stamps at face value, the Company also sold most of them in 'used' condition. This was, in fact, a convenient way of disposing of the remainders of issues after their period of validity had ceased. Such stamps were cancelled with a barred obliterator and then sold at a large discount below face value. Not only were they 'cancelled to order'—a term used by philatelists to denote stamps apparently used but with their gum still intact—but they had never been anywhere near the country for whom they were ostensibly produced to prepay postage. Here then was a philatelic agency which served to exploit collectors rather than help them, and, in the long run, did North Borneo's stamps more harm than good. Not until the Crown Agents assumed control for North Borneo's stamps after the Second World War and these nefarious practices were stamped out did these attractive pictorials recover something of their former popularity.

In 1889 Nicholas F. Seebeck negotiated contracts with the governments of Honduras, Nicaragua and Salvador to provide them with new definitive issues each year, printed by the Hamilton Bank Note Co. of New York. Article 8 of this contract gave Seebeck the right to 'use the plates to make such *Reprints* as the Engraving Company may want to sell again to stamp dealers and collectors'. In the ensuing decade these three countries released a fantastic number of stamp issues:

	Honduras	*Nicaragua*	*Salvador*
Period of Seebeck Contracts	1890–5	1890–9	1890–8
Stamps Issued	55	127	217

Even today none of these issues is worth more than a few shillings while many of them can be picked up for a few pence. Nor was this all. Under the terms of Article 8, Seebeck exploited the printing plates to the full and the Hamilton Bank Note Co. produced countless thousands of 'reprints' similar to those stamps which had been produced for legitimate postal use. Fortunately is is possible to identify the reprints fairly easily since they were printed on paper of a different thickness and texture and in many cases the colour and the watermark also differed from the genuine stamps. Innumerable schoolboy collections even to this day are well salted with the fruits of Mr. Seebeck's misplaced efforts in Central America at the very end of the last century. For this reason most collectors still shun the 'Seebeck countries', even though this episode barely lasted a few years: though I should perhaps add that *used* Seebecks on cover are much sought after by specialists and bring substantial prices.

Philatelic agencies thus have an awful power in their hands: they can soak the collector for a year or two and make a lot

of money in so doing; but they can also very effectively kill
philatelic interest in a country for generations after their
activities have ceased.

For ill or good, the 1960s are the decade of the commercial
philatelic agency, with at least thirty stamp-issuing entities
directly or indirectly under their control. At one end of the
scale there are the sales and publicity services performed by
the Intercontinental Philatelic Agency on behalf of Pakistan
and Nigeria in much the same way as the Crown Agents act
for Papua or Botswana. Some countries, whose stamps are
controlled by the Crown Agents, have appointed a commercial
philatelic agency to act for them in certain areas, such as North
America. At the other end of the scale we find Ecuador whose
most recent stamps, allegedly honouring Sir Winston Churchill,
John F. Kennedy, Dr. Albert Schweitzer and Dag Hammarskjöld, were apparently never intended for postal use in that
country, but were produced by an external philatelic agency
purely for philatelic sales—the non-postage stamp has arrived
at last! Of Paraguay, *Gibbons Catalogue* states at the end of the
latest stamps listed (1962): 'The listing of later commemorative
issues has been suspended pending the receipt of satisfactory
evidence that they have been in regular use. The G.P.O. are
unable to supply these issues or state if any are on sale and,
having given authority to an agency to print and issue stamps
on their behalf, they appear to have lost control over their
stamp issues.'

The most dramatic increase in the output of new issues of
stamps has been seen in the Middle East, particularly in Arabia
where eleven new postal administrations have sprung up almost
overnight, like the oil derricks in that part of the world. I have
listed below the numbers of stamps issued by some of these
countries since their postal service was established, up to and
including their last entry in *Gibbons Catalogue*:

Ajman	1964–5	72	
Dubai	1963–4	142	(no stamps listed after that date)
Fujeira	1964–6	64	

PLATE VI
Foreign Rarities.

(1) Iceland, Balbo flight, 1933 (£110, $375), (2) Mexico, 20p. airmail, 1934 (£100, $375), (3) Sweden, 80ö., 1918 (£90, $300), (4) San Marino 2l., 1903 (£165, $900), (5) Turkey, 500k., 1923 (£50, $135), (6) Russia Sports, 1935 (£10, $40), (7) Spain, Montserrat 4p., 1931 (£50, $150), (8) Thailand, Red Cross 20b., 1918 (£30, $90).

Qatar	1964–6	53	(since the British postal ad-
			ministration was closed)
Ras al			
Khaima	1964–5	23	
Sharjah	1963–6	202	
Umm al			
Qiwain	1964–6	77	

In each case, however, a vast number of new stamps has been released since the 1967 catalogue was published and the figures for the older-established post offices, such as Dubai and Sharjah, are an ominous indication of the direction in which the others are going. Nor is this all. There is a tendency in these and many other 'agency countries' to issue limited quantities of each set in imperforate condition, sometimes in colours differing from the normal stamps, and to release miniature or souvenir sheets. These and other gimmicks which tend to have a detrimental effect on philately and are of doubtful investment value are treated in greater detail in Chapter IX.

A phenomenon of post-war philately is the 'band wagon issue'. By this I mean that for one reason or another a number of countries release, more or less simultaneously, stamps honouring a common subject. They had their origins in the portmanteaux or omnibus issues released in France and its colonies in 1931 (to mark the great Paris Exposition Coloniale), and in the British Commonwealth four years later to celebrate the Silver Jubilee of King George V. These issues were confined to the respective Empires, but just after the Second World War not only did the British Commonwealth issue a large number of stamps in honour of the 75th Anniversary of the Universal Postal Union but many other countries released stamps for this purpose at the same time. It became fashionable for collectors all over the world to collect U.P.U. stamps and for a time they enjoyed tremendous popularity; but once the event was no longer topical, interest in the stamps waned and it would be difficult to recommend them now as a good investment.

Perhaps the theme represented by these stamps has not held lasting interest for collectors. In the years immediately preceding the U.P.U. commemoration many stamps were issued throughout the world in memory of the late Franklin D. Roosevelt, President of the United States, and this theme has had a more enduring appeal for collectors. There is even a philatelic society and a stamp magazine devoted to the President who was himself a keen philatelist. Following the death of his widow, Eleanor Roosevelt, in 1965, a number of stamps were released in her memory and this had the effect of reviving interest in the F.D.R. stamps—if, indeed, that interest had been flagging.

In the same way the death of John F. Kennedy has led to a spate of stamps, many from countries which had little or no connection with the United States. But they or the philatelic agencies which control their stamp production and sales have realised that there is a tremendous vogue in America for any stamps relating to him, and thousands of collectors will fall over themselves to acquire the latest novelty if it should happen to portray or allude to the assassinated President. More than three years after his death there seems to be no diminution in the output of new stamps commemorating Kennedy. Some of these countries (or rather the agencies controlling the stamps), realising the attraction of other themes such as Space, have incorporated them with the Kennedy theme. Thus the Yemen Arab Republic's Kennedy series not only portrayed the President but depicted various American space rockets and satellites. For the same reason, Panama's *second* series in memory of Sir Winston Churchill bore, in addition to his portrait, Britain's more modest attempts to get into the Space Race— Blue Streak and Honest John.

This combination of themes was, perhaps, manifest in its most extreme form in the miniature sheet issued by the sheikh-dom of Qatar in 1966 to mark International Co-operation Year. Each sheet consisted of 25 subjects (5 × 5) arranged in four blocks of four 40 n.p. stamps, one block in each corner of the sheet. Each block contained four different stamps featuring respectively the symbols of the United Nations and International Co-operation Year, Kennedy and the U.N. Building, Dag Hammarskjöld and the U.N. General Assembly and Pandit

Nehru and a dove of peace. These stamps were additionally overprinted U.N. 20TH ANNIVERSARY. The remaining nine subjects, forming a cross separating the four blocks, consisted of five 5 n.p. stamps with coupons between them—these five stamps were all different and depicted the following: a rocket and telecommunications satellite, Kennedy facing right, laurel leaves, Kennedy facing left, and the Flame symbol of the Alliance for Progress (an organisation incorporating the countries of Latin America for their material advancement under the aegis of the United States). Four of these stamps and also the four coupons interspersed were overprinted with the following inscriptions respectively:

'Towards the Peaceful Development of Peace' (*sic*).
In Memoriam John F. Kennedy 1917–1963.

'In Victory, Magnanimity, In Peace, Goodwill'—Sir Winston Churchill.

20th Anniversary of the United Nations (in Arabic).

20th Anniversary of the United Nations (in English).

'Freedom can prevail—and peace can endure'—John F. Kennedy.

(The same, but in Arabic).

'Our problems are man-made, therefore they can be solved by Man'—John F. Kennedy.

Any avid collector of no less than twelve different themes* would not feel that his collection was complete unless it contained this sheet. Moreover, inasmuch as the sheet was issued both perforated and imperforate and overprinted either in red

---

* These were Alliance for Progress, Birds, Churchill, Flora, Hammarskjöld, International Co-operation Year, Kennedy, Nehru, Peace, Space, Telecommunications and United Nations.

or black, four sheets would have to be purchased instead of one. The retail price for this remarkable sheet in all its variations at the time of issue was about £60, although the total face value of the four sheets was only Rs. 26.60, or less than £2.

Needless to say, remarkably few of these curious stamps were ever postally used and their supply to the world market was so carefully controlled by the philatelic agent that the price fetched bore no relation to the value of the postal duty for which they were ostensibly produced. Designed in London and printed in Switzerland, inscribed mainly in English and depicting subjects of little interest to the Arabs who inhabit this sheikhdom, it is no wonder that the cynics regard with amusement those philatelists who paid large sums for this material.

There is no escaping from the fact that nowadays it is the subject of a stamp which is its biggest selling factor. Once a subject develops in popularity and acquires a serious following it is exploited to death by the 'agency countries'. This has, for instance, sickened many collectors from forming thematic studies of Space and Sport. As I write this, the theme which has suddenly attracted the unwelcome attentions of the philatelic agencies is Art.

Art has been inextricably linked with postage stamps since the Penny Black reproduced William Wyon's finely sculpted portrait of Queen Victoria, but in its narrower context Art stamps may be defined as those depicting paintings. France led the way in the current vogue for stamps reproducing masterpieces of this sort, especially since the modern multicolour processes permitted reproduction in the full colours of the original paintings. The first Art series from France appeared in 1961, and since then many others have been released. Beautifully engraved and printed, these stamps are masterpieces in their own right. This, coupled with rather restricted sales periods, resulted in unexpected increases in their commercial value and by 1965 they had gained enormously in international popularity.

In 1966 several other countries emulated France; both Czechoslovakia and Hungary began issuing annual sets of stamps featuring paintings and even the United Kingdom has now joined in. These stamps, like the French, have concentrated on the art of their respective countries, having as their legitimate aim the encouragement of a greater awareness of the artistic heritage in each case.

So far so good. But simultaneously a number of the 'agency countries' decided to cash in on the sudden popularity of Art stamps. The Cook Islands in the Pacific released six Christmas stamps in December 1966, each depicting a famous 'Old Master'. Then the Kathiri State of Seiyun in South Arabia issued eight gaudy, multicoloured stamps early in 1967 showing well-known paintings, framed in gold and—as if this was not enough—also issued a set of eight stamps commemorating Sir Winston Churchill and featuring *his* paintings!

Although some themes such as Churchill, Kennedy, Art and Sport will always be a sound investment in general, one must exercise rigid self-control and refuse to pay inflated prices for the band wagon issues of the less scrupulous agency countries. Such issues are bought dear and are unlikely to produce a reasonable, let alone a handsome, dividend when one comes to dispose of them eventually. If collectors would rid themselves of the obsession to be 'complete', and would boycott the more blatantly speculative emissions of the 'agency countries', rackets of this sort would inevitably die out.

The idiotic thing is, however, that when sales of such issues dwindle from around the 50,000 set average to less than a tenth of that, philatelic interest in the country of issue wanes for the present—but such stamps will have a nasty habit of soaring in value in years to come when their true scarcity becomes more important than their questionable antecedents.

CHAPTER VII

STAMP CATALOGUES

TAKEN IN their simplest form, Stamp Catalogues are dealers' price lists. In the hands of the intelligent philatelist, however, they become indispensable tools—enabling him to classify and arrange his stamps according to their date of issue, their watermark and their perforation. Moreover, most catalogues nowadays have graduated beyond being merely the retail price list of a dealer and are regarded as valuable reference works. They have been compiled very carefully over the years, subject to constant revision. Though one man may ultimately be responsible for editing a catalogue, behind him there is inevitably a galaxy of leading specialists who have contributed towards ensuring that the listings are as accurate and informative as possible.

The infant hobby was hardly under way when the earliest catalogues made their appearance. The first of these was the modest *Catalogue des timbres-poste creés dans les divers Etats du globe* compiled by Alfred Potiquet in December 1861 and published in Paris by Eugène Lacroix. It was preceded by three months by the even less prepossessing list reproduced from handwriting, by Oscar Berger-Levrault of Strasbourg. The very first catalogues bore no prices, but in May 1863 Messrs. Zschiesche and Koder began the serialisation of their priced catalogue in the pages of *Magasin für Briefmarken-Sammler* published in Leipzig.

In November 1865 the youthful Edward Stanley Gibbons published his first modest price list. Priced at a penny, it consisted initially of a mere sixteen pages and listed 1,613 stamps. The early Gibbons price lists appeared at monthly intervals—in much the same way as many dealers today circularise their clients with their latest offers. But right from the very beginning Gibbons strove to give his customers a list which was not only as comprehensive as possible, but gave its readers a realistic basis for valuing their possessions. Two years later, on the other side of the Atlantic, the coin and stamp dealer, John Walter Scott, brought out his first catalogue. Several dealers (Pierre Mahé, Jean B. Moens, P. L. Pemberton, Mount Brown and Frederick Booty) and at least one private collector (Dr. John Gray of the British Museum) had already published catalogues, but not only are Gibbons and Scott still going strong, they are in a class of their own. Between them their catalogues are used by two-thirds of all collectors in the world—ranging, of course, from the philatelist who buys the latest editions as soon as they appear each year, to the 'philatelist' who relies on an edition ten years out of date (bought second hand at a club sale) with occasional glances at a slightly more up-to-date edition in the local public library.

As I am writing this, Gibbons have just announced that they are breaking into the North American market, with a special catalogue containing the British Commonwealth, the United States and its Possessions, and the United Nations Organisation. This venture is being launched in conjunction with the well-known numismatic publisher, Whitman of Racine, Wisconsin. But that is nothing new, for, sixty years ago, Gibbons had an office in New York and published an edition of their catalogue, priced in U.S. cents and dollars. In the three years immediately prior to the First World War Gibbons even had a branch in Buenos Aires and produced a South American edition of the catalogue, written in Spanish and priced in decimal shillings.

The earliest catalogues were unpretentious little manuals, devoid of illustrations and usually confined to the items which the dealer-publisher actually had in stock. Often their descriptions (colour, method of printing, design) were inaccurate and few bothered in the early days to make any distinction in perforation or watermark. Gibbons' earliest lists did not bother to differentiate whether stamps were perforated or imperforate and it was many a long year before the catalogues deigned to list the different plate numbers on the British line-engraved and surface-printed issues. Few collectors of the present time realise the great debt they owe to the catalogue editors and compilers of the past century. True, these gentlemen are only human, and errors occasionally occur, but for every slip that occurs there are ten thousand facts presented correctly. A few years ago the perennial problem of the production of a 'collectors' catalogue' was raised again; and no doubt it will be raised many times again, for philatelists will never be satisfied with the catalogues they use.

L. W. Fulcher gave a paper on this subject at the very first Philatelic Congress of Great Britain, held at Manchester in 1909. His principal complaint he set out as follows: 'The catalogues now in existence . . . are all published by dealers and are, in fact, price lists of what they have to sell. As a result they are unduly slanted in their presentation and in pricing according to their country of origin, and are both incomplete and inaccurate.' On the subject of pricing in the catalogues, he went on, 'It is not adequately realised that these prices are based on trade requirements, and . . . this is not always in accordance with what the true value of the stamp in the market really is. As all collectors well know, the sudden inclusion in *Stanley Gibbons Catalogue* of a variety which had not been recorded there before has a very remarkable effect upon the price of that variety in the market.' He concluded, 'It would be very desirable if we could really have a catalogue, a good reference catalogue, for collectors, compiled by collectors'.

Fulcher's views were heartily endorsed by Kenneth R. Lake, in his paper on the same subject, given before the Philatelic Congress held in 1965. He made a plea for a catalogue which would list 'all stamps which fulfilled a genuine postal requirement', illustrate all stamp designs, figures of stamps printed, issue and withdrawal dates. It should list the 'side lines' such as postal stationery, postal history items and proofs—ignored by most of the standard catalogues.

Mr. Lake summed up the purpose of the ideal catalogue as 'to instruct the learner, guide and lead on the student collector, and act as a work of reference for the more advanced researcher and the man who "has 'em all". Like a collection itself, it should illustrate and describe, be infinitely expandable and never slow to correct its errors of omission and commission. It should be selective only in a meaningful way—by emphasising major varieties over minor ones, not by ignoring all those things it does not wish to accept for reasons of prejudice or considerations of trade. It should be standardised throughout in scope, numbering, illustrations and layout, and indeed in every way necessary for easy comprehension and use.'

An interesting example of a catalogue which attempted to please the collector, while being entirely independent of the philatelic trade, was the short-lived *Reliant* which ran to several editions in the 1940s. It was, however, tied to a printed album for British Commonwealth stamps and thus could never be entirely objective and all-embracing. In fact, it listed a great deal less than the *Gibbons Part I Catalogue* (though more detailed than the *Gibbons Simplified Catalogue*). The aims of the publisher were clearly set out in the opening preamble: 'The chief object in publishing this catalogue is to provide a semi-simplified catalogue at a price within the means of every collector, with an Album to go with it arranged on the same lines. The *Reliant* is an independent catalogue and not a house-organ of any one firm but rather a price-list that can be used by all.' On the subject of prices the editor stated, 'These have been fixed by a group of dealers with very many years of experience of the trade behind them, and represent prices for stamps in good condition. The prices constitute the average retail market valuation, and have no grossly inflated values, and are about those charged by the MAJORITY of dealers.'

An innovation, which will be of particular interest to readers of this book, was an attempt to predict those stamps which were regarded as having the most investment potential. Such stamps were indicated by asterisks. Regarding the tipped stamps, the compiler wrote, 'Many of those so marked in earlier editions have already shown considerable rises. The prices quoted for such stamps are considered as market value at the time of publication. These "tips" have proved very popular and collectors who have followed them and procured the stamps will not regret their purchases.'

The validity of tips is discussed at greater length in Chapter X.

If the perfect catalogue has not yet made its appearance, it is nevertheless true to say that never before has the collector had such a bewildering array of catalogues to choose from. Only a few of these are published by people who do not deal in the stamps so that catalogues are still predominantly the price-list of their publisher. The world of catalogue-publishing being a highly competitive one, however, this means that every publisher tries to outdo his rivals as he thinks best. In the end, the collector is faced with a choice between several catalogues, all possessing many good points and some bad, and he has to select the one which he thinks will serve him best.

Catalogues range from those which embrace the whole world in one volume, arranged on a simplified basis, to highly special-ised 'priced handbooks' covering selected issues of one country. There are catalogues devoted to groups of countries, either geographically (by Continents) or politically (British Common-wealth, France and Colonies, United States and Possessions). Reflecting public demand, there are catalogues for airmail stamps, thematic catalogues, and catalogues for postal station-ery, local stamps and revenues.

There are several publishers who cover more than one of these facets in their catalogues. Pre-eminent in this field is Stanley Gibbons, already referred to. Gibbons' catalogues have their champions and their detractors. There are inconsistencies and foibles about Gibbons that the philatelist finds exasperating, but I know of no other English-language catalogues which give the same amount of detail.

Gibbons' catalogues exist nowadays in three categories. The *Simplified Whole World Catalogue* gives a straightforward listing of the world's stamps and is designed mainly for the beginner, the general collector and the thematic or topical enthusiast. Watermarks, perforations, shades and paper variations are ignored. Dates of issue are confined to the year and the names of designers and printers are not given. Stamps of the British Commonwealth are illustrated in actual size; those of the rest of the world have been reduced to ¾ linear. The heading for each country or postal administration includes the political status and the various currencies used (together with their dates) —information which is curiously omitted from the much more comprehensive '*Big*' *Gibbons* series.

The '*Big*' *Gibbons* volumes are familiarly referred to by collectors by the colour of their bindings: red for *Part I* (*British Commonwealth*), green for *Part II* (*Europe and Colonies*) and blue for *Part III* (*America, Asia and Africa*). These volumes together cover the entire world in much greater detail than the *Simplified Catalogue*. Information is given on the designers, engravers and printers of stamps, so far as the information is available. Regarding miniature sheets, Gibbons could be seen at their most arbitrary. Shortly before the Second World War Gibbons became alarmed at the increasing profusion of these issues (about which I have more to say in Chapter IX) and decided not to list any issued after 1937. Consequently editions of the '*Big*' *Gibbons* until recently listed miniature sheets up till 1937 in full but made only occasional mention of these thereafter, and usually confined comment to those cases where stamps might be found which could only have emanated from miniature sheets. The spate of miniature sheets has steadily grown rather than diminished, so that Gibbons might have been expected to stick to their principles even more steadfastly than ever. But, bowing to popular demand, they have now given way, and from this year onwards all new editions of the '*Big*' *Gibbons* will list these sheets and price them. One cannot but admire Gibbons for their lonely boycott of what represents one of the most parasitic aspects of modern philately, but, since all the other leading catalogues continued to list miniature sheets, it was inevitable that Gibbons should come into line with the rest.

In many respects the best catalogues of world stamps at present are those published by Eugen Berlin GmbH of Munich. I refer, of course, to the famous *Michel* series. The highlight of the Michel range is the *Europa Catalogue*, while the rest of the world is treated in the three-volume *Ubersee Catalogue* arranged alphabetically. Basically the Michel catalogues list the same information as the '*Big*' *Gibbons*—details of printer, designer,

perforation and watermark. In the case of the British Commonwealth territories they do not go into the same detail
as Gibbons, but their European catalogue is in many respects
more comprehensive. *Michel* has the edge over *Gibbons* in the
meticulous footnotes liberally sprinkled throughout. *Michel's*
illustrations are smaller and of questionable value to the collector who wishes to check a dubious specimen against a picture
of the genuine article. On the other hand *Michel* illustrates
every type of stamp issued—a tremendous boon for the thematic
collector. *Gibbons* illustrates the stamps of the British Commonwealth in entirety, but the rest of the world is illustrated on a
selective basis only, so that the thematic collector is likely to miss
items unless he carefully studies the verbal descriptions of sets.

Of the American catalogues the leader is still *Scott*, though
Minkus has many advantages, particularly for the thematic
collector who can derive a great deal of useful information
from the captions of the latter. Scott's *Whole World Catalogue*
may be purchased in one large volume, or, more usually, in
two volumes. *Volume I* is devoted to the United States and the
United Kingdom and their respective possessions, together
with the United Nations and the Americas. *Volume II* covers
the rest of the world (with the obvious exceptions of Communist
China, North Korea, and North Vietnam, and Cuban issues
after mid-1961).

Volume I is not as detailed as *Gibbons* in its listing of the British
Commonwealth, though marginally more comprehensive for
United States issues. Illustrations are smaller and less representative, if anything, than *Gibbons*. In this way *Scott's* listings
are marshalled into four columns, whereas *Gibbons* gets only
three in a volume of the same quarto format. A major failing
of the *Scott Catalogue* is its omission of such elementary details
as the printer and designer. On the other hand, the *Scott
Catalogue* is much more detailed and advanced than the *Gibbons
Simplified Catalogue*, whose place it occupies in North America.

The *Minkus Catalogue* follows the same division as *Scott*, into
two volumes (America and the British Commonwealth, and
the Rest of the World respectively) and is designed on the lines
pursued by the celebrated *Minkus Global Stamp Album*.

French-speaking philatelists are catered for by the *Yvert* range of catalogues which consist of *Volume I* (France and Colonies), *Volume II* (Europe and Colonies) and *Volume III* (Rest of the World). Their arrangement is more convenient in this respect than *Gibbons*, whose political grouping of postal administrations has tended to be rather arbitrary in recent years. For example, anyone foolish enough to specialise in the stamps of the Cameroons will find the U.K.T.T. series of 1960 and the British occupation issues of 1915 in *Part I*, the stamps of the German colony of Kamerun and the French mandatory period in *Part II* and the issues since independence in *Part III*. There are many other examples which one could cite. On the other hand Gibbons have recognised that European collectors are interested in countries which are geographically in Europe though politically in the Commonwealth, by listing Malta, Gibraltar, Cyprus, the British post offices in the Levant, Heligoland and the Ionian Islands in both *Part I* and *Part II*. Conversely, Ireland, though not part of the Commonwealth, is listed in *Part I* as well as *Part II*, for the convenience of collectors of the British Isles.

Apart from the exclusively European catalogues, *Michel*, *Gibbons* and *Yvert*, there is an excellent one published by Zumstein of Berne, Switzerland. It is printed in German and in many respects resembles the *Michel Catalogue* though it lacks a great deal of information given by the latter (designers, printers and major varieties). It is more on the level of the *Gibbons Simplified*, but lists watermark and perforation varieties, and of course, miniature sheets.

THE LANGUAGE PROBLEM

Zumstein's introductory pages contain copious notes in German, French and English. *Gibbons*' concession to foreign users consists of a three-page glossary of colours and philatelic terms in English, French, German, Spanish and Italian. *Michel*'s introduction is predominantly in German, but has tables of abbreviations in English, French, Spanish, Portuguese and Italian and a philatelic glossary in German, English, French, Spanish and Portuguese. The American catalogues, however, are 'all-American' and no attempt is made to help the European or Latin American user whose English is not very fluent. Stamp collectors, however, by the nature of their hobby, tend to have less trepidation about picking up a catalogue in a language other than their own, and soon find their way about the text. Pictures are worth thousands of words and the ingenious use of symbols, which are gradually winning international acceptance, is making the whole-world catalogues acceptable everywhere.

COLOURS

The question of colour is a vexed one. So long as it remains impossible for stamps to be illustrated in full colour, catalogue-users must rely on written descriptions to sort out the various stamps. Since the value of a stamp can vary considerably according to its colour, this is an important point, but it is amazing how much variation there is between one catalogue and another in the colour nomenclature for the same stamps. A comparison of the various listing of France's first 10c. stamp illustrates this clearly.

Gibbons	Scott	Yvert	Zumstein	Michel
yellowish bistre, £40	bistre, $165	yellow-bistre	light olive-brown	yellow-brown
greenish bistre, £100	dark bistre, $175	greenish bistre brown-bistre		olive-brown
brownish bistre, £45				

The 1 franc stamp in the same series is even more confusing:

orange-vermilion, £1,100	vermilion, $5,000	vermilion	orange-red	orange-red
light orange-vermilion, £300	pale vermilion, $1,200	pale vermilion	vermilion	vermilion

Gibbons	Scott	Yvert	Zumstien	Michel
orange-brown, £600	dull orange-red, $3,000	{ bright vermilion / chalky vermilion }	bright red	pale red
carmine-brown, £300	brown-carmine, $1,100	brown-carmine	brown-carmine	brown-carmine
carmine, £175	carmine, $700	{ dark carmine / light carmine }	carmine	carmine

I have included the prices stated in *Gibbons* and *Scott* merely to give some idea of the different values attached to the various shades. Reds and yellows are always tricky colours to distinguish, but the task of the poor philatelist is not made any easier by the catalogue descriptions. Incidentally, Gibbons publish a splendid *Colour Guide* containing a hundred different colours corresponding to the descriptions given in their catalogues.

SPECIALISED CATALOGUES

Collectors nowadays are tending to concentrate on the stamps of one country or a small group of countries, so catalogues have appeared in recent years to provide as much information as possible in a limited field. It used to be said that true philately began where the catalogues left off. This is no longer valid in view of the many erudite catalogues which are available to the collectors today.

These catalogues are dealt with below, according to the countries they cover.

The best-served country, so far as these catalogues are concerned, is GREAT BRITAIN, though scarcely four years ago it ranked among those countries totally unprovided with a specialised catalogue, reflecting, perhaps, the fact that British stamps were neglected to a large extent by the majority of collectors. The growing interest in British stamps, however, encouraged Gibbons to publish, in 1964, their monumental *Great Britain Specialised Catalogue, Volume I*, which was devoted to the issues of the reign of Queen Victoria. Some idea of its infinitely more detailed nature, as compared with the '*Big*' *Gibbons, Part I*, has been given in Chapter V. On the one hand it lists such items as proofs, colour trials, imprimaturs, specimen overprints, re-entries, plate flaws, Mulready wrappers (pictorial stationery issued at the same time as the 1d. black in 1840) and scarce postmarks which the ordinary catalogue ignores; while its notes are positively encyclopedic. In 1967 *Volume II* appeared covering the stamps of King Edward VII, King George V, King Edward VIII and King George VI in a similar fashion.

These two volumes are complemented by another catalogue which made its debut in 1967—the *Woodstock Catalogue of British Elizabethan Stamps*, edited by Dr. John Sugden. As its title implies, this deals exclusively with the postage stamps of the United Kingdom from 1952 onwards. Each issue is followed by detailed notes which other catalogues would do well to emulate. Cylinder blocks, 'traffic lights', photogravure flaws and retouches, watermark and perforation varieties are treated in minute detail. In addition the *Woodstock Catalogue* lists the by-ways of modern British philately—the 'local carriage labels' of Herm and Lundy, the People's League postal service, the Talyllyn Railway stamps and British European Airways labels.

At the other extreme, two small catalogues, the *Tudor* and the *G.B. Netto*, have been published for the benefit of those who merely wish a simplified listing of British stamps from 1840 to the present time.

Giving a much more detailed listing than *Part I* is Gibbons' *Elizabethan Catalogue* which, as its name implies, covers the Commonwealth stamps of the present reign (1952 to date). This grew out of the old *Two Reigns Catalogue* which was little more than the King George VI and Queen Elizabeth periods of *Part I* catalogue printed separately. The *Elizabethan* made its

PLATE VII

FOREIGN RARITIES.

(1) Austria, Dollfuss, 1936 (£150, $500), (2) Japan 10s., 1916 (£35, $125), (3) Saar, Charity 10fr., 1928 (£85, $350), (4) Belgium, Red Cross 10fr., 1918 (£55, $200), (5) France, 50fr. airmail, 1936 (£48, $175), (6) Egypt, Port Fuad 50p., 1926 (£150, $275), (7) France, Orphans 5fr., 1917 (£100, $375), (8) Italy, Philatelic Congress 40c., 1922 (£50, $250), (9) Germany, Chicago flight 1m., 1933 (£60, $225), (10) Bulgaria, Balkan Games 50l., 1933 (£30, $125).

début in 1965 during the celebrations marking the centenary of Gibbons' first catalogue. It lists booklets, some of the more prominent flaws and varieties and gives dates of printings, plate numbers and quantities printed.

Gibbons have now been overtaken in this field, however, by the *Commonwealth Catalogue of Queen Elizabeth Stamps*, which was formerly published by the Commonwealth Stamp Co., of Liverpool, but has recently come under the control of Urch, Harris and Co. Ltd. of London and Bristol. The first edition of the catalogue under new management appeared in 1967 and already is far superior to anything else on the market, in spite of a few printing errors inevitable in a first edition. It lists everything that the *Elizabethan* does and a great deal more, such as First-Day Covers, and is much more detailed in the information it gives on varieties and stamp booklets.

For the variety enthusiast the *Catalogue of Varieties on Queen Elizabeth II Postage Stamps*, formerly published by John Lister (hence its popular name, the '*J.L.*' *Catalogue*) and now published by the Shelley Stamp Co., is ideal. At the other extreme, for those who want a simplified listing of the present reign only, there is the *Catalogue of Queen Elizabeth II Postage Stamps* published by John Lister.

The UNITED STATES is catered for in *Scott's Specialised Catalogue of the U.S.A.* It covers the issues of the Confederate States, Hawaii, the Philippines, the Danish West Indies (U.S. Virgin Islands) and the other territories which now comprise the United States. An important feature is the illustration of every stamp larger than life size. All the varieties are listed and priced, and include stamps on cover, blocks of four, plate numbers, the Farley imperforates, postal stationery, revenues, savings stamps and even Christmas seals. The *Minkus American Catalogue* is also useful, though not quite so detailed.

Testifying to the fanatical popularity of German stamps there are no less than five catalogues devoted to GERMANY. Only one of these, published by Minkus and priced in cents and dollars, is written in English, but it lacks the detail which is to be found in the others. Michel, Muller and Borek publish German catalogues on a semi-advanced basis, but Michel also publish a specialised catalogue which is in the same class as Gibbons' British counterpart. Their *Simplified German Catalogue* is pretty detailed and would satisfy most moderate specialists, but the *Specialised Catalogue* is the ultimate in Teutonic thoroughness and anything omitted from its pages would hardly be worth knowing. Across the Wall, in East Germany, a fairly competent catalogue is published by Lipsia of Leipzig, though it allows politics to obtrude into its pages by omitting all the stamps of the Hitler period (1933–45).

FRANCE is currently catered for by five catalogues. The oldest established is the *Maury Catalogue*, direct descendant of the *Liste des timbres-poste* of 1863. The most detailed, however, is that published by Yvert et Tellier. Apart from the stamps themselves and their varieties, this catalogue includes the imperforates and *épreuves de luxe* (presented to high officials, but invariably finding their way on to the philatelic market), *millesimes, coins dates* (corner blocks bearing the date of the printing), specimen overprints, parcel stamps, First-Day Covers, and *Ballons Montés* (covers flown by manned balloon during the Siege of Paris). Monaco, Saar, Andorra and the countries and territories comprising the former French colonial empire and the present-day independent countries of the French Community are also included. Much the same ground is covered by the catalogue published by Thiaude, though not in the same detail. The two other French catalogues are published by Berck and Ceres respectively and it is difficult to choose between them. The *Berck Catalogue* is distinguished by its small format, which enables the collector to carry it around in his pocket, and its thumb-indexing by which the various sections can be located instantly.

SWITZERLAND is covered by four catalogues, two of which, published by Amateur Collector Ltd. of London, and Minkus of New York, are in English—a sure proof of the popularity of this country beyond its own boundaries. *Amateur Collector's Catalogue* is more detailed than the Swiss sections of *Gibbons Part II*, with chapters on *se-tenant* pairs and strips, *interpanneau* pairs, special flight postmarks and cachets, miniature sheets, telegraph stamps, franks, railway stamps and the vignettes used by the Hotel posts. Of the two indigenous catalogues the more comprehensive is the *Müller-Katalog* published by Basler-Taube Verlag of Basle, though the *Zumstein Catalogue* is printed in French as well as German throughout. Both include a section on the neighbouring principality of Liechtenstein. *Müller* includes a section on First-Day postmarks.

Unlike the majority of the Continental catalogues both the *Sassone* and the *Bolaffi* catalogues of the stamps of ITALY illustrate each stamp in full, natural size. They cover the issues of the old Italian kingdoms and principalities, San Marino, the Vatican and the former colonial possessions of the Italian Empire (including the British occupation issues of the Second World War and after). If Italian is beyond you, however, there is a good English-language catalogue of the Italian group of countries published by Minkus.

SCANDINAVIA (Denmark, Norway, Sweden, Iceland, Finland and their dependencies) is covered by the *Facit Catalogue*. Here again, Minkus provide a competent catalogue in English (pricing in U.S. dollars) while, for the more advanced collector, AFA of Copenhagen publish an excellent-priced handbook on Denmark, Iceland, Greenland, the Faeroe Islands and the former Danish West Indies.

Most of the other 'popular' countries have a specialised catalogue devoted to them, usually published in the country of origin. These are listed below:

Australia: *The Australian Commonwealth Specialists Catalogue* (The Hawthorn Press, Melbourne).
Australian Dependencies: *Catalogue of the Stamps of the Australian Dependencies* (Sterling, Dubbo, N.S.W.).
Austria: *Österreich Netto-Briefmarken Katalog* (Herinek, Vienna).
Argentina/Brazil: *Borek Netto Katalog*, Brunswick.
Belgium: *Belgique* (Prinet, Brussels).
Canada: *Specialised Philatelic Catalogue of Canada & British North America* (Holmes, Toronto).
Czechoslovakia: *Borek*.
Ceskoslovensko Katalog Znamek (Pofis, Prague).
Minkus (includes Hungary).

Egypt (and Sudan): *Catalogue of Postage Stamps of Egypt and the Sudan* (Zeheri, Cairo).

Hungary: *Borek.*

Magyar Belyegek Arjegyzeke (Magyar Filatelia Vallalat, Budapest).

Minkus (includes Czechoslovakia).

India: *A Specialised Priced Catalogue of Indian Stamps* (either 1852–1966 or 1947–1966) (Jal Cooper, Bombay).

Borek.

Israel: *Catalogue of the Postage Stamps of the State of Israel.* (Mosden, London).

Catalogue of Israel Stamps (Simon, Tel Aviv). (Text in English; prices in U.S. dollars.)

Borek.

Japan: *Borek.*

Luxembourg: *Catalogue Speciale Illustré des Timbres-Poste du Luxembourg* (Banque du Timbre, Luxembourg).

Netherlands: *Speciale Catalogus* (Nederlandsche Vereeniging van Postzegel-Handelaren).

New Zealand: *The C.P. Specialist New Zealand Loose-Leaf Catalogue* (Campbell Paterson, Auckland).

Portugal: *Catalogo de Selos Postais, Portugal* (Simoes Ferreira, Porto).

Poland: *Borek.*

Russia: *Borek.*

Minkus.

South Africa: *Handbook/Catalogue of Union of South Africa* (Philatelic Federation of Southern Africa).

Spain: *Catalogo Unificado y Especializado de Espana* (Galvez, Madrid).

Turkey: *Turk Pulari* (Pulhan, Stamboul). *Borek.*

Yugoslavia: *Borek.*

Most of these catalogues are available from Harris Publications, 27 Maiden Lane, London, W.C.2, or Lindquist Publications, 153 Waverley Place, New York, or direct from the publisher concerned.

SUBJECT CATALOGUES

So far I have dealt only with those catalogues whose contents are arranged on a territorial basis. There are also several which contain stamps according to their subject—either types of stamps or themes on stamps.

Some of these catalogues are collectors' gems in their own right nowadays and, because of their specialised interest, seldom ran to more than two or three editions at most and consequently contain information which has never been improved on. In this category come such works as Forbin's *Catalogue prix-courant de timbres-fiscaux* (1905) and Cazin et Rochas' *Catalogue des Timbres Commemoratifs* (1914), or L'Estrange Ewen's *Priced Catalogue of Railway Letter Stamps of the United Kingdom* (1904) and Walter Morley's *Catalogue of the Revenue and Fee Stamps of Great Britain and Ireland*.

But the most popular and enduring group of special stamps have been the airmail issues. Theodore Champion pioneered the airmail catalogue with his *Catalogue Historique et Descriptif des Timbres de la Poste Aerienne* which first appeared in 1921. David Field of London published two editions of his *Airmail Catalogue* in 1932 and 1934 and there is still a great deal of useful information to be gleaned from its pages. The leading aero-philatelic catalogue in Britain today, however, is that published by Francis J. Field of Sutton Coldfield. His series of 'Aero Field' priced handbooks gives up-to-date market valuations not only on stamps, etiquettes and vignettes, but also on cachets, special postmarks and souvenir flight covers. The principal catalogue, covering the airmail stamps, both official and semi-official, of the whole world is published annually by Nicholas Sanabria and entitled *The World Airmail Catalogue*.

Between 1899 and 1904 Stanley Gibbons published special catalogues devoted to postal stationery and local stamps respectively. Unfortunately they discontinued these publications when they ceased to trade in those branches of philately and interest has suffered accordingly. Nowadays both stationery and locals have become fashionable once more, but though there is a fair amount of literature on these subjects there is a dearth of sound, priced catalogues to give the collector an indication

of relative values. Very few of the 'one country' catalogues
cited above list stationery, though many deal with local stamps
(i.e. those stamps issued by a town, a province or a private
company, and whose validity is limited within the country of
origin).

Since thematic or topical collecting is all the rage at the
moment, it is hardly surprising that a number of catalogues
has appeared in this field. They range from the modest catalogue
of Scout and Sports stamps published by Henri Trachtenberg
of Paris, to the sumptuous, hard-bound *Catologo Specializzato
Europa* published in Rome by Aldo D'Urso. This magnificent
volume, printed on art paper, is copiously illustrated with the
stamps, covers, postmarks and cachets whose theme is European
Integration. Lollini of Italy publishes a priced catalogue of
stamps whose theme is Space Travel. While Sieger of West
Germany publishes a catalogue of Olympic Games stamps.
Animals, Sport and Flowers are each covered by catalogues
published by Brun (in French) and Torrens (in Spanish). The
American Topical Association has published an admirable
series of handbooks setting forth check-lists of stamps arranged
according to the subject depicted on them, but these are not
priced.

CHAPTER VIII

SOUND INVESTMENTS, A TO Z

WHAT ARE the 'Top Twenty' countries, whose stamps are worth collecting as a sound investment? This difficult question has often been posed and invariably a different answer is given each time. The answer also depends on the country in which the question is asked since it is axiomatic (in Europe and America at any rate) that that country will head the list.

Recently a poll was conducted in Italy* to determine the most popular countries with Italian collectors (probably the most investment-conscious collectors anywhere in the world). Naturally, Italy, San Marino and Vatican headed the list but it is interesting to note that the most popular *foreign* countries were (in order of preference): Great Britain, France, West Germany, Sweden, Switzerland, Denmark, Norway, United States, Austria, Finland, Netherlands, Spain, Canada, Portugal, Luxembourg, Greece, Australia, Iceland, New Zealand, Argentina, Brazil, India, Libya, Malta, Monaco, Somalia and the United Nations. Since this poll was taken, Malta has soared in the Italian charts and it is now fast attaining the popularity already enjoyed by San Marino and the Vatican.

For collectors in Britain and the United States the order of popularity would be different, but basically the same countries would be listed. It must not be forgotten, however, that philately is a *hobby* not a business proposition, and many of the most valuable collections have been devoted to countries which would come at the bottom of the popularity poll. Besides, by tipping certain countries or themes as worth collecting I am,

---

* See *Il Boom della Filatelia*, by Gianni Castellano (Capelli editore 1966).

to some extent, defeating the object of the exercise. If everyone rushed out tomorrow to buy French stamps or stamps featuring Kennedy there would be a tremendous boom in these issues for a while, but sooner or later this would be followed by the inevitable depression when speculators started to unload their holdings. In the survey which follows I can do no more than make a few general observations on the past and present performance of the stamps of most countries and leave it to the reader to weigh up the future prospects in each case. Space limitations prevent me from mentioning every country, but most of those which are catching attention at the present are referred to below.

ABU DHABI. The largest of the Trucial States on the coast of the Persian Gulf, Abu Dhabi has only been issuing stamps since 1964 and until fairly recently its postal system has been under the control of the Overseas Mails Branch of the British Postal Services Department in London. Up till now issues have been restricted to a definitive series with a face value of just over Rs. 20 (30s. or $4.20) and a set of three stamps depicting Falconry. This conservative outlook is a refreshing contrast to the perpetual flood of new issues emanating from several of the other states in this area. Its stamps are nicely designed pictorials, not too plentiful in used condition and worth searching out.

ADEN. This has formed the Federation of South Arabia since 1963. It did not begin issuing its own distinctive stamps till 1937. Worth a handsome premium, especially on cover, are Indian stamps bearing Aden postmarks. The first series, the 'Dhows' of 1937, had a relatively short life of less than two years. Originally available for 30s. this set could be bought in the 1950s for £12 ($36) but now rates £39 in *Gibbons* and $105 in *Scott*. Among the later issues the most interesting are the colour and perforation changes to which the Elizabethan series of 1953–9 was subject. None of them is really elusive—as yet. The first ½ anna stamp of Qu'aiti State is usually found in blue-green, but the December 1946 printing appeared in a distinctively olive shade. Fine used copies of the ½ anna are fairly

plentiful, but though the blue-green is priced in *Gibbons* at
9d. the olive variety now rates £2, so it is worth looking for.
Since 1966 the two states in the former Eastern Aden Protectorate—the Kathiri State of Seiyun and the Qu'aiti State in
Hadhramaut—have had their stamps produced and distributed
by philatelic agencies. Thus we have had stamps for the
Olympic Games, Kennedy, Churchill, the World Cup Football
Championship and Famous Paintings, none of which can have
the least possible bearing on the states concerned, except, for
the moment, to line their coffers with much-needed sterling
and dollars. The stamps of the FEDERATION OF SOUTH
ARABIA come under the aegis of the Crown Agents and are
a sounder proposition, but, with the political situation in that
area deteriorating rapidly, their long-term prospects are
problematical.

AFGHANISTAN. The early 'Tigers', with their circular
design, outlandish inscriptions and primitive appearance, have
a certain appeal, though many of them are expensive to acquire
nowadays. The middle issues, however, are singularly unattrac-
tive while the modern stamps have been subject to a certain
amount of 'funny business'. Between April 1961 and March
1963 the production of new stamps was in the hands of a
philatelic agency acting under the authority of a contract
granted by the Afghanistan Government. To quote *Gibbons
Catalogue*, 'It later became evident that token supplies were only
placed on sale in Kabul for a few hours and some of the sets
contained stamps of very low denominations for which there
was no possible postal use. Moreover, the prices at which some
of these stamps were released bore no relation to their face
value and appear to have been quite arbitrary.'
  These stamps were released perforated, imperforate and in
miniature sheets and were produced with an eye to thematic
sales. Gibbons does not list them and this has effectively damned
them, in the eyes of British collectors at least. Things are
reputedly back to normal in Afghanistan again, but caution
should be the watchword in collecting its stamps. The late
Major Hopkins of Bath formed an outstanding collection of

Afghanistan stamps, but although it would fetch a very large sum if it were sold, this country can hardly be recommended as a general rule.

AJMAN, another of the Trucial States. This has been controlled by a philatelic agency since its first stamps appeared in 1964. Handsome, large-sized, multicoloured though they be, they are distinctly 'collector-bait'. No less than 26 stamps appeared in 1964 (from June to December) while 46 were issued in 1965 and the spate of new issues since then shows no sign of slackening. These have been imperforate as well as perforated, and miniature sheets have accompanied all but the definitive series. It would be difficult to recommend Ajman as a steady prospect for investment and yet its stamps have tremendous thematic appeal which will probably ensure their popularity for some time yet. The Kennedy stamps (featuring pictures of J.F.K. from boyhood to President) and the Churchill series (depicting famous London landmarks) were among the most interesting of all in these respective themes.

ALBANIA. Never philatelically fashionable, ranks as one of the world's least popular countries today. Too many poorly-designed and poorly-printed stamps of the present time have an outright political bias to merit their getting serious attention in the West. They have a certain following behind the Iron Curtain, but elsewhere they rouse little interest. Most of the moderns exist imperforate and many of them are known in different colours from limited printings done specially for the collector. The pre-war issues had little appeal, on account of their seemingly interminable overprints—yet the earliest issues would repay the astute philatelist prepared to delve into the tortuous political background and the postal history of the country from 1912 till 1920.

ALGERIA. Not as popular as it deserves to be, though assured of a large following in France. It issued its own stamps from 1924 till 1958 and these, particularly the later ones, possess the charm for which the stamps of the mother-country are renowned. From 1958 till 1962 French stamps were issued in Algeria and these, with legible Algerian postmarks, are worth a premium to specialists. The issues since independence in 1962 are colourful, of reasonable face value and not too frequent, so that Algeria is a country whose stamps should improve steadily as a financial prospect.

ANDORRA, the Pyrennean principality, jointly controlled by the Spanish Bishops of Urgel and the head of the French state. The outward symbols of this dual sovereignty are the twin postal systems, one Spanish, the other French, which exist side by side and each issue their own stamps. Since the late 1920s only about 300 stamps altogether (including Postage Due labels) have been issued and none is very expensive. The modern issues of both post offices are beautifully produced and this, coupled with the romantic remoteness of Andorra, puts them high in the affections of collectors. A collection of Andorran stamps definitely offers scope for investment, provided one gets on to it before everyone else thinks of it.

ANGOLA. This country has not excited much attention, on account of the rather dreary colonial key-type designs of the period from 1870 to 1931. But there is no doubt that the stamps issued in the past two decades have attracted a lot of attention with their bright colours and thematic appeal. These remarks apply equally well to Cape Verde Islands, Mozambique, Macao and other Portuguese colonies, all of which have a strong following in their mother country and which are rapidly increasing in popularity abroad.

ANTIGUA. Like all the British islands of the West Indies, this is a good country to collect for a sound investment. Apart from the watermark and perforation variations in the Victorian line-engraved issues, none of them is difficult to acquire. The Tercentenary series of 1932 is a good property which will undoubtedly go far, while interest in the modern issues is increasing, as more and more American and Canadian tourists discover this island.

ARGENTINA. In spite of the blatant use of stamps for political ends, continues to be popular with British collectors. One of the best sets, from the point of view of future appreciation, was the trio of 1964 showing maps of the Falkland Islands and British Antarctica clearly marked with the Argentinian flag! Argentina's stamps have greatly improved in quality and subject matter in recent years and, were it not for the rather unstable economy of the country just now, would be a serious proposition for the investor. The early issues, the Buenos Aires stamps of 1858–62 and the 'Rivadavias' which followed, were among the blue chips of philately, but even now it is possible to pick up unconsidered trifles which turn out to be worth a great deal more. The middle issues include some of the best stamps for steady financial growth—the Centenary sets of 1910 and 1916 and the Revolution commemoratives of 1930, not to mention the Zeppelin stamps of the latter years.

ARMENIA. One of those 'dead' countries which on first sight would appear to hold out little prospects to the philatelist. Every schoolboy collection contains some of the Mount Ararat pictorials printed in Paris in 1920 but never issued in Armenia which by that time had fallen under Bolshevik control. For that reason Armenia tends to be regarded as a country whose stamps cannot be taken seriously. Nevertheless the legitimate issues of this ephemeral state, which had a precarious existence between 1918 and 1923, are now eagerly sought after and in recent years Gibbons have extensively revised their listings (and prices!) for many of these stamps. Most of the surcharged stamps have been forged, so caution is required when purchasing Armenians.

ASCENSION. For many years under the control of the British Admiralty (all births on this South Atlantic island were at that time registered in the London parish of Wapping). Prior to 1922 British stamps were used, with distinctive postmarks which now command a good price. Apart from the 1922 series of St. Helena stamps overprinted for use in Ascension, none of the island's issues is expensive, but they are gradually becoming more elusive, especially used on cover. This is definitely a country worth collecting; its stamps are few as yet, but many of them have thematic appeal and the fact that Ascension now has a tracking station manned in connection with National Aerospace Association projects has brought it within the orbit of American philatelists.

AUSTRALIA. A vast number of indigenous philatelists stimulate interest in every aspect of its stamps, quite apart from its devotees in Britain, Europe and America. Many of the greatest rarities and the best classics emanate from the old Australian states—the 'Sydney Views' of New South Wales, Tasmania's 'Chalon Heads', Western Australia's 'Black Swans' and the 'Half-Lengths' of Victoria are outstanding examples. These are now in the millionaire class, but it is not too late for the collector of relatively modest means to put together a reasonably representative collection of the Commonwealth issues from 1913 onwards. Even in this group the prices are hardening and the 'Kangaroo' £2 of 1913 may soon top the £100 mark, though as little as two years ago it was valued at only half that figure. Even the Navigators stamps of 1963–4 in Australian shillings and pounds are proving singularly difficult to find, especially in lightly cancelled condition.

AUSTRIA. High among the desirable countries to collect. Its earliest issues include several of the world's greatest rarities (the 'Red Mercury' of 1851 is now priced by *Gibbons* at £4,000 mint and £4,500 used), but most of the later issues are still within the reach of the average collector. The better stamps have a steady market and prices are continually rising as the demand grows. Sets such as the 1930 Rotary Convention and the pre-war Charity issues have soared enormously in value in recent years, while the 1936 Dollfuss memorial stamp, priced by *Gibbons* in 1938 at 10s. 6d. rose to £20 in 1950 and £150 in 1967.

BAHAMAS. A very popular country to collect since it is usually bracketed with the British West Indies (though geographically it lies outside that area). You would need a large pocket-book to make a reasonable collection of the 'Chalon Heads', with their intricacies of perforation and watermark, but the later issues are fairly straightforward. There are several elusive stamps in the George VI series—the colour changes of 1941 and the various shades of the 5s. In 1942 and 1948 the Bahamas were guilty of issuing long commemorative sets (½d. to £1) marking the 450th Anniversary of Columbus' Landing and the Tercentenary of Eleuthera. Unpopular at the time of issue, these sets are now steadily creeping up in value and should be good investments. The 1965 definitive series had a very short life, being replaced by a decimal surcharge issue in 1966, so this set also should go far. A good little set to watch out for is the definitive pair overprinted BAHAMAS TALKS 1962. Because of their association with the late President Kennedy this set has already rocketed from a face value of 1s. 6d. to 18s. 6d. (*Gibbons*) and $3.75 (*Scott*).

BAHRAIN. Has been issuing stamps longer than any other sheikhdom in the Persian Gulf area and yet has issued fewer than 150 different varieties in the past 45 years. Probably because all the stamps up till 1960 consisted of contemporary Indian or British issues suitably overprinted, Bahrain has not received the attention from collectors that it deserves. Yet many of these stamps were released in ridiculously small quantities and once collectors wake up to that fact the existing catalogue quotations will be seen to be quite unrealistic.

BARBADOS. Always a firm favourite in Britain, this island has grown in popularity with American collectors in recent years. Here again many of the Victorian stamps, particularly the provisional 1d. on 5s. of 1878, are decidedly rare. In the 1907 Nelson Centenary series *Gibbons* lists the 2½d. black and bright blue at 35s. mint, while the shade variety in indigo rates £75—quite a difference! It pays to be able to distinguish shades of this sort and it is cases like this that enable the knowledgeable philatelist to profit from the ignorance of others. In the 1938 series the ½d. green can be worth anything from 6d. to £5 unused, depending on its perforations, the scarce variety being one of the 'Blitz perfs.', so-called since the printers, De La Rue, were bombed out of their premises during the Second World War and had to have some of their stamps perforated by other firms.

BASUTOLAND (now renamed Lesotho). Has issued only a moderate number of stamps since they first appeared in 1933 and none of them is particularly pricey. There was some speculation in the Victory series of 1945 (this remark applies also to the issues from Bechuanaland and Swaziland) but after they were dumped on the market their price fell below face value and it will take a long time for them to recover. A sensation was created in 1961 by the provisional surcharges converting the stamps to South African cents and rands, and there are some good varieties, though not in the same class or variety as those of Bechuanaland and Swaziland.

BECHUANALAND (now Botswana). Would repay the student prepared to delve into its earliest issues, particularly the stamps of Britain and the Cape of Good Hope overprinted. The 1961 decimals include the first type of the 1 Rand on 10s. which some lucky collectors received in their New Issue packets for 11s. 6d.; once the dealers cottoned on to the fact that this overprint differed from the subsequent printing, the price rocketed and now stands at £110 in *Gibbons* ($275 in *Scott*).

BELGIUM. A good country to collect since it appeals to philatelists rich and poor alike. One could spend a fortune, making a plating-study of the 'Epaulettes' or the 'Medallions' (the epithets given to the beautifully engraved stamps of 1849–65) or derive a lot of pleasure and profit from the humbler Montenez issues of the 1920s. The modern stamps are well designed and produced, still moderately priced, but rapidly rising in value as their popularity increases in the Common Market countries. The erstwhile Belgian territories of the CONGO and RUANDA-URUNDI (now the Republics of

Rwanda and Burundi) will always retain a considerable following in Belgium and the issues since independence are colourful,
interesting and not unduly prolific. The stamps of Mr.
Tshombe's ephemeral regime in KATANGA have already
risen in value and are not so easy to come by.

BERMUDA.   Another British territory usually (though
wrongly) classified with the West Indies. Actually sited off the
coast of North Carolina, it has long been popular as a holiday
resort for American and Canadian tourists and it is hardly
surprising that its stamps are eagerly collected in North
America where there is a ready market for the great 'primitives',
the Perot and the Thies postmaster issues of 1848–61. Prices
for these range from £1,750 to £4,500 (*Gibbons*) or $25,000
(*Scott*). There is plenty of variety among the later issues to keep
the philatelist busy—the King George VI high values
especially.

BHUTAN. A country which I find difficult to take seriously.
A set of four fiscal stamps appeared in 1954 and these apparently
served such postal purposes as were required in this backward,
remote kingdom in the Himalayas. In 1962, however, it began
issuing stamps which, though undoubtedly used in Bhutan,
were only available to the philatelic trade through a 'Philatelic
Trust' based in Nassau, Bahamas. Stamps for World Refugee
Year (two years late!) and a belated set of three in March 1964
in honour of the Winter Olympic Games—held in Innsbruck
the previous November—set the trend for subsequent issues
designed to raise as large a philatelic revenue as possible.
Commercially used stamps and covers from Bhutan *are* desirable, but gaudy pictorials from the Bahamas are a risky
investment.

BOLIVIA.   A country worth collecting. Fewer than 800
different varieties of stamps have appeared in the past hundred
years and there are not many which cost pounds rather than
pence.

PLATE VIII
POST-WAR RARITIES.

(1) Luxembourg, Europa 2fr., 1956 (£12, $50), (2) Netherlands, airmail 25g., 1951 (£12, $60), (3) United Nations, Human Rights 3c., 1954 (£5, $18.50), (4) Saar, Stamp Day, 1950 (£9, $37.50), (5) Vatican, airmail 500l., 1948 (£135, $550), (6) West Germany 90pf., 1952 (£20, $90), (7) West Berlin, Goethe 20pf., 1949 (£14, $75), (8) West Berlin 1m., 1949 (£20, $100), (9) San Marino, airmail 1,000l., 1951 (£90, $400), (10) Switzerland, Peace 5fr., 1945 (£25, $70).

BRAZIL. The first country in the Western Hemisphere, officially, to issue postage stamps.* The famous 'Bull's Eyes', which made their debut in August 1843, may still be purchased for as little as £20 (*Gibbons* price for a used 6or. worn impression). This is a complex country, where a knowledge of the various papers, perforations and watermarks in the middle issues rewards the *cognoscente*.

BRITISH GUIANA (GUYANA). Boasts the most expensive stamps anywhere in the world, so this is a country which you can never hope to complete unless you have a bottomless purse. Apart from the fabulous 1 cent black and magenta of 1856, there are a round dozen stamps of the 1850s in the four-or-five-figure bracket (depending on whether you count in sterling or dollars). But leaving aside the 'Cottonreels' and the Baum and Dallas type-set stamps there is plenty of good material which is always assured of a steady rate of appreciation. In the King George VI series the $1, perf. 12½, is worth 8s. but the last printing, made in 1951, was perforated 14 × 13 and now rates £25 in *Gibbons* ($75 in *Scott*).

BRITISH HONDURAS. Does not enjoy as much popularity as many other small British colonies do, probably because new issues are, as yet, 'few and far between'. Nevertheless, the earlies have plenty of scope for the discerning collector, particularly in the complicated provisional surcharges of 1889–91.

BRITISH SOLOMON ISLANDS. Began issuing stamps in 1907 when a series of rather crudely lithographed 'locals' were produced. They had a short life, being superseded the following year by a set engraved by De La Rue, and are much scarcer than their catalogue values would seem to indicate, especially used on cover. Solomons' stamps have not so far begun to enjoy the great upsurge in popularity now enjoyed by those of other Pacific groups, but their time could be coming soon. Meanwhile, the provisional decimal surcharges of 1966, and

---

* The City Despatch Post in New York City issued a 3c. stamp in 1842 and there were many other 'Carriers' and 'Postmasters' stamps prior to the government issues of 1847.

the 1965 series which they replaced, are worth purchasing before the inevitable rise in price.

BRUNEI. Also something of a 'sleeper' though interest in this sultanate is beginning to grow. Few catalogues list the local series of 1895 which not so long ago could be picked up for a few shillings, but which are now extremely elusive. The monotony of the 'Brunei River' design (which was used from 1907 to 1952) militates against these stamps ever becoming very popular, though a more liberal policy on new issues might change all this.

BULGARIA. Scarcely more popular than Albania, already referred to, and for the same reasons. Its stamps, never very interesting or well designed at the best of times, tend to be too 'political' to make them acceptable in Western Europe or America.

BURMA. A small band of devotees remember the country in the palmier days of the British Raj. But many were the ex-Servicemen who got their fingers burned over the Military Administration overprints of 1945 in which they invested heavily and have then been trying to unload on to an unwilling market ever since. Although this set was in use for a few months only it is still listed by *Gibbons* at little more than face value and can usually be purchased for a great deal less. This *should* have been a good set (the 1938 series, in use for more than three years, now rates about £13) but it was so heavily over-bought by speculators as to ruin eternally its future prospects. Post-independence Burma has provoked little response among philatelists and yet its stamps are well designed on the whole and not too frequent in issue.

CAMEROONS. A country with interesting possibilities, its varied political career being reflected in its stamps over the past seventy years. From German colony to Anglo-French mandated territory, independent state and now federal republic—each stage in the development of the country is represented by stamps, some of which, particularly those of the British and French occupying forces in the First World War and the short-lived issues of the Southern Cameroons, are becoming increasingly scarce.

CANADA. One of the really 'safe' countries whose stamps show a steady upward trend guaranteed by the large body of collectors in the country itself. In the United States its stamps rank second in popularity only to those of the U.S.A. Some of the early issues are for millionaires only but the later issues offer immense scope. The Victorian 'Large and Small Cents' and the George V 'Admirals' are fertile fields for study, while the coil stamps (imperforate on two opposite sides) usually rate a good premium and are worth the time and trouble in sifting through Canadian accumulations. Also worth watching out for are the stamps perforated or overprinted for Official use, Though the Canadian provinces are politically 'dead countries'. philatelic interest in them remains as lively as ever.

THE CAYMAN ISLANDS. Fewer than 200 different stamps have been issued since they first appeared in 1901 and none of them should be too difficult to obtain. But prices for the stamps of this popular West Indian group are soaring rapidly. *Gibbons* have advanced many of their Caymans' quotations in the past year or two. The 1966 catalogue listed the 5s. and 10s. of the Centenary set at £7 and £22 respectively; the corresponding prices in the 1967 catalogue are £9 and £30. An even greater increase was shown by the 10s. of 1935 which rose in one year from 95s. to £7. The 1967 *Scott Catalogue* lists these three stamps at $25, $75 and $20 respectively.

THE CENTRAL AFRICAN REPUBLIC. Stamps have only been issued since 1959. (Though the 'forerunners' when this country was the French colony of Oubangui-Chari are admissible.) A hundred stamps in eight years is not unduly excessive, while the colourful designs have attracted many new collectors who never bothered with the rather dull French colonial issues.

CEYLON. Renowned for its classic 'Pence' issues, but apart from the 'earlies', little interest seems to be shown in its stamps generally. A more liberal policy on new issues has been introduced recently and this, together with more colourful designs, should result in Ceylonese stamps becoming more popular. The George VI series is noted for a number of very scarce wartime perforation varieties—the 3c., for example, normally worth only 3d., can be worth up to £12 mint if it is perf. 13 × 13½ (though this variety rates only 3s. in used condition).

CHILE. Like most South American countries, Chile enjoys immense popularity in the United States and has a vigorous following in the country itself. With the exception of the Gillet and Desmadryl printings of the early Columbus issues, there are few expensive stamps, yet there is plenty of variety in the middle issues, particularly the 1911–29 definitives which include some elusive items. Some of the airmail stamps take searching for—especially the overprinted issues of 1927 and 1928–33.

CHINA. Like the curate's egg—'good in parts'. The local stamps of the Treaty Ports were overdone and undoubtedly owed their existence in large measure to philatelic demand, but nowadays they have a steady following. The Imperial issues and the early issues of the Republic are still popular, but collectors are in the main deterred from studying the later emissions on account of the complexity of surcharges and provincial overprints. The stamps of post-war Formosa are popular, particularly with American philatelists, but the issues of Communist China excite little interest *anywhere*. They are not listed in *Scott* 'because the U.S. Treasury Department (Foreign Assets Control Section) has prohibited their purchase abroad and importation'. There is a virtual ban on reporting them in American magazines and their collection is frowned on in the United States. Because of their fanatically political undertones and generally poor production they are unpopular in Britain and Western Europe, though they enjoyed some esteem in the Communist bloc. Now, however, they are presumably in bad odour there as well, following the rift between

Moscow and Peking. Finally their collection and study is even frowned on in Red China which has recently declared philately to be a decadent bourgeois habit and closed down its philatelic bureau!

CHRISTMAS ISLAND. Has only issued stamps since 1958 but already the first definitive series has begun to creep up in value. Together with Australia's other dependencies, the Cocos Islands, Nauru, Norfolk Island and Papua-New Guinea, this is a territory whose stamps are worth collecting. Unlike most of the others, however, the stamps of Christmas Island are still available in reasonable quantities. Do not overlook the forerunners, the stamps of the Straits Settlements and Singapore, used in the island from 1906 till 1948.

COLOMBIA. Plenty of scope here to offer the philatelist, but the classics of the United States of New Granada (1861) are on the expensive side, while many of the semi-official air stamps of SCADTA and the Compania Colombiana de Navegacion Aerea are in the millionaire class now. *Gibbons* ignores these fascinating issues, but they are listed by *Scott* and *Sanabria*.

COMORO ISLANDS. One of the latest territories in the French colonial empire. Definitely worth investigating. Its stamps are beautifully designed pictorials which are not too frequently issued (fewer than 60 since they first appeared in 1950). The forerunners from the component islands of this Indian Ocean archipelago—Anjouan, Grand Comoro, Mayotte and Moheli—take some finding, especially used on covers. If the Comoros ever equalled the popularity of similar island groups in this area, such as Mauritius or the Seychelles, values would soar correspondingly.

THE CONGO REPUBLIC (formerly the French colony of Middle Congo). Like all the countries of the French Community, this has fairly good investment prospects, so long as the flow of new issues is reasonably controlled. Its stamps, designed and printed in France, have the same quality which is associated with the erstwhile motherland. These countries are slowly growing in popularity outside the French area since the achievement of independence.

THE COOK ISLANDS. Have enjoyed a fair amount of popularity till now. There is something about the romance of the South Pacific which has always lured collectors towards its stamps. But since 1966 the postal affairs of the Cook Islands have been controlled by a philatelic agency and some rather peculiar things have happened which have already had a detrimental effect on the popularity of its stamps. Too many 'errors', deliberate or otherwise, on the overprinted Churchill and Airmail stamps have made collectors extremely suspicious.

COSTA RICA. One of the more conservative of the Latin American countries as regards philatelic output, and thus deserves a better following than it enjoys at present. Many of the middle issues, particularly the higher denominations, are far scarcer than their catalogue prices would indicate.

CUBA. Formerly very popular with American collectors, but since the advent of the Castro regime the strained relations between the United States and Cuba have militated against philatelic interest. On the other hand Cuba has acquired a large following in the Communist countries, for whom the naïvely 'political' slant of the recent issues is more palatable. *Scott* does not list any Cuban stamps issued after January 1961, and they are at present under interdict in the United States, even though a series of three stamps commemorated Ernest Hemingway in 1963.

CYPRUS. Since independence was granted in 1960, Cyprus has boomed in popularity. The stamps are no more attractive than previously (the reverse is true, if anything) but on the other hand, this island which, though geographically part of Asia is politically part of Europe, has acquired a large following among Continental collectors. Although it has taken part in most of the international 'band-wagon' issues, Cyprus has some-how or other managed to imbue them with its own classical spirit. The set of three stamps honouring the Tokio Olympic Games in 1964, for example, depicted athletes from the ancient Olympics. Cypriot stamps thus combine the appeal of the ancient world with the topicality of the modern. The earlier issues have a steady following in Britain and some of the George V high values fetch hundreds of pounds nowadays.

CZECHOSLOVAKIA. One of the few Communist countries whose stamps are universally popular. The political overtones are there—but this is more than compensated for by the ex-quisite engraving and delicate artistry of the designs. Czecho-slovakia's first stamps, the Boy Scout issues of 1918, are in great demand on account of their thematic interest, while many of the earlies, particularly the overprinted Austrian and Hungarian stamps of 1919, are very expensive nowadays.

DENMARK. An ideal country for the 'modest' philatelist, with plenty of variety in every period from 1851 to the present day, yet without any very costly items. This is one of the few countries still relying mainly on recess-printing—a major factor contributing to their attractiveness. The Danish dependencies include some elusive stamps, particularly the wartime pro-visionals from the Faeroes and the Liberation Commemoratives issued by Greenland in 1945.

DOMINICA. Another of those popular West Indian countries which, with fewer than 200 different varieties in almost a century of stamp-issuing, gives the collector a reasonable pros-pect of completion, though some of the surcharged provisionals of the 1880s are difficult to find now. The mint 1d. on 6d. green of 1886, for example, now rates £1,500 in *Gibbons* and $5,000 in *Scott*, but most of the others are within the reach of the less wealthy philatelist. The last King George VI series was highly tipped when it became obsolete in 1954 after a life of three years, but it has not lived up to expectations, having shown only a moderate increase in the past fourteen years. On the other hand the original 48c. in the first Elizabethan series was replaced rather unexpectedly by another design in October 1957—after a life of three years also. Many collectors were caught napping, having bought the 1954 series only as far as the 24c. (the equivalent of the shilling, which is the maximum for many New Issue subscribers) and in the resulting scramble to get the obsolete 48c. its price rose rapidly. Now it stands at 55s. mint and 60s. used in *Gibbons* ($8 mint or used in *Scott*) while the Georgian 48c. of 1951, which had a comparable life, rates only 5s. mint and 7s. 6d. used in *Gibbons* (80c. mint or used in *Scott*). Why should it be worth only a tenth of the Elizabethan stamp? Because investors and speculators had ample opportunity in 1954 to purchase it, when the impending Elizabethan series was announced. Consequently there are more than enough to go round—for the moment—though in the long run this set may improve as the demand increases.

THE DOMINICAN REPUBLIC.   Modestly popular in America just now, though it has not such a strong appeal to collectors in Britain or Europe. Apart from the issues of 1865–74 there are few stamps in the rarity class, but many in the price-bracket from £1 to £3 ($3 to $10). The modern stamps tend to be somewhat on the gaudy side and some of the recent sets, particularly the various issues commemorating Olympic medallists past and present, have rather detracted from the soundness of this otherwise 'clean' country.

DUBAI.   Referred to by me in Chapter VI in not very favour-able terms. Although this is a sheikhdom with a large volume of commercial mail, there is no doubt that many of its emissions of stamps are philatelically inspired. If the stamp-issuing policy were reduced to more sensible proportions, Dubai might improve as an investment possibility, but at present it cannot be safely recommended.

ECUADOR.   Like most countries of Latin America, Ecuador is reasonably popular in the United States but hardly excites any interest at all in Europe and Britain as yet. Nevertheless its stamps are attractive and until recently were freely available at no great cost. Such popularity as it enjoys may be killed by the present policy of Ecuador's philatelic agency, to which I have referred in Chapter VI.

EGYPT, now known as the United Arab Republic. Still popular —philatelically at least—in Britain where its bright and attractive stamps are worthy successors to the issues of the Farouk era and earlier. There are many philatelists, however, who are content to concentrate on the stamps only up to the time of the British evacuation of Egypt in 1947, or up to the time of the withdrawal from Suez in 1954. Conversely—and perversely —the various propaganda issues of 1956–7 which followed the abortive Suez operation, found a ready market in Britain and France because of their topicality. Among the post-war stamps, the various issues of 1953 with the erstwhile King Farouk's portrait obliterated contain a number of quite rare and highly-priced stamps which, at the time they were current, could be picked up for a song among commercially used accumulations.

ESTONIA, LATVIA and LITHUANIA may conveniently be grouped together. These three Baltic states issued stamps only between 1918 and 1940 when they were 'absorbed' into the Soviet Union whose stamps they now use. There is little general interest shown in their stamps nowadays, in spite of the fact that there is plenty of scope for the serious student. The first issues of Latvia were printed on the backs of German military maps and unissued banknotes either of the Bolsheviks or the White-Russian regime of Colonel Bermondt-Avalov and complete sheets of such stamps are highly prized by collectors.

ETHIOPIA (formerly known as Abyssinia). There was little to interest most collectors at one time on account of the monotony of the design and the bewildering profusion of Amharic overprints. Since the restoration of Haile Selassie in 1942, however, the stamps of Ethiopia have attracted many enthusiasts. The changeover from French to English as the alternative language to Amharic in the inscriptions has subtly stimulated

interest in America in the past fifteen years. Now, even the
pre-war sets are beginning to creep up in value.

THE FALKLAND ISLANDS and their DEPENDENCIES.
Popular with stamp collectors on account of (a) their remoteness
(b) their association with the Antarctic (one of the biggest
philatelic attractions at the moment) and (c) their perennial
topicality in view of the chauvinistic claims of Argentina and
Chile. Add to this their attractive designs, tastefully recess-
printed, and you can begin to understand the appeal of these
stamps. The early issues are always in demand, while the 1933
Centenary series is experiencing something of a boom just now.
In 1966 I myself purchased the £1 denomination for a thematic
collection of Scotland (King George V is portrayed in the
uniform of the Black Watch, a Scottish Highland regiment)
and was forced, rather reluctantly, to pay the full catalogue
price of £60 for it. True, it was a superb, nicely-centred, unmounted mint specimen, but I had hoped for a discount off
the *Gibbons* quotation. Scarcely a month later, however, *Gibbons*
revised their price, increasing it to £90. I began to realise my
good fortune when two copies came up at auction not long
afterwards and both fetched £120. *Gibbons* 1967 catalogue
raised the price to £125 and, as I write this, I note in the March
1967 issue of *Gibbons Stamp Monthly* that a few of these scarce
stamps are being offered at this price. Cyril Andrews, describing
them, says, 'Do I hear you say "Phew!" at this price? In five
years' time you will look back at this and say "Phew"—but
in a different tone.' This stamp (and the series as a whole) will
undoubtedly go farther, but who can foretell just how far.

FINLAND. Included in the very popular Scandinavian group,
yet its stamps are still plentiful at little cost. This is an ideal
country for the philatelist of limited means who wants stamps
which can yield a great deal of interest in the way of shade,
paper and printing varieties. The stamps issued under Tsarist
rule, however, are in the millionaire bracket. The prices in
Gibbons and *Scott*, high as they are, are no real indication of
the rarity of the early stamps in superb condition. The stamps

from 1860 to 1875 were 'perforated' by a serpentine roulette and the resulting teeth on the separated stamps were often broken or torn off. Thus stamps with the teeth intact are worth a substantial premium.

FRANCE. One of the world's most popular countries with stamp collectors of all kinds and degrees of wealth. Only a millionaire could hope to form a decent collection of the classics, from the 1849 Ceres type to the first emissions of the Third Republic. General Robert Gill of Baltimore managed to achieve this by purchasing the French collection of Maurice Burrus intact and amalgamating it with his own, which had won a gold medal at FIPEX in 1956. The combined assemblage decisively won the International Grand Prix of SIPEX in 1966. The Burrus-Gill France is being auctioned by the Uncommon Market—Robson Lowe, Jacques Robineau and Urs Peter Kaufmann—during 1967, and it is estimated to fetch more than a million dollars. At the other end of the scale there is a moderate boom in French pictorials just now, particularly the very popular Art series. Those who purchased the Art stamps when they were current have seen their holdings increase in value. The first series, when current, could be purchased for 7s. ($1) but is now listed by *Gibbons* (1967) at 46s. This 600% increase does not reflect the present market value—*Scott* lists the set at $20.50, which is almost *three times* the *Gibbons* price.

GABON, a West African republic within the French Community. Has the same prospects as those other countries in this area, provided that its present policy is adhered to. Many of the stamps from the colonial period are already priced in hundreds of pounds.

GAMBIA. Evinces great interest for British philatelists who were first attracted to it by the beautifully embossed 'Cameos' of the nineteenth century. Apart from the imperforates of 1869–74 and embossing varieties in the later 'Cameos' the stamps are moderate in value. One stamp to look out for is the slate-purple shade of the 1922 3s. which rates £32 mint and

£35 used in *Gibbons* (*Scott* $90 mint or used) compared with 35s. mint, 40s. used (*Scott* $5.50 and $5 respectively) for the commoner bright aniline violet shade. Once again is demonstrated the advantage in being able to distinguish colours and spot the rare shades which other collectors have overlooked. Incidentally, the 10s. denomination of the 1966 definitive series contains a spelling error: MUSAPHUGA instead of MUSAPHAGA (the Latin name of the Plantain Eater) and if this were withdrawn and replaced by the amended version it could put up the value of this stamp. Of course, by drawing your attention to this instead of sitting back on a stock of the error, I am spoiling my own chance of making a profit out of this stamp. As there is (at the time of writing) no sign of the error being corrected the would-be speculator will probably have plenty of time in which to lay in ample supplies!

GERMANY. Nowadays rates as one of the soundest philatelic investments there are. There are literally hundreds of stamps among the middle issues which can still be bought for pennies and every schoolboy collection has a good showing of the cheaper sets. On the other hand, the stamps of the old German States and the early issues of the German Empire include many expensive stamps which few people could hope to possess. The immediate post-war stamps, particularly those of West Berlin, could be obtained easily at new issue rates while current, but now cost almost as many *pounds* as they once did *pence*. The West German Parliament pair, which cost 8d. (9c.) in 1949 are now catalogued at £6 10s. (*Gibbons*) or $38.50 (*Scott*); the Lubeck Church pair cost 1s. (14c.) in 1951 and today rate £12 (*Gibbons*) or $55 (*Scott*); while the top values of the 1951 'Posthorns' definitive series, from 40pf. to 90pf., cost 8s. when current but today they are listed at £68 (*Gibbons*) or $292.50 (*Scott*). These are but a few examples, but the same fantastic increase in value has been exhibited by most of the issues of the Federal and Democratic Republics and West Berlin between 1948 and 1953. This phenomenon may be explained by the fact that, in the years just after the Second World War, the Germans were too busy getting back on their feet to bother about collecting stamps—even if they could have afforded them at the time. By the mid-fifties philatelic activity had begun to pick up again in Germany (regarded as having more stamp collectors in proportion to its population than any other country) and there just were not enough of these obsolete issues to go round. The stamps of the Democratic Republic, with a few notable exceptions such as the Oder-Neisse pair and the Chinese friendship series of 1951, are not such good property and the business of 'blocked values' (see Chapter X) has tended to deter philatelists from collecting them seriously.

GHANA. Scarcely taken seriously anywhere nowadays though it went through a period of high popularity in the late 1950s. Too many new issues with a high face value and devious practices such as flooding the market with cancelled-to-order remainders virtually killed off philatelic interest before the bankrupt Nkrumah regime was finally discredited. A change of regime and the long, slow climb back to respectability may eventually rehabilitate the stamps of Ghana. The stamps of the former GOLD COAST, however, have maintained their interest.

GIBRALTAR. Britain's only colony on the continent of Europe is popular with British collectors as part of the Commonwealth and with European collectors because of its geographical position. Thousands of G.I.s passed through this Allied naval base during the Second World War and countless American tourists have visited it since then. All this adds up to Gibraltar being one of the fashionable countries to collect. The boom in the Lady of Europa Commemorative last year is symptomatic of this. Few of the early issues are very pricey as yet, but already the values of some of the Edward VII and George V stamps are soaring.

GILBERT AND ELLICE ISLANDS. Have not issued very many stamps since the first series appeared in 1911, but such as there are take a good deal of finding in fine used condition —particularly on commercially used covers. The issues of the last few years show a certain amount of promise. Two stamps of the 1956 series appeared with a new watermark in 1964–65, shortly before the series became obsolete. The 1965 definitive series, which was released on 16th August, was superseded the following February by a decimal surcharged series, which in turn is merely a stop-gap pending the production of an entirely new set. A second printing of the 1965 ½d. stamp differed markedly in colour from the original. Both shades of the ½d. should have good prospects, though at the moment the second shade is priced far more highly than the first.

GREAT BRITAIN. As I have illustrated in Chapter I, we are booming at the moment. The present upsurge in interest may be likened to the boom in Germany a decade ago. British stamps are rising fast and will go even further in price before their true levels are found. Already many of the early issues are beyond the pocket of all but the very rich. Concentrating on the 'moderns', however, I would recommend all the phosphor-line varieties, both in the commemoratives and the definitive series, *all* the regional stamps from 1958 to the present time, and the various printings of the line-engraved 'Castles' high values. It may come as something of a surprise to the layman to realise that in the past twelve years the high values have been printed on two different watermarked papers, by three different printers. Four sets can be formed and already the De La Rue printing on E2R paper has risen to over £40 —not a bad increase over the face value of £1 17s. 6d. in ten years.

GREECE. For a long time in the doldrums, Greece has been gaining in popularity in the past ten years and consequently the prices of many of the post-war sets have gone up by leaps and bounds. This sudden rise in price has also affected the earlier issues—not only the classic 'Hermes Heads' and the once-notorious Olympic commemoratives—but many of the stamps released between 1912 and 1941. In spite of many fakes and forgeries, the stamps of the ephemeral administrations of

Crete, Epirus, Icaria and the other territories now assimilated into Greece are also sharing in the boom just now.

GRENADA. One of the more expensive of the West Indian countries; the beautiful 'Chalon Heads' of 1861–83 include many minor rarities. But there is a great deal of interest to be found among the later issues—the various tints of the George V series, the watermark changes in the Edwardians and, most of all, the perforation and shade varieties of the George VI series. The 2½d. stamp of this series is normally priced at 6d. (7c.) but one small printing was made in 1950 with perforations gauging 12½ × 13½ instead of the usually 12½ all round, and this stamp is now priced by *Gibbons* at £200 mint and £12 used (*Scott* $500 mint, $35 used) so it is worth hunting for, especially in accumulations of commercially used copies.

GUATEMALA. No especial interest in Europe at present, though there is a vigorous band of devotees in the United States and a growing indigenous body of philatelists to stimulate the home market. Many of the early issues were printed by American Bank Note Co., Waterlows, Perkins Bacon or De La Rue in the best traditions of these fine printers and perhaps some day this fact will help to revive interest in this country. Under the Ubico regime of the 1930s there were, perhaps, too many issues, but at the present time they are not so frequent.

GUINEA. Almost 500 stamps have been issued since 1959— far too many if collectors are not to be frightened off. Most of these, however, are either very attractive 'thematics' (butter-flies, fish, birds, etc.) or 'band-wagon' issues commemorating Kennedy, Olympic Games, Red Cross and so forth, so that a fair amount of philatelic revenue inevitably accrues from those who do not necessarily collect all the stamps of the country, but only those whose particular subject is appealing.

HAITI. Fairly respectable until recently, but there is obviously some kind of chicanery going on just now. Collectors began to lose faith when there was a rash of overprinted issues (one way of using up unsold stocks of obsolete stamps) for all manner of events, ranging from Alphabetisation (literary campaign) and the inauguration of Dr. Duvalier, to 'Mothers' Festival' and the Innsbruck Winter Olympics—usually bearing a hefty surcharge in aid of one or other of the many charities sponsored by 'Papa Doc's' regime. The stamps originally commemorating the Century 21 World's Fair at Seattle in 1962 were re-issued the following year with an overprint dedicated to the 'peaceful uses of outer space'. The stamps overprinted in purple or violet were available in reasonable quantities, but, overprinted in *black*, they could not be bought at less than four times face value. A series of diamond-shaped stamps commemorating Sir Winston Churchill were allegedly issued in 1966, but no one seems to be able to purchase them, nor have enquiries of the Haitian postal administration elicited any satisfactory explanation. In the circumstances, therefore, Haiti is not a country whose stamps can be recommended at present.

HONDURAS. One of the most conservative countries in the world at the moment—so far as issuing stamps is concerned. Few stamps have made their appearance in the past decade, and none at all in 1960, and 1962–3. In spite of the Seebeck period (see Chapter VI) the stamps of Honduras have a good record in the past and deserve to be more popular than they are.

HONG KONG. The same monotonous design (apart from changes in the sovereign's portrait) appeared from 1862 till 1962, the only relief being occasioned by the bi-coloured issues of Edward VII and George V. In recent years, however, the stamps have brightened up considerably, the current high values depicting the Annigoni Portrait of the Queen in full colour. This has helped to awaken interest in these stamps in Europe and America, although they have always had some indefinable appeal for British philatelists. Worth watching out for are the early issues used in the Chinese Treaty Ports and in various towns in Japan.

PLATE IX

POST-WAR RARITIES.

(1) South Korea, Olympic Games 5w., 1948 (£11, $37.50), (2) Spain, Canary Islands Visit 25p., 1950 (£33, $135), (3) Liberia, UNICEF, 1954 (£18, $45), (4) Israel, 1,000m., 1948 (£32, $175), (5) Ireland, Europa 1s. 3d., 1960 (27s. 6d., $7). This is an example of a stamp which dropped in catalogue price by 50% in the past year!

HUNGARY. Not particularly worth recommending at present. Apart from the political slant of many of its stamps, one has to contend with imperforate 'proofs' which are often sold at prices bearing absolutely no relation to their face value. Yet there is no denying that the modern issues have great thematic appeal and many of them have risen considerably in value. In 1953 the 2fo. Football Stamp was overprinted to celebrate Hungary's crushing victory over England at Wembley. At the time of issue it could be obtained for 2s.; the 1967 catalogue lists it at 25s. (*Scott* $5) and after the spectacular interest created by the 1966 World Cup series it is likely to go much higher since this is one of the 'plums' which every collector of soccer stamps needs to be complete.

ICELAND. Has always had a strong following in Scandinavia; now it is enjoying a much wider popularity in the rest of Europe and in America and certain sets, which are of particular interest elsewhere, have shot up enormously in value recently. Italian collectors have forced up the value of the Balbo Transatlantic Flight trio of 1933: *Gibbons* raised the price for the mint set from £117 to £190 in 1967 alone—a considerable mark up (*Scott* now prices this issue at $750). The modern issues are attractively produced, not too frequently issued— and have a nasty habit of going up rapidly in value when they become obsolete, so it always pays to get them while they are current.

INDIA. Retains its popularity in Britain despite twenty years of independence. With a vigorous home market and increasing interest in Europe and America, India is definitely on the up and up. Few of the stamps are basically expensive, but they offer plenty of variety for the specialist. For investment the Scinde Dawks of 1852, which vary in price between £120 and £600, can be recommended as rarities in the medium range which are steadily increasing in value all the time.

IRELAND. Has stagnated philatelically for many years. The typographed designs of the definitive series, with their appearance more in keeping with medieval monasticism than twentieth-century commercialism, have been in use for forty-five years—a record for conservatism that would be hard to beat. But all this has begun to change in the past seven years. More attractive stamps and more frequent commemoratives have led to the sudden growth in popularity in Europe and America. The Europa pair, issued in 1960, rose rapidly from a face value of 1s. 9d. to their present rating of £2 (*Scott* $11) and even the earlies, which could be bought at face value not so long ago, have increased considerably in price lately.

ISRAEL. One of those post-war states whose popularity was immediate and world-wide, largely helped by the national sentiment of Jews everywhere. Consequently the first 'Coins' series of 1948 ranks as one of the most expensive sets anywhere in modern philately. Israel takes an almost fierce pride in the quality of its stamp design and production and this has contributed to the universal interest shown in its emissions. Though they are essentially modern in concept they often allude to Biblical subjects, hence their great appeal for Jew and Gentile alike. The first 'Coins' excepted, few of the stamps are beyond the reach of the average collector, though prices are rising continually.

ITALY. Probably the most philatelically-conscious country in the world. Philatelic speculation affects the population as a whole much in the way that football pools have a hold in Britain. There have been some spectacular increases in the prices of some Italian issues in the past few years but somehow I am inclined to feel that it is all a bit artificial. Much of the philatelic trade is in the hands of two powerful dealers who juggle with the prices in ruthless efforts to oust each other from the top position. Many Italians have invested heavily in stamps in complete sheets and, if there were a sudden loss of faith in them and these speculators began to unload their holdings, 'il boom' could easily become 'lo sboom (slump)', as the Italians succinctly put it. At least, now that the 'Stock Ministeriali' has been consigned to the incinerator, confidence in the early and middle issues could improve.

JAMAICA. Popular without being pricey. None of its stamps since 1860 are unduly difficult to secure and there is a great deal of interest in the middle period. The Arms series of 1903–11 are worth careful scrutiny for the missing 'V'—a variety which occurs once on every sheet. The letter 'V' missing in the word SERVIET in this error rates a hefty premium. Many of the Queen Victoria types have a curious error in the inscription showing the $ sign instead of an 'S' in SHILLING and these also will repay the observant philatelist, if he can find it.

JAPAN. A philatelically conscious populace periodically hit the headlines by besieging post offices on the day of issue of new stamps. Not a great deal of interest was shown outside the country, however, until after the Second World War, when American servicemen sparked off the current craze for Japanese stamps in the United States. Like Germany, Japan has a booming economy, and this post-war prosperity is demonstrated in the way that a large amount of choice philatelic material has been drained out of Europe and America back to Japan itself. The early issues with their syllabic alphabet 'plate numbers', and the subtle plate varieties of the 'mon' series, are extremely complicated, but this probably accounts for their appeal to the philatelist who loves the challenge of these difficult stamps.

JORDAN. A great deal of interest arises for the serious student who wishes to sort out the varieties and overprint errors on the early issues. The recent sets have unfortunately pandered to the world-wide thirst for brightly coloured thematically inspired stamps in which Jordan demonstrates its equivocal political position (e.g. stamps commemorating President Kennedy one moment and others celebrating Soviet space achievements the next). In spite of the religious animosities which have made them the deadly enemies of the Israelis, the Jordanians have shown a remarkable predilection for stamps with religious themes such as the Dead Sea Scrolls and the Fourteen Stations of the Cross. The 'Holy Places of Jerusalem' series of 1963, for example, depicted the Holy Sepulchre and the Omar el Khatab Mosque with equal impartiality.

KENYA may be bracketed here with UGANDA and TANZANIA (Tanganyika and Zanzibar). For very many years these countries had a common issue of stamps and even now have a common postal system and usually issue uniform commemorative stamps throughout the territories covered by East African Posts and Telecommunications. New issues are confined to moderate proportions—one or two commemorative sets a year—so they have retained the popularity they enjoyed in colonial times while gaining many adherents in Europe and America. Kenya's high values of the 1922 series, produced primarily for fiscal use though inscribed for postage, have come into prominence lately and prices have risen fantastically. The £100 denomination, the stamp with the highest face value ever issued, was listed by *Gibbons* in 1966 at £5,250 and in 1967 at £10,000—a record for any twentieth-century stamp.

KOREA. A land of sharp political and philatelic cleavages. South Korea, firmly entrenched in the Western camp, is popular in America where its early stamps fetch fancy prices nowadays. The Olympic Games pair of 1948, with a face value of 15 weun (about 9d.) is now listed by *Gibbons* at £14 and by *Scott* at $45.50. There are still a few bargains left—if you can find them. The stamps of North Korea are currently under the ban of the U.S. Treasury Department and it cannot be said that they have any great appeal to philatelists in Western Europe on account of their generally poor designs, political bias and the fact that many of them are circulated in 'cancelled-to-order' condition.

KUWAIT. One of the few Arab countries *not* to have succumbed to the temptation of the stamp collector. This oil-rich state does not have to bother about philatelic revenue and consequently its stamps are confined to issues commemorating Kuwaiti events. The stamps may be designed in Kuwait, but they rely on the cream of the world's printers for their production. Many of the earlier issues, overprinted on the stamps of India or Britain, are more elusive than their catalogue prices would indicate and if interest were to revive in these 'fore-runners' their value would soar considerably.

LAOS. Some handsome, line-engraved stamps have been produced since the first issues appeared in 1951. None of these is difficult to procure, though already some of them are priced in pounds rather than shillings. An elusive item is the short-lived 2p. in the 1951 series, now listed by *Gibbons* at 45s. and *Scott* at $9, though not so long ago it could be purchased for a shilling.

LEBANON. Could easily be fashionable—and then prices would rise sharply. Unexplicably, however, it does not seem to excite much interest at the moment; the stamps are well-enough designed with more than a modicum of topicality and they are not over-prolific. Perhaps a more aggressive sales drive by the Lebanese postal administration would stimulate interest.

LEEWARD ISLANDS. With their monotonous typographed key-plates their designs have never been very popular. The last series, issued in 1954 and withdrawn on 1st July 1956 when the Leeward Islands Federation was dissolved, was tipped to the skies shortly before they became obsolete. The result is that they are not particularly uncommon today and, with no new issues coming along to entice new collectors, will show only a very slow appreciation in value, if even that.

LIBERIA. Seems to have settled down somewhat, after a dubious career in the early years of this century marked by cancelled-to-order 'pretty pretties' produced solely for the stamp collector. The modern issues have a good following in the United States which may be explained by their predilection for subjects of American interest: Idlewild Airport, the UN Building, the New York Coliseum and the Statue of Liberty are but a few of the landmarks depicted on them, while no fewer than five U.S. Presidents have been portrayed on Liberian stamps.

LIBYA. This ex-Italian colony, British occupied territory and now flourishing North African kingdom has a philatelic history which faithfully records its turbulent politics in the past fifty years. It is popular, for nostalgic reasons, in Italy, while growing contact with Britain and the United States in recent years has served to increase its popularity in these countries. Most of the stamps are fairly plentiful, but the stamps of Cyrenaica, overprinted during the transitional period in 1951 when the kingdom was unified, are very expensive nowadays. Grouped with Libya are the stamps of its component territories, the governorates of Cyrenaica and Tripolitania and the former French colony of Fezzan—all of which add up to a fascinating group offering much to interest the philatelist.

LIECHTENSTEIN. It would cost a fortune to complete this tiny principality nowadays though fewer than 500 different varieties have appeared in the 55 years that it has had its own stamps. Few relatively modern issues could vie with the Agricultural Exhibition pair of 1934–5 which *Gibbons* increased in the 1967 catalogue from £245 to £600—a fantastic jump in twelve months (*Scott* currently lists these two stamps at $1,800).

LUXEMBOURG. One of the best countries of which to commence a collection at the moment, since its stamps are still reasonably priced. But here also the price of popularity is becoming a high one. The 10 frs. green of 1923—the world's first miniature sheet—was increased by *Gibbons* in 1967 to £175 —a jump of £100 over the previous year's figure (*Scott* lists it at $450).

MADAGASCAR, now independent as the MALAGASY REPUBLIC. Much to interest the stamp collector and the modern issues are exceedingly attractive without overdoing the frequency of release. Apart from the 1896 surcharged provisionals, which are now priced in three figures (sterling), most of the pre-independence stamps are not too expensive or too difficult to find, though fine commercially used covers are scarce.

MALAYA. Never widely popular, on account of the monotony of the key-plate designs used by the various states which formed the Federated Malay States, then the Malayan Federation, and now Malaysia. The recent Orchids issues, however, are very colourful, and the appearance of the commemorative stamps has improved lately so that interest in Malaysia, now confined to a dedicated few, may improve. In a different category altogether is SINGAPORE which seceded from the Federation of Malaysia recently and has always pursued an independent, and more colourful, line as far as stamps are concerned.

THE MALDIVE ISLANDS. Very conservative at one time, only 42 stamps between 1906 and 1960. In the latter year it was taken over by a philatelic agency, however, and in the ensuing five years released more than three times as many new stamps. Kennedy, Churchill, Olympics, the Temples of Nubia and Boy Scouts are only a few of the subjects commemorated by this Indian Ocean archipelago. Significantly *Gibbons* does not price any of the modern issues in used condition.

MALI. Many attractive stamps have been produced since it graduated from French colonialism and changed its name from Senegal. These are philatelically inspired, however, and aim their appeal mainly at the topical collector, so that they have no great stability for the 'one-country' philatelist.

MALTA. On the crest of the wave philatelically with Italians falling over themselves in a mad scramble to complete the issues since independence. The Independence series itself, available at the time of issue in 1964 for 7s., is currently priced by *Gibbons* (1967 edition) at 11s. 8d. mint and 13s. 6d. used and by *Scott* at $1.95 mint and $1.77 used; both quotations are quite unrealistic and this set changes hands just now at around the £5 mark. In spite of a certain amount of speculation in some of the recent issues (and even a determined effort by an Italian syndicate to corner the Trade Fair 2s. 6d. stamp) Malta is a good country to collect and its stamps, reflecting more than 3,000 years of colourful history, are deservedly popular in Britain, America and Europe generally.

MAURITANIA. This former French colony in North Africa and, since 1960, independent Islamic Republic has followed the same pattern as most of the ex-French Community countries in Africa. Its stamps figure somewhere in most thematic collections but there must be few serious philatelic studies of this country as a whole.

MEXICO. A 'difficult' country where the early issues are concerned, complicated by the bewildering array of district names and numbers which were overprinted on the stamps from 1856 till 1883. The numerous Civil War provisionals of 1914–15 are also complicated but nevertheless have a large band of devotees. In spite of the fakes and forgeries perpetrated by Raul de Thuin, who specialised in doctoring Mexican stamps and covers, confidence in the classic issues is still fairly strong. The modern issues are often mediocre in design and poor in production otherwise Mexican stamps would be more popular in the United States than they are.

MONACO. Formerly scorned as one of those tiny principalities which produced new issues by the dozen for the collector. But it must be admitted that interesting designs coupled with high quality printing (usually line-engraved) has made Monaco very popular with philatelists. Prince Rainier is, himself, a philatelist of no mean stature and the Monegasque postal administration knows exactly what collectors want and how to cater to them without overdoing it. Among the recent issues the annual Monte Carlo Rally stamps have shown the most promise, whereas the much publicised Wedding set, which all patriotic Americans (and cinema-goers) bought as a memento of Grace Kelly, has scarcely moved up in value.

MONGOLIA. The issuing of stamps began in 1924 and the early emissions, up till 1959, were quite respectable and nowadays rate a heavy premium. Since then, however, Mongolian stamps have been printed in Budapest and are rather suspect, the great majority of the used specimens now in circulation having been cancelled to order in Hungary. In this context may be mentioned the stamps of Mongolia's neighbour, the erstwhile state of Tannu Touva which was absorbed into the Soviet Union in 1944. During the 1930s the philatelic market was flooded by large numbers of pictorial stamps which are thought to have originated in Moscow. There is no real evidence that these stamps ever did genuine duty in Tannu Touva and they are, quite rightly, ignored by the stamp catalogues; but they still turn up in boys' collections and are offered from time to time in junior approval packets, despite the efforts of philatelic trade associations to expose the activities of their less reputable colleagues.

MONTSERRAT.   Another of these popular West Indian territories whose stamps, particularly the early issues, are always in demand. The ones to watch are the high values in each series, especially the 5s. denominations of 1903, 1907 and 1914. Montserrat was one of those colonies which issued lengthy commemorative sets (in this case, to mark the Tercentenary of the Settlement in 1632) at a time when the world in general was in the middle of an economic depression. Consequently few could afford to pay out the 10s. required to secure a set at the time of its release in 1932; nowadays it rates £21 14s. 6d. in *Gibbons* and $75.70 in *Scott*. An even better investment, however, was the top value in the 1953 definitive series, the $4.80 depicting the badge of Montserrat. Originally this was inscribed BADGE OF PRESIDENCY, but, on the dissolution of the Leeward Islands Federation in 1956 and the elevation of Montserrat to a crown colony, this inscription was altered to BADGE OF COLONY in 1958. Although the original version had a life of three years (long enough for most people to have secured the original version) it has now risen from a face value equivalent to £1, to *Gibbons'* estimate of £9, while *Scott* prices it at $32.50.

MOROCCO. A country with an extremely interesting history,

reflected in its past postage-stamps. Prior to 1956 it was divided between France and Spain, while two other powers, Britain and Germany, maintained their own post offices in certain cities. In addition there were the Sherifian postal services whose stamps, though not listed in the standard catalogues, are worthy of study. The stamps issued since the kingdom gained its independence in 1956 are well designed and printed. This is not a very popular country at the moment, and its British and German overprinted stamps are in the doldrums, but if they were to become more fashionable, Morocco's stamps would undoubtedly rise rapidly.

NEPAL. The collector has the vicarious pleasure of intimacy with a country which he could seldom hope to visit. The more remote it is, the more its stamps are in demand. Unlike neighbouring Bhutan, Nepal has a 'clean' philatelic record. In the early years, from 1881 till 1949, it was ultra-conservative—the Siva design of 1907 lasted for forty-two years—but in the past two decades Nepal has issued more stamps, with the accent on pictorialism, so that collectors' interest has now been stimulated. *Gibbons* lists Nepal in its *Part III Catalogue*, whereas *Scott* puts it with the British Commonwealth issues. Were *Gibbons* to follow *Scott*'s policy the interest in these stamps would increase enormously in Britain.

THE NETHERLANDS. One of the best countries which any collector could adopt today. Its stamps are plentiful at the moment, and most of them can still be obtained for a reasonable sum. They are also among the best-designed stamps and, with the development of the Common Market, Dutch stamps are being taken up by philatelists in France, Italy and West Germany. Thus they are now enjoying a moderate boom which is beginning to extend to the United Kingdom, and prices, especially for the pre-war charity (semi-postal) sets, are rising.

NEWFOUNDLAND. Described as 'a dead country which refuses to lie down'. In other words, although its stamp-issuing career ended in 1949 the issues prior to that date contain so much allure for the collector that their popularity will never wane. Newfoundland, as well as all the other provinces of Canada which collectors group together as 'British North America', has always had a large following in Canada and Britain; now it has been adopted by American collectors as well and prices have begun to soar. In fact, it is probably true to say that the cream of the Newfoundland material passing through the London auction rooms in the past two years has all gone across the Atlantic.

NEW ZEALAND. One of the 'gilt-edgeds' of the stamp world. The beautiful 'Chalon Heads' of the last century will always find a ready market wherever fine classic stamps are appreciated. This is an exceedingly difficult country to collect, on account of the complicated paper varieties in the Penny Universal and later definitive issues, but this is one of the best examples to prove that knowledge pays off. For this purpose a thorough perusal of the four-volume handbook on New Zealand stamps by Messrs. Collins and Fathers, plus constant reference to the Campbell-Paterson catalogue, will enable the keen student to make some very good bargains among the otherwise unconsidered trifles in many dealers' stocks. Among the more recent issues I would recommend the definitive stamps of the past ten years, particularly the 1958 thick white paper varieties. Check carefully the backs of all stamps of the 1882–97 series; those which bear commercial advertisements on them are worth a substantial premium over the catalogue price.

NICARAGUA. In spite of being one of the 'Seebeck countries', Nicaragua is moderately popular in America today. There is, however, very little interest shown in its stamps in Britain or Europe in general. Apart from the general apathy towards Latin American stamps, British collectors may well be put off Nicaragua by the seemingly interminable surcharged and overprinted issues which characterise the philately of this country up till 1939. Nevertheless this is a sound country, which has not sunk to some of the shady practices of some of its neighbours and the tendency in recent years has been to release fewer, rather than more, stamps. It could hardly be *less* popular, and, as it might well become *more* popular, a collection of its stamps might be worth forming at the present time.

NIGERIA. Like many other Commonwealth countries in Africa, Nigeria was popular until it became independent. Many collectors ceased collecting its stamps in 1960, fearing that they might proliferate unnecessarily as had Ghana's, but such fears have not been justified by subsequent events. On the other hand, the present state of flux in that unhappy country has created a lack of confidence abroad and this is reflected in the general lack of interest shown in its stamps. If the political situation improves, current Nigerian stamps may gain the popularity at present enjoyed only by the pre-1960 issues. Here again, the most startling price increases have been shown in the high values, particularly the Northern Nigeria £25 which has shot up within the past decade from £800 to £7,000 in *Gibbons* (*Scott* lists it at $15,000), which makes it one of the most valuable twentieth-century stamps.

NORFOLK ISLAND. Stamps have been issued only since 1949 but this is now one of the most popular of the Pacific group. For years the first series, depicting Ball Bay, was a drug on the market but, with the upsurge in the popularity of Norfolk Island stamps in general, this series has boomed dramatically. *Gibbons* increased its listing for this set from £1 mint, 25s. used, to £7 mint, £10 used in 1966 and now that it has been belatedly discovered that there were two distinct printings (somehow overlooked up till now) the prices will no doubt rise even higher. This boom in Pacific material is also shared to a greater or lesser extent by the stamps of Pitcairn, and the Australian dependencies of Papua, New Guinea, Christmas Island, Cocos Islands and Nauru.

NORWAY. In the past never one of the most popular countries. Now it rates high on the list. The reason for this is partly because *any* country in Western Europe is philatelically popular nowadays and partly because Norway's stamps, like Britain's,

have increased in output and improved in design of late. This
is a gross oversimplification, since Norway's commemoratives
have always been more frequent and more attractive than their
British counterparts, and as they improved their popularity has
increased correspondingly. Incidentally, Norway holds the
world record for the longest period in use of a stamp design;
the Numeral and Posthorn design, introduced for the 1 to 7
skilling stamps of 1872, has been used for the low values of
the definitive series ever since, having been typographed,
photogravure and recess-printed in turn.

PAKISTAN. A good example of an independent Commonwealth country whose stamps, issued only since independence,
have maintained their popularity with British collectors, while
gaining many adherents in America and Europe. Interest was
generated initially by the overprinted provisionals of the
obsolete series of the Indian Empire and maintained by the
steady flow of high-quality pictorials, both definitive and commemorative, ever since. While there have been no dramatic
increases (the best set is the U.N. pair of 1955 which, available
originally for 1s. 6d., now rates £1) a collection of all the stamps
of Pakistan from 1947 to date, bought at new issue rates, would
show a reasonable profit. With Pakistan, I would include the
ephemeral stamps of BAHAWALPUR which appeared in
1945–9. Some of these, particularly those designed for government use, range from the elusive to the exceedingly rare.

PANAMA and PARAGUAY may conveniently be treated
together. Both of them were fairly respectable—and consequently reasonably popular—until the late 1950s when their
stamps came under the control of extra-territorial philatelic
agencies. Since then almost every issue has been accompanied
by imperforate 'varieties' and souvenir sheets. Both countries
have climbed on every band wagon possible, resulting in such
farcical issues as 'Europa' stamps from Paraguay and a series
commemorating medallists from the Innsbruck Winter Olympic
Games of 1964 from Panama. Neither country is recommended
as a good investment. *Scott* and *Gibbons* have not listed any

Panamanian stamps produced since 1964, nor any Paraguayan stamps since 1962, since they are not satisfied that stamps since those dates have been brought into regular use.

PERSIA. Never popular, partly because of the rather obscure designs and unintelligible (to a Westerner) inscriptions in Arabic which characterised the early issues, and partly because many of the middle issues (1900–24) were reprinted or cancelled-to-order for the benefit of collectors. Confidence in the issues up till the advent of the Pahlavi regime in the 1920s has been further shaken by the great numbers of forged and faked over-prints and surcharges which abound. Nevertheless, there is a hard core of enthusiasts in Europe and America and the gradual improvement in the quality of the design and printing of Persian stamps in recent years is awakening a more general interest.

PERU. An interesting country with a respectable past and a bright future. New issues are kept to a moderate figure. The classic issues of 1858–60 are rather expensive nowadays and the provisional overprints from the period of the war between Chile and Peru, 1881–4, have been very popular with philatelists and postal historians for many years and fetch high prices in many instances. Nevertheless there are still many cheap stamps which would amply repay study.

THE PHILIPPINES. Still very popular in the United States, though there has naturally been some falling-off of interest in the stamps issued since independence, a situation which is not improved by *Scott* grouping the post-1946 issues in *Volume II* of the catalogue instead of in *Volume I* along with the stamps of the United States administration (1899–1946). The chief interest lies in the airmail sets of 1926 to 1939, especially used on special flight covers.

POLAND. This country divides into three distinct periods, each popular with different categories of collectors for different reasons. The first period covers the 10 kopeck stamp and its variants, used in the Russian-protected Kingdom of Poland from 1860 till 1865. The cheapest variety in this interesting stamp is now listed by *Gibbons* at £60 mint and £20 used (*Scott* $150 and $65 respectively). This stamp—'Poland Number One'—has long been popular in the United States and Western Europe, but recently there has been evidence to suggest that collectors in Poland and even Russia have been buying these stamps back from the West—a situation which would have been incredible five, let alone ten, years ago. Second came the stamps of independent Poland (1918–39), plus the issues of the London Government in Exile, which have a strong following in Britain and America, where there are large Polish communities. Undoubtedly there was a great deal of speculation in the wartime London issues but they are attractive pictorials which are gradually creeping up in price again, after the inevitable post-war slump. Finally, the issues of the Communist regime, like those of most of the other Iron Curtain countries, suffer from (a) cancelling to order for re-sale below face value, and (b) an overdose of irrelevant pictorialism aimed at the 'packet trade'. Recent issues have included, for example, a number of animal thematic sets covering dogs, cats, reptiles and prehistoric monsters of the world! One cannot take them very seriously, though some of the stamps issued in 1944–6, as the Lublin Government gradually took over the territory yielded by the retreating Germans, are more elusive than their catalogue prices indicate.

PORTUGAL.   Always the possessor of a select following. Probably the monotony of the Ceres issues (*Gibbons* lists no fewer than 213 examples of this design for the mother country, let alone the corresponding sets for the colonies) and the portrait key-type designs of the Monarchy has militated against their wider acceptance. Portugal also had a penchant for excessively long commemorative sets in the 1920s—a policy hardly calculated to endear its stamps with collectors. In more recent years, however, commemorative sets have been short, more frequent and more colourful, so Portugal is beginning to share in the general popularity of European stamps. At the

same time, the stamps issued by Portugal's colonial territories
—Angola, Cape Verde Islands, Macão, Mozambique, Guinea,
St. Thomas and Prince Islands and Timor—have swung from
the monotonous to the colourful in the post-war years and the
key-plates of yesteryear have given way to bright thematic
issues. As a group they have distinct possibilities.

RHODESIA comprises the stamps of the British South Africa
Company (1890–1925), Northern and Southern Rhodesia
(1924–54), Rhodesia and Nyasaland—the abortive Central
African Federation (1954–63) and the stamps since 1963 issued
by Southern Rhodesia, which changed its name to Rhodesia
in 1965. These stamps have a strong following in Rhodesia
itself and are popular in South Africa, the United Kingdom and
the United States. The political events since the Unilateral
Declaration of Independence have served only to whet philatelic
appetites, particularly in Britain where information on new
issues has been sporadic on account of the inability of dealers
to trade in them to any great degree. The various experimental
papers and the local (Salisbury) printings of stamps formerly
printed in Britain have given philatelists plenty to occupy them;
and when the 'dust of battle' has settled and more detailed
information on these stamps becomes available, it will be seen
that many of them are quite scarce and prices are bound to
harden.

ROUMANIA. Its earliest stamps are some of the world's
greatest rarities—the Moldavian 'Bulls' of 1858—and the
Prince Charles issues of Roumania proper (1866–72) have
been collected and studied by philatelists all over the world.
The later issues, however, are unlikely to be a worthwhile
investment. Some of the pre-war sets, such as the Scouts issues,
are not cheap, but the stamps issued since the Second World
War have little to commend them. Roumania is one of the
world's most prolific producers of new stamps, many of which
are aimed at the thematic collector and all are invariably found
cancelled-to-order.

PLATE X

'UNDESIRABLE' STAMPS OF YESTERYEAR.

(1–2) New South Wales, Diamond Jubilee charity stamps, 1897, (3) San Marino, Regency, 1894, (4) Greece, Olympic Games, 1896, (5–7) Diamond Jubilee Commemoratives from Mauritius, Leeward Islands and Canada, 1897, (8–9) United States commemoratives for the Columbian Exposition (1893) and the Trans-Mississippi Exposition (1898).

RUSSIA. The output of new issues is second to none. *Scott's* 1967 edition lists no fewer than 3,369 different stamps, not counting varieties and shades, and omitting postage dues— more than the total of U.S. and French stamps issued over a longer period. The issues of the Tsarist period will always hold their own, but those produced from 1917 onwards are more problematical. Russian stamps are unpopular in the West because of their number, their propaganda element and the fact that the export of stamps, controlled by the State organisation Mezhdunarodnaja Kniga, is not as free and easy as that of, say, the Crown Agents. Some Western dealers have given up handling Russian stamps as a result of Mezhdunarodnaja Kniga's practice of selling off remainders in package deals at the end of each year. Most Soviet stamps are also available cancelled-to-order, a fact which does nothing to improve confidence in them.

THE RYUKYU ISLANDS. These islands have been under U.S. military administration since the end of the Second World War and consequently their stamps have been very popular with American collectors. The Ryukyuans rather exploited this situation, with the result that there was a decline in American interest. Since 1962, however, this tendency has been remedied by a change in stamp-issuing policy; long commemorative and thematic sets with a high face value have given way to single stamps or small sets consisting of low denominations only— usually the 3c. letter rate. A total of 173 stamps in twenty years is not excessive and it is still possible to pick up most of them —though some of the earlies are very expensive today. The 100 yen provisional of 1952, which could be bought for less than 10s. fifteen years ago, is now priced by *Gibbons* at £150 mint, £100 used (*Scott* $375, $200).

RWANDA. This former part of the Belgian mandated territory of Ruanda-Urundi, has issued almost 200 stamps since independence in 1962. Although this number is a trifle excessive, the stamps are attractive and topical and therefore fairly popular. Provided that the output of new stamps does not increase drastically, Rwanda should be worth considering.

SAAR. Stamps of the Saar territory have appeared only on two occasions in its history: in 1920–35 when it was under the control of the League of Nations and from 1947–57 when it was again administered by the French. Subsequent to which stamps in designs similar to contemporary German ones, but inscribed in French currency, were issued in the Saar for a further two years. Both periods are popular with European collectors; and many stamps, now priced in pounds, could once have been bought for pence. The boom in Saar stamps has now come to an end and prices appear to have levelled out. For example the 1950 Stamp Day Commemorative, available at the time of issue for 3s. 6d., is now priced at £9 by *Gibbons* and $37.50 by *Scott*. Of late there has been more attention paid to the 1920–35 issues and prices for many of them have increased whereas the later stamps have tended to remain stationary.

SABAH (formerly North Borneo) and SARAWAK now comprise States of the Malaysian Federation. Both have a large following in Britain and America, as well as a strong local appeal to philatelists in the Far East. North Borneo was under a cloud for many years, on account of the gaudy pictorials of the turn of the century which could be had at a discount off face value if they were cancelled-to-order. Things have been infinitely more respectable under the aegis of the Crown Agents. The stamps of the past thirty years are all good properties, particularly the definitive sets of 1939, 1961 and 1964. The last-named, consisting of the 1961 series overprinted with the new name of the country, was replaced the following year by the Orchids designs common throughout the Malaysian states and by the high-denomination Birds set of Malaysia. The prices of the first Sabah series have gone up already and will probably go much higher yet.

ST. CHRISTOPHER-NEVIS-ANGUILLA (or St. Kitts-Nevis, as the stamps of 1903–51 were inscribed). One of the best West Indian territories of which to have a collection at the moment, though it would cost a small fortune to put one together now, starting at present-day prices. The most striking increase is seen in the high values of the George V period, particularly in the Tercentenary series of 1923. The 1964 *Gibbons* priced mint examples of the 5s., 10s. and £1 at £6, £18 and £38 respectively; now the 1967 figures have shot up to £25, £50 and £175 respectively. If one had bought these stamps at *Gibbons'* figure in 1964 and sold them at *Gibbons'* quotes (which are actually based on recent auction realisations) a profit of £188 would have been made—an average increase of 100% per annum.

ST. HELENA. There is plenty of scope in the Victorian issues, particularly in the numerous surcharge varieties. This was one of the colonies to issue a lengthy commemorative series in the shape of the Centenary issue of 1934. The three top values (2s. 6d., 5s. and 10s.) have doubled in value in the past three years, from £16 5s. to £33, thus proving that Georgian high values are the blue chips of Commonwealth philately. When Tristan da Cunha was evacuated in October 1961 a quantity of the Tristan 2½c., 5c., 7½c. and 10c. held at St. Helena were promptly overprinted 'ST. HELENA Tristan Relief' and surcharged with sterling premiums equivalent to their decimal postal value. The set was thus sold for 5s., 2s. 6d. of which was to be credited to the special fund for the refugees. This step was highly irregular and, as soon as news of it reached London, the Colonial Office ordered that the Tristan Relief stamps must be withdrawn. The set was on sale for only seven days, but even so only 434 complete sets were sold. The remainder were then destroyed. Some sets quickly found their way to Britain where they were readily snapped up at about £50 a set. (It is ironic to note that the proceeds of this misguided issue netted for the Tristanians little more than £50 altogether!) Prices rose rapidly to £100 and two years later had doubled again. By 1966 an unmounted mint set was fetching £500 and the following year a price of £750 had been reached. Has this set reached its ceiling yet? I wonder.

ST. LUCIA.   Would have been recommended as a good country to collect, had it not blotted its copybook (or rather, its stamp album) immediately after achieving Associated Statehood status in March 1967. The full story of the way in which a country, having been philatelically respectable for more than a century, could lose the confidence of collectors overnight is recounted in Chapter IX. The issues from 1860 till 1967 will retain their popularity, however, and some of these are worth looking out for. In the 1949 series the 4c., perforated 12½, rates 10d., while the rare perforation 14½ × 14 is unknown in mint condition and priced by *Gibbons* at £250 used. It *might* just be possible to turn up one of these rarities in a large accumulation of commercially used stamps.

ST. VINCENT.   One of the more 'difficult' West Indian countries with a range of surcharge varieties in the Victorian period which deter all but the more determined (and wealthy) collector. Otherwise quite straightforward.

ST. PIERRE AND MIQUELON.   These last remnants of France's erstwhile colonial empire in North America, were in the doldrums until the 1950s when more attractive pictorial stamps began to appear. At the same time the stamps of these two little islands in the Gulf of St. Lawrence suddenly began to interest collectors in Canada and the United States. Apart from the first series, which made its début in 1885, the stamps of St. Pierre are still not too difficult to find.

SALVADOR.   Not very popular on account of the Seebeck issues of 1890–8 and the welter of provisional overprints and surcharges which have appeared from the earliest times right down to the present day. For that reason the prices of these stamps are reasonable, and the philatelist seeking an interesting country with plenty of scope might find it profitable to collect Salvador.

SAMOA High in popularity with collectors of the Pacific area. The issues of the *Samoa Express* (1877) have been reprinted and forged so that the prospective purchaser of these elusive stamps should exercise caution. There was a great deal of speculation in the stamps of the native kingdom and of the Provisional Government which followed it and consequently these stamps are too plentiful ever to be a good investment. On the other hand the 'G.R.I' overprints on the German colonial series, brought into use after the territory was invaded by British Imperial troops, are very expensive nowadays and prices show no sign of levelling off yet. The issues of the New Zealand Administration and the independent state are good, solid property—nothing dramatic, but showing steady appreciation.

SAN MARINO. The pocket republic whose stamps used to be derided by the old school of collectors, because of their obviously philatelic inspiration. In the past ten years, however, there has been a fantastic boom in the stamps of San Marino, especially the high-value airmails issued since the Second World War. There are indications, however, that this boom is now at an end; it would appear that the market for San-Marinese stamps was somewhat artificially pegged by the big Italian dealers.

SAUDI ARABIA. For many years very respectable, but deadly dull. Its stamps were poorly designed and their obscure Arabic inscriptions excited little interest. The quality of design and production has now improved, but the popularity of the stamps has not gone up correspondingly. This could be a 'sleeper' which might amply repay the discerning collector who takes it up now.

SIERRA LEONE. Now fallen into the hands of an agency and some of the results are enumerated in the next chapter. The issues prior to independence, however, have retained their popularity. The high values of the King George V period, particularly the £1, £2 and £5 denominations, have soared in value recently. The two £5 stamps fetched about £60 in 1964 but by 1967 were fetching five times that sum. The 1933

Centenary of the Abolition of Slavery series is also much sought after and has rocketed in value in the past decade.

SOUTH AFRICA. In spite of the political climate, is still very popular with collectors in Europe and America, while the existence of a large philatelic public in the country itself will always insure its stamps against fluctuations in world opinion. Of the four territories which make up the Republic each issued its own stamps prior to 1910. The Cape triangulars, especially the 'Woodblocks', the Natal embosseds, the Transvaal *tête-bêches* and the 'V.R.I' surcharges of the Orange Free State—all rank among the great rarities of Commonwealth philately and are mostly in the millionaire class today; yet there is much to interest the philatelist of more moderate means.

SOUTH WEST AFRICA. Not perhaps as popular as it once was. Nevertheless its stamps are attractive and free from any taint of being produced for philatelic motives. The majority of the earlier issues consisted of contemporary South African stamps suitably overprinted and some of the errors and varieties in the typesetting of these overprints are worth looking for.

SPAIN. Currently enjoying unparalleled popularity. This is on account of an extremely attractive thematic series, depicting the arms of the provincial capitals, which was released between 1962 and 1966. These stamps caught the imagination of collectors who had never bothered about Spanish stamps before. Now a series depicting provincial costumes is being released in instalments and everyone is rushing to purchase these stamps as they are issued, so they are unlikely to be such a good investment. Many of the pre-war sets, particularly the Goya, Catacombs, Red Cross, U.P.U. and Montserrat Monastery issues, have soared enormously in value over the past ten years.

SURINAM (or Dutch Guiana). Flirted with a philatelic agency for a few years before returning, like the prodigal son, to the aegis of the Netherlands Philatelic Service in The Hague. Little harm was done, fortunately, and its stamps have shown a good rate of appreciation.

SWEDEN. Like the other Scandinavian countries, Sweden has always had a fairly large following, but this has inevitably become more widespread in recent years as the number of new issues has increased. Swedish stamps include some of the world's greatest rarities, the unique 3 skilling-banco error of colour and the 'TRETIO' (thirty) error on a 20-ore stamp of 1872, but there are plenty of more modest items which would repay investment.

SWITZERLAND. Well established as one of the most popular countries in the world, due to its stable economy and the attractiveness of its stamps. While it is unlikely that any philatelist, embarking on a collection of Swiss stamps today, would make a fortune, there could be few safer countries to take up. The annual Pro Juventute stamps, in aid of Child Welfare, are among the most popular issues, with their great thematic appeal.

SYRIA. Still has its devotees in France where the stamps of the mandatory period (1919–36) find a ready market; but otherwise it seems to have little appeal at the moment. This state of affairs is difficult to explain, since the modern issues are reasonably attractive and plentiful in commercially used condition. Fashions in philately are often capricious and unpredictable and Syrian stamps may suddenly interest the collecting public in just as inexplicable a fashion.

TCHAD. One of those countries of the French Community which have not overdone the spate of new issues since receiving its independence in 1959. Fewer than a hundred have appeared and they have covered a wide variety of subjects of international thematic appeal. None of these is unduly expensive as yet, but several of them (Kennedy, Churchill, Nubian Monuments and Olympic Games) may well turn out to be good investments in their own right.

THAILAND (Siam). Worth a second glance since, in spite of the present lack of interest shown in it by philatelists in general, it has all the criteria of the country with good investment prospects. New issues are infrequent and inexpensive; the early issues are not too dear; and they offer plenty of variety for those who care to seek it out. The Scouts' Fund sets of 1920, by virtue of their thematic interest, are fairly expensive nowadays, but they will always be a good investment.

TOGO. Burst on the philatelic scene in 1960 with a set of four stamps honouring the Four-Power 'Summit' Conference which never took place! Since then about fifty stamps on average have been issued annually, honouring all manner of people and events of little relevance to Togo. Togo's ambivalent attitude towards East and West is best seen in the Space stamps which depict Leonov and White, Gagarin and Shepard, with equal impartiality. It would be hard to take Togolese stamps seriously.

TRINIDAD and TOBAGO. Little attempt to exploit independence by issuing stamps; the 1960 definitive series is still current and there has only been a handful of commemoratives in the past five years. This is one of the soundest of the Caribbean countries to collect, the best items being the 'Britannias' of the 1850s and the Georgian high values. There was quite a lot of panic buying of the provisional 1c. stamp which made a hurried appearance in time for use on the Christmas cards of 1956 and prices rapidly rose to 15s.—where they have remained ever since. Local speculators bought this provisional stamp by the sheet and thus there are more than enough to go round.

TRISTAN DA CUNHA. Perhaps the most romantically remote of all British colonies. The dramatic events of its evacuation, in the shadow of the volcano, contributed to an enormous boom in Tristan stamps late in 1961. Six definitive sets (½d. to 10s.) in thirteen years is a formidable record but some of these have shown a good appreciation. The first series (1952) consisted of St. Helena stamps suitably overprinted, and gave way in 1954 to a Tristan pictorial set. This was replaced, in the fullness of time (1960), by a series depicting marine life of the South Atlantic. It was superseded in 1961 by a similar series inscribed in South African rands and cents, but this was abruptly withdrawn from use when the island was evacuated in October of that year. The resettlement in 1963 was marked by a second provisional series overprinted on St. Helena stamps and this was followed in 1965 by the present set depicting Historic Ships. Now several denominations are being dropped or their designs altered, as new postal rates are introduced, so it is advisable to secure this series (especially the obsolete 4½d. and 10s.) before prices rise again.

TUNISIA. Its present popularity is due to the whimsical designs of Hatem Elmekki, who has had a virtual monopoly in this field since independence was achieved in 1957. There have been no startling increases in value, but the stamps are full of interest. Tunisian stamps, both before and after independence, are popular in France primarily, but are gaining ground in America, Italy and elsewhere. This is definitely a country to watch.

TURKEY. Such a vast and complicated country from the philatelic point of view that most philatelists tend to limit their interest to a specific period, e.g. the Ottoman period (1863–1922), the Kemalist regime (1922–38), and the modern issues from 1939 to the present day. All three periods are full of interest and all show bright prospects for the shrewd collector.

THE UNITED NATIONS. The only non-governmental organisation whose postage stamps are universally recognised and accepted. The stamps consist basically of those issued at the U.N. Headquarters in New York, but U.N. enthusiasts usually take an interest in the stamps of the various specialised agencies in Switzerland, the erstwhile League of Nations, and the International Court of Justice in The Hague. Probably for political reasons, U.N. stamps are not very popular in Britain, but everywhere else, and particularly in the United States, they

are avidly collected. Many of the earlier commemorative sets
have shown a good increase in value over the years.

THE UNITED STATES. The appeal is primarily to American
collectors, but stamps of the U.S.A. have a strong following
everywhere else. Commemoratives are usually confined to the
prevailing letter rate and are not too frequently released. In
1948 no fewer than twenty-eight new stamps were released—
the maximum ever released in any one year—but it was felt
that this was excessive and in more recent years the number of
new issues has dropped to half that figure. While the United
States is pre-eminent in the world popularity stakes, no one is
likely to make a big profit out of American stamps. Because of
their low face value, these stamps have habitually been bought
by the sheet by avid collectors and many of these sheets are
still salted away by their hopeful owners against the day when
they can be sold for a handsome profit. Since everyone is in
on the racket, there will always be plenty of stamps to go round.
One consolation is that no U.S. stamp since 1847 has ever been
invalidated, so one is always safe in the knowledge that nothing
(other than interest) is lost on money laid out on these stamps
—they can always be used for postage! Very few American
commemoratives since the White Plains 2c. of 1926 have shown
a profit to investors. Prior to that the story is quite different,
but, even so, those who invested in the Columbus and Omaha
sets of 1893 and 1898, for example, had to wait a long time
before their investments paid off. With the definitives knowledge
pays off, time and time again. The ability to distinguish the
rare printings from the common, in the issues from 1908 to
1932, is a valuable asset.

URUGUAY. A solid following in the United States and South
America generally, while interest is beginning to pick up in
Europe. The Montevideo 'Suns' of 1856–62 rank among the
world's greatest rarities and the collector should treat specimens
(especially used ones) with great caution. Of particular interest
are the Football sets of 1924 and 1928—the forerunners in any
collection devoted to the World Cup, since Uruguay were the

original champions in the series. These stamps will not remain long at their present quotes.

THE VATICAN. Often cited as the philatelic investor's paradise, because of the way in which its stamps have risen astronomically in value. A recent advertisement extolling the virtues of Vatican stamps has claimed that if one had invested £5 a month on new issues of Vatican stamps from 1947 to the present date (1967) one would now own £50,000 worth, for an outlay of only £1,200. When one examines the current market value of such sets as the Gratian, Tobias, the 1949 airmails and the Stamp Centenary the truth of this claim becomes all too apparent. But it must be emphasised that these values are due to the fact that the proud possessors of these stamps do not believe that the summit has yet been reached and consequently they are not yet inclined to sell. The market in Vatican stamps is somewhat artificial, since a sizeable fortune is tied up in them. For years Italian collectors, investors and speculators have been buying up Vatican issues in blocks and sheets and many a religious order is reputed to have its surplus cash invested in this way. There was a partial slump in 1966 when one of the largest Italian dealers suddenly reduced his prices and some panic selling resulted. Vatican, like San Marino, must be treated with some caution at the moment.

VENEZUELA. Not among the most popular of Latin American countries. This is on account of the rather dreary Bolivar portrait issues which were once the backbone of the packet trade. Today these stamps may be found in every schoolboy collection. Interest developed suddenly in the late 1950s when Venezuela began to increase its material wealth and prosperity as a result of the exploitation of its vast oil and mineral resources. The appearance of a long series depicting the arms of the provinces (a full-length series for each province) seems to have stimulated collectors' interest rather than weakened it. Apart from the Arms series, which numbered 389 stamps all told, Venezuela's new issue programme tends to be a modest one.

VIETNAM. Here are two extremes in philately as well as politics. The stamps of the People's Democratic Republic of NORTH VIETNAM are poorly printed and, at the moment, almost entirely political in motive. Recent stamps have commemorated the 1,000th and 1,500th U.S. aircraft shot down (both figures denied by the Pentagon) and paid tribute to Norman Morrison, a young American who burned himself to death as a protest against his country's participation in the Vietnam war. North Vietnamese stamps are currently taboo in the United States, but they excite little interest in Britain or Western Europe where trade in them is permitted. SOUTH VIETNAM on the other hand has its stamps beautifully recessprinted in France and its overseas sales and distribution handled by a highly competent philatelic agency in America. New issues are none too frequent, which makes it all the more desirable. Always popular in France, South Vietnam is rapidly gaining in ground with American collectors, though obsolete issues are still moderately priced.

YEMEN. Here is another example of two political regimes resulting in two lots of stamps to contend with. But as the issues of the YEMENI ARAB REPUBLIC and the guerrilla Mutawakellite KINGDOM OF YEMEN are both handled by philatelic agencies, backed by American 'know-how', they do not appear so terribly different in character. Aside from the more obviously propaganda-slanted issues aimed against each other, the two governments have resorted to thematic sets in great profusion—Kennedy, Space, Sports and even Cats. These sets invariably include denominations of $\frac{1}{8}$, $\frac{1}{4}$ and $\frac{1}{2}$ bogash, although the Yemeni letter rate is 2 bogash. These fractional denominations have no postal use, but are handled by the thousand by the manufacturers of stamp packets for department stores, and Yemeni pictorials have now ousted Mongolian triangles from the average schoolboy collection. The Yemen's early issues from 1926 till the end of the Second World War are scarce, and command a good premium if genuinely used on cover. After the War, however, a vast quantity of stamps purporting to have been issued in the Yemen flooded the

American philatelic market. They are ignored by the majority of the catalogues, yet fetch astonishingly high prices nowadays on account of their thematic appeal.

YUGOSLAVIA. Now beginning to improve steadily as a country worth collecting, after the post-war depression of its philatelic market. A large body of well-organised philatelists within the country itself, plus an ever-increasing number of Western tourists buying stamps as souvenirs of their visits, are the cause of this. The pre-war issues are full of interest and the famous 'Chain-breakers' of the early twenties have been keenly collected and studied for many years. There is plenty of interest, too, in the forerunners, the issues of Bosnia-Herzegovina, Montenegro, Serbia and Trieste, not to mention the wartime issues of the German and Italian puppet regimes.

ZANZIBAR. A brief spell of notoriety occurred at the time, shortly following Uhuru (independence), when the Sultan was deposed by the Afro-Shirazi party and union with Tanganyika was subsequently proclaimed. The Sultan's portrait on the definitive series and Uhuru commemoratives was first defaced with a ballpoint pen, subsequently handstamped 'Jamhuri' (Republic) and latterly overprinted in London to the same end. Three distinct issues in as many months had the philatelic world in a whirl and they were eagerly bought up because of their dramatic topicality. Subsequent issues, however, have been printed in East Germany and have pronounced left-wing over-tones, while their all-Swahili inscriptions have not exactly helped to make them more acceptable to European and American collectors. Among the earlier issues the ultra-high values (200 rupees) of 1908 and 1913 have been in the limelight lately, and have been climbing steadily in price.

CHAPTER IX

UNNECESSARY ISSUES

O NCE UPON a time postage-stamps were produced solely as a convenient method of indicating the prepayment of postage —and nothing more. New issues were necessitated by changes in postal rates, the death of a ruler or some other political change.

This was in the uncomplicated period when no one considered purchasing postage-stamps for their own sake. Sooner or later, however, people began to collect the various different kinds of stamps and philately as a hobby was born. It is impossible to say when 'timbromania', as stamp collecting was originally known, came into being, but it was probably established by the early 1850s. The genesis of the hobby is discussed in a fascinating manner in *The Postage Stamp: its History and Recognition* by L. N. and M. Williams, and need not concern us here. Certainly by the mid-1860s it would appear that some postal administrations were beginning to produce stamps with an eye on philatelic revenue. One of the earliest attempts in this direction was reported in September 1866 by *Le Timbre Poste* under the title 'An Unattended Birth'. The magazine had heard rumours concerning a series of provisional stamps of Uruguay of whose status the editor was rather sceptical. Eventually the editor, Jean B. Moens of Brussels, received from the Administrator-General of Posts in Montevideo a circular which contained the following curious information:

'The undersigned . . . certifies that, on 1st January of the present year, there was placed in circulation four denominations of postage stamps with new values overprinted in black ink; these stamps are the same as those which were in use up till 31st December 1865 and which were superseded by the stamps shown in this present certificate. These stamps, provisionally released on this date, were withdrawn from circulation on 10th January of the present year and have been replaced by others which are now in circulation. I have drawn up this certificate at the demand of those interested, at the Central Post Office of Montevideo, 13th June 1866.'

Moens commented on this astonishing document that it was a matter for some regret that the Administrator General failed to inform the public of this decision at the time the stamps were issued. Apparently the Uruguayan authorities decided to make a provisional surcharged issue on 29th December 1865. The stamps were brought into use three days later—too short an interval of time to permit all the post offices in the Republic to be made aware of the issue, communications at that time being decidedly irregular. They were allegedly valid for ten days only and were withdrawn when a consignment of new definitive stamps arrived from Glasgow. The new stamps were in denominations of 5c., 10c., 15c. and 20c. and the temporary series consisted of 5c. on 12c., 10c. on 8c., 15c. on 10c. and 20c. on 6c. of the previous series. It will be noted that a provisional 10c. was created, though this denomination already existed and, in fact, was in turn utilised to produce the provisional 15c.

Nor was this all. The surcharges were subject to all manner of errors, which included *tête-bêche* pairs, inverted surcharges, three sets of figures instead of two, double and even treble surcharges. Used copies are extremely rare and many of these provisional varieties are not known in used condition. As if this were not enough, dangerous forgeries of the surcharges were later manufactured in both Montevideo and Paris. Nowadays a 'straight' set of the surcharges (the cheapest variety of each denomination) is listed by *Gibbons* at £8 12s. 6d. and by *Scott* at $26, whereas, ironically, the set of four stamps which superseded the surcharges and had a legitimate usage over a period of several months, is now listed by these two catalogues at £11 7s. 6d. and $36. The motive in producing the short-lived surcharges was to make money for the Uruguayan Administrator-General, but it is obvious that in the long run the stamp collector did not profit from them.

This was an unnecessary issue, since the proper 5c., 10c., 15c. and 20c. arrived only a few days later (if they were not actually in the Administrator-General's safe at the time!). One could cite numerous examples of similar issues from many countries throughout the past hundred years. At the time of their issue such stamps have not always been seen in their true light, or controversy has raged over them when first they appeared on the scene. The first issues of the Transvaal in 1869 were purely 'philatelic' in conception and genuinely used copies are almost unheard of; yet today they have achieved an aura of respectability and are eagerly sought out by specialists. The first issue of Brunei, however, though it undoubtedly served some postal purpose, is still ignored by most catalogues.

At one time, moreover, when world communications were not so swift as they are today, it was possible for certain plausible individuals to manufacture a stamp and pass it off as genuinely issued by some far-off country. Samuel Allan Taylor of Boston was a past-master at the art of producing bogus stamps. Among his many masterpieces were stamps purporting to have been issued by Santo Domingo, Guatemala, Paraguay and Prince Edward Island, but which were entirely the product of his fertile imagination. Fred Melville's book, *Phantom Philately*, describes most of the bogus stamps of this early period when collectors could not rely on the efficient New Issue notes conducted by most philatelic periodicals nowadays.

COMMEMORATIVE STAMPS

The idea that stamps could be made to serve two purposes— to prepay postage and commemorate an event—was slow to take root. The earliest postal items of a commemorative nature were the 3c. stamped envelopes issued by the United States in 1876 to celebrate the centenary of the Declaration of Independence. The first adhesive stamp of a commemorative nature was a 2pf. stamp produced by the Privat-Brief-Verkehr (local postal service) of Frankfurt-am-Main in July 1887, in honour of the ninth German Federal and Jubilee Shooting Competition. The first commemorative series produced by a government

PLATE XI
OMNIBUS ISSUES.

(1) French colonies, Colonial Exhibition (1931), (2) British colonies, Silver Jubilee (1935), (3) French colonies, Revolution sesquicentennial (1939), (4–7) British colonies, Victory (1946), Freedom from Hunger (1963), International Telecommunications Union (1965) and Red Cross (1963).

postal administration was the set inscribed 'ONE HUNDRED YEARS' which New South Wales issued in 1888 to mark the centenary of the British settlement at Sydney Cove. The series consisted of ten values, from 1d. to 20s. and, though issued for a commemorative purpose, was retained in use for twelve years, undergoing numerous changes in colour, watermark and perforation.

Though the idea of commemorative stamps was slow to catch on, those countries which did produce them at the end of the nineteenth century did so in no uncertain fashion. One of the worst offenders at this time was the United States which, on 2nd January 1893, released a set of sixteen stamps to publicise the Columbian Exposition in Chicago and commemorating the quatercentenary of Columbus' first visit to America. The stamps ranged in denomination from 1c. to $5 and had a total face value of $16.34. The series was greeted by protests from the philatelic public and for many years they were under a cloud. They were largely responsible for the creation, early in in 1895, of The Society for The Suppression of Speculative Stamps, a body which aimed at the boycotting, by dealers and collectors, of certain issues, mainly commemorative, but sometimes including an unnecessary definitive stamp which came under their interdict. At first prominent dealers as well as collectors subscribed to the 'Four S'd League', but, inevitably, there were those collectors who would not be dictated to in respect to what they put in their albums, and so long as these collectors perversely demanded the forbidden stamps, there would always be a dealer or two who did not scruple to supply them. Other dealers, putting self-interest before the good of philately, gave up their boycott when they observed their less scrupulous brethren handling the banned but highly lucrative stamps and eventually, and inevitably, the Society fell apart when the support of the trade began to vanish.

Nevertheless, sufficient apprehension was felt in official postal circles for the Congress of the Universal Postal Union, meeting at Washington in 1897, to pass a resolution stating that 'stamps issued for a special object peculiar to the country of issue, such as stamps called commemorative stamps and available for a limited time only, should no longer be valid for international postage'.

This resolution was never implemented, however, and postal administrations continued to do as they pleased. This was also the hey-day of the 'Seebeck' issues, referred to in Chapter VI. In this same year of 1897 Canada issued a marathon series of sixteen stamps, from ½c. to $5, to celebrate the Diamond Jubilee of Queen Victoria. There was a considerable amount of speculation in these stamps at the time of issue and several denominations, including the ½c., speedily disappeared from the post office counters.

In 1896 Greece blotted her copybook by issuing a set of twelve stamps in honour of the resurrected Olympic Games, ranging from 1 lepton to 10 drachmae in value. All of these long and very expensive sets came in for world-wide denunciation by collectors who felt that they were not only unnecessary, but exorbitant in price. Nowadays they represent the 'plums' of the early commemoratives as their current catalogue quotes show:

	Face value	Gibbons	Scott
U.S.A. Columbus	$16.34	£318 13s. od.	$1,072.65
	(£3 5s. 7d.)*		
Canada Jubilee	$16.20½	£187 4s. 6d.	$700.85
	(£3 5s. od.)*		
Greece Olympics	19.63dr.	£178 5s. 6d.	$707.20
	(£1 os. od.)*		

* The sterling equivalents are based on the rates of exchange current at the time the stamps were issued.

Their rise in value was very gradual for many years, but after a decent passage of time they have achieved a respectability which was denied them seventy years ago. What is condemned today has a nasty habit of turning into a highly desirable item tomorrow.

Not only the long sets were criticised, however, and it is amusing, in a way, to note the annoyance with which collectors sixty years ago regarded so innocent a stamp as America's 2c.

commemorating the Hudson-Fulton Celebration of 1909. This was the third 2c. commemorative to appear that year—sufficient for one eminent American philatelist to declaim bitterly, 'We already have the reputation of issuing a new stamp every week and we seem to be living up to it, I am sorry to say'. Nowadays we are accustomed to a vast out-pouring of new issues—almost 6,000 were released in 1966 alone—and few are the voices raised in protest.

Strictly speaking, *all* commemorative stamps are unnecessary since the ordinary definitive issues are quite sufficient for the mundane business of prepaying postage, but everyone acknowledges that the commemorative has its honourable functions, whether it be to acquaint a country's inhabitants with their history and traditions, or to pay homage to famous men, or to propagate the image of a country or political regime.

CHARITY STAMPS

Charity stamps, or semi-postals as they are termed in America, combine in one label an indication of postal prepayment and a premium in aid of some good cause. Surprisingly they had their origins in the United Kingdom which has never made a charity issue since. In 1890 a stamped pictorial envelope was issued in Britain to mark the Golden Jubilee of Penny Postage. It was sold for a shilling, but only paid 1d. postage, the remaining 11d. being credited to the Rowland Hill Benevolent Fund for Post Office Widows and Orphans. Seven years later New South Wales produced two stamps in aid of a Consumptives' Home (T.B. Sanatorium). These were sold for 1s. and 2s. 6d. but prepaid postage of 1d. and 2½d. only, the balance being given to the Home. This idea was speedily adopted by another Australian state, Victoria, which issued two Hospital stamps in October of the same year, also priced at 1d. (1s.) and 2½d. (2s. 6d.). Three years later 1d. (1s.) and 2d. (2s.) stamps were issued on behalf of the Boer War Patriotic Fund. But in spite of this ominous beginning, neither Australia nor her states have since resorted to this practice.

The idea of making money out of stamp collectors for charitable purposes spread to Europe in 1905 when Russia issued four stamps with premiums in aid of a War Charity at the time of the Russo-Japanese War. Neighbouring Roumania adopted this practice the following year, releasing no less than four separate Charity sets, each consisting of four stamps. In the same year the Netherlands issued three stamps on behalf of the Amsterdam Anti-T.B. Federation.

The early Charity stamps were roundly condemned by the philatelic public; in some cases the stamp catalogues refused to list them, and collectors boycotted them. They almost died out, being largely superseded by non-postal labels such as the Christmas seals which had been introduced in Scandinavia in 1905. They were given a new lease of life, however, with the advent of the First World War when many countries on both sides, as well as several of the neutrals, issued Charity stamps with premiums for the Red Cross, war relief, the widows and the orphans. Hungary was the worst offender, with sets of seventeen stamps bearing hefty premiums produced in 1914 and 1915. The most bizarre series emanated from neutral Sweden in 1916—a set of ten stamps with a premium to purchase clothing for the Landstorm (army reserve)! Many British colonies and protectorates issued stamps surcharged in aid of the Red Cross.

In spite of this welter of War Charity issues a solitary stamp from Switzerland, released in 1913, went almost unnoticed. Yet this was the first of a long line of Charity stamps which endures to this day and is now the most popular Charity issue made anywhere in the world. This was a 5c. stamp inscribed in Latin 'Pro Juventute' (for youth) and it bore the exorbitant premium of 10c. No Children's stamp appeared in 1914 but in 1915 two stamps were issued. In 1916 there were three and by the 1920s there were four. Now collectors are faced each year by five Pro Juventute stamps, which are eagerly snapped up. In spite of their present popularity, few of them have shown much financial appreciation over the years.

The Children's Charity issues of Netherlands and Luxembourg between the wars have gone up in value more rapidly. New Zealand's Health stamps, issued annually since 1929, have a steady following among the world's stamp collectors, but not all of them have shown the same rate of increases in value. The stamps issued prior to 1935 are priced in as many pounds as they once were in pence, the best known being the 1931 pair, known to philatelists as the 'Smiling Boys', which had a face value of 5d. (including 2d. in premiums) and are now priced by *Gibbons* at £10 (*Scott* $40).

By and large, however, charity stamps are not regarded benevolently by stamp collectors. No other hobby has been made to pay in the way that philately has. Stamp collectors have, in effect, paid for the restoration of an abbey (Orval, in Belgium), provided Health camps (New Zealand) and T.B. sanatoria (from the Philippines to Fiji), subsidised 'unemployed intellectuals' (France) and contributed handsomely to Hitler's Culture Fund (Germany). With the exception of the last-named, all of these are or were worthy causes, but it seems to be taking an unfair advantage for postal administrations to raise money for charity in this way.

Premiums are not as high nowadays as they were at one time, due mainly to the recent threat of the Fédération Internationale de Philatelie to blacklist semi-postals bearing an excessive premium. A premium is held to be excessive when it amounts to more than half of the postal value of a stamp. The Dutch Children's series of 1965, for example, was blacklisted by F.I.P. since two denominations, the 8c. and 10c., bore premiums of 6c. each—more than 50% of the postal value in both cases. An exception to this interdict was Samoa's 8d. stamp which was put on sale in 1966 with a 6d. premium for hurricane relief. The F.I.P. relaxed its ban in this instance in view of the grave national disaster which hit Samoa the previous year and necessitated the issue.

MINIATURE SHEETS

There is a third category of unnecessary issue which requires special mention—miniature sheets. They originated in the Low Countries, in the 1920s, making their début in Luxembourg in 1923 where a small sheet containing a single stamp of 10frs. denomination was released in honour of a philatelic exhibition.

Belgium followed in May 1924 with miniature sheets, containing a block of four of the 5frs. definitive stamp, but in altered colours, also as a souvenir of a philatelic exhibition. Within fifteen years this insidious practice had grown to dangerous proportions and in 1937 *Gibbons* announced that henceforward they would not list miniature sheets in their catalogues.

Sheets up to that date, however, continued to be listed by them. None of the other leading catalogues omitted them and though, thirty years afterwards, miniature sheets seem to be more prolific than ever, *Gibbons* have bowed to the apparent dictates of the collecting public and have now begun to list them again, including all those which had been ignored in the intervening period.

A recent phenomenon is the souvenir sheet as distinct from the miniature sheet (though stamp collectors rather haphazardly apply both terms indiscriminately to each category). This term should be applied to the large imperforate labels, too large to be regarded as a stamp in themselves, but not containing a stamp with a broad margin all round. Examples of this sort of thing would be the souvenir sheets produced in 1965–6 by the Mutawakelite Kingdom of the Yemen in memory of Kennedy, Churchill and 'Builders of World Peace', the Space Vehicles sheet from Sharjah (1964) and Hungary's 10 forint sheet depicting the painting 'May Picnic' (1967).

Somewhere midway between the two are those miniature sheets which contain 'stamps' surrounded by imitation perforations (e.g. Jamaica's 'Miss World', 1964, and Malawi's Christmas, 1965). Theoretically the stamps in a miniature sheet should be capable of being detached for postal use in the normal way, but where no real perforations exist the implication is that the sheet has to be used on an envelope in its entirety—or not at all (probably the latter). Admittedly I have seen commercially used miniature and souvenir sheets on correspondence, but as their average size is 6″ × 6″ they are really too ungainly to be of practical postal use.

In most cases, where a miniature sheet contains a stamp or group of stamps, the collector has to pay well over the face value of the stamp or stamps—in other words, the marginal paper is made to take on a value in itself. This must surely be the ultimate in the unnecessary.

PHILATELIC ABUSES

Commemorative stamps, semi-postals and miniature sheets are all, strictly speaking, unnecessary to the business of pre-paying postage. Though all three were condemned at one time, provided they are not seen to exploit the collector too obviously, they are now tolerated and even welcomed (since the present boom in British stamps is due largely to the recent increase in the spate of commemoratives). Where once they were de-nounced out of hand, these stamps are now avidly collected and provide the principal vehicle for the man who wishes to make a philatelic investment.

On the other hand, commemoratives and miniature sheets in particular have been abused by certain postal administra-tions and philatelic agencies, and stamps have been issued bearing a premium on behalf of no cause other than that of the post office selling them.

One of the worst, though by no means the earliest, attempts to exploit not only collectors, but the country issuing the stamps, occurred in 1930 when Iceland celebrated the thou-sandth anniversary of its parliament, the Althing. Some time before the anniversary the Icelandic authorities were ap-proached by a mysterious body, located in Vienna, calling themselves the 'Friends of Iceland', who undertook to supply the Post Office with a series of fifteen commemorative stamps, *free of charge*. The Icelanders showed a surprising degree of naïveté in agreeing to this astonishing proposal and in due course negotiations with the 'Friends' were concluded, arrang-ing for the issue of the stamps and the sale of any remainders. The issue, according to the contract, was fixed at 25,000 sets— a figure which was sufficiently low as to encourage collectors to buy a set, with reasonable hopes that it would increase in value. The Elbemuhl printing works in Vienna, however, apparently produced considerably more than were stipulated in the contract and it is obvious that the 'Friends of Iceland' were selling sets direct to dealers without going through the

Icelandic Post Office. Moreover, the various errors and mis-
prints—wrong colours and imperforates—which should have
been regarded as printers' waste and consequently destroyed,
were vended to the philatelic public as genuine varieties at
very high prices. An outcry in the philatelic press led to the
Icelandic Government investigating the matter, whereupon it
was discovered that the 'Friends' had altered the figure in the
contract, from 25,000 to 1,025,000, to cover their production
of a million sets for their own use. Eventually the 'Friends of
Iceland' were prosecuted and punished.

Fortunately, Iceland's philatelic reputation soon recovered
after this lapse, but it is amazing to think how other postal
administrations have succumbed to the blandishments of
agencies and have lost their reputations overnight. Perhaps the
most staggering scheme ever foisted on stamp collectors was
that announced early in 1956 by a Panamanian syndicate
which planned to issue a series of stamps portraying all the
Popes since the time of St. Peter. This would have entailed an
issue of no less than 261 different stamps, released in groups of
twelve every four months over a seven-year period. Rumour
had it that the Vatican itself had backed the scheme to the
tune of $10,500,000. It was expected that the profit from
philatelic sales would amount to at least $100 million. The
promoters were obviously confident of large sales, since 15 to
30 million copies of each stamp were to be printed. Collectors
would have had to pay about £10 a year or a total in excess
of £70 for the complete series. But only the first group of twelve,
portraying all the Popes with the title 'Pius', ever saw the light
of day. It was roundly condemned, not only by the F.I.P., but
by the St. Gabriel World Federation (which caters for collectors
of Religion on stamps) whose members unanimously boycotted
it. The 'Pius' series does not even rate a mention in *Gibbons*,
Scott or most of the other major catalogues, in the belief that,
as one film magnate once said, 'there is no such thing as *bad*
publicity'. It is, however, listed by *Michel* and priced at 300
Michel-marks (which in terms of real money, amounts to about
£7 10s. or $22).

The anniversaries which are made the occasion for stamp

issues are usually in nice round figures—a golden jubilee, perhaps, or a centenary. Occasionally one finds a 75th or a 125th anniversary being celebrated and, for political reasons, Robert Burns was belatedly honoured by Britain seven years after his bicentenary. But the oddest anniversaries ever commemorated by stamps were the 110th anniversary of the oldest post office in West Africa and the 104th anniversary of adhesive stamps in Sierra Leone (the centenary of stamps, funnily enough, passed unnoticed four years earlier). They were celebrated simultaneously by overprinting six stamps of the obsolete definitive series of 1961, which were released for this purpose in November 1963. As if this were not enough, there were many errors in the typesetting of the overprints which appear to have been deliberately contrived and in a very short time these errors were being touted in the philatelic trade at ridiculous prices.

This set came hard on the heels of a similar series of overprints, released in April 1963, to mark the second anniversary of independence. The independence set, likewise, was marked by a number of constant 'varieties', the chief being that five stamps in every sheet of the 3d., 4d. and 6d. had the third line of the overprint in a narrower setting.

Sierra Leone was also one of the first countries to indulge in philatelic gimmicks, such as the 'free-form', self-adhesive stamps described in Chapter II. Sierra Leone subsequently overprinted the unsold remainders of this issue in memory of the late President Kennedy—an example of an insidious practice whereby those countries, which cannot produce a historic event or famous person from within their own frontiers worthy of commemoration, resort to honouring the events and celebrities of other lands.

In the matter of unusual stamp shapes Sierra Leone was anticipated by the Polynesian kingdom of Tonga whose 'Beer-mats' have been described on page 21.

Tonga later reissued several of these coin stamps provisionally surcharged by the time-honoured numismatic method of 'counter-marking'. The basic set consisted of 1s. 3d., 1s. 9d., 2s. 3d., 2s. 6d., 2s. 9d., 4s. 6d. and 5s. denominations, and cost

Also regarded in this category are the so-called 'blocked values' (*sperrwerte*) of East Germany. These are certain denominations in a commemorative series which can only be obtained if the would-be purchaser is a state-registered philatelist. Even then the philatelist is rationed to a limited number. There is usually no ban on the remaining values in the set, but the fact that one or more denominations are 'blocked' effectively prevents East Germans from trading in sets (which have to be complete, to be commercially marketable). It has been claimed that this scheme was introduced to eliminate the smuggling of stamps to the West in exchange for dollars and sterling. This practice began with the Schiller sesquicentennial series in April 1955. The 10pf. and 20pf. stamps were freely available but the 5pf. was 'blocked'. Consequently it is now priced at 2s. 6d. by *Gibbons*, while the other stamps are listed at 4d. and 5d. respectively. *Gibbons* does not indicate the *sperrwerte*, though their much higher pricing is sufficient to identify them. *Scott* lists their prices in italic numerals.

The F.I.P. also frowns on stamps issued imperforate in a limited edition. One of the worst offenders in this respect is Hungary, which has issued nearly every stamp in the past twenty years in a limited quantity imperforate, as well as the normal release with perforations. Prior to 1958 these imperforates were sold to collectors at five times their face value, but since then they have been released at only four times face value. Afghanistan has done likewise, but only charged twice their face value for these 'curiosities'. Other countries, such as Albania, Panama and Paraguay, have issued imperforates in colours differing from those of the normal perforated stamps. This has been done, perhaps, with some misguided idea of passing them off as 'proofs' or 'colour trials', a class of material which, when authentic, has begun to harden in value and attract more attention from serious collectors.

Other categories considered objectionable by F.I.P. are:

(1) Stamps or miniature sheets issued by advance subscription and which cannot be purchased direct over the post office counter.

(2) Stamps or miniature sheets in restricted supply from the moment of their issue, and thus offered for sale at a price appreciably above face value.

(3) Stamps carrying either an overprint or a perforation applied by a private organisation.

(4) Stamps or miniature sheets of which the conception or realisation have been assigned in whole or in part to a private organisation, or in the issue of which a private organisation has participated.

There is nothing to prevent collectors from purchasing these items, so long as dealers continue to stock them; and dealers, for their part, will continue to handle such material so long as collectors demand it. What the F.I.P. has succeeded in doing is to lay down regulations governing competitive entries in international philatelic exhibitions, by which collectors who exhibit any banned stamps are automatically disqualified. Lists of banned stamps are circulated to all intending entrants prior to every international exhibition in order that they should have due warning. Some postal museums refuse to exhibit to the public any stamps banned by the F.I.P., even though these items are forwarded from the country of origin, via the headquarters of the Universal Postal Union in Berne.

The American Philatelic Society goes even further and actively blacklists the offending countries; lists of new issues are accompanied where necessary by a 'black blot', thereby drawing the collectors' attention to the abusive issue. It is a case of 'Caveat Emptor' and yet collectors must obviously be buying these speculative items since their number is increasing alarmingly. The worst example has occurred as this book is being written, and concerns the West Indian island of St. Lucia which decided to dispense with the good offices of the Crown Agents, following the assumption of Associated Statehood status in March 1967. A decree by the Ministry of Works and Communications of St. Lucia authorised the release on 1st March of the definitive series (minus the 4c.) bearing the commemorative overprint 'Statehood 1st March 1967'. The overprint was done in red, but 300 copies of the $2.50 denomination were also issued overprinted in *black*. In addition the 25c. value of the recent UNESCO series was released with the commemorative overprint, in black or blue. For good measure a special 15c. Statehood commemorative was also produced, both perforated and imperforate, and including a miniature sheet whose marginal embellishments included telecommunications satellites (thus making it a Space thematic item).

Of the 300 examples of the 'black' $2.50, 268 were allegedly available to the philatelic trade in mint condition and were rapidly touted at about £70 on the London market. The 'straight' set was changing hands at £6 for the thirteen denominations while the UNESCO overprints fetched 55s. (blue) and £6 (black). The 15c. commemorative offered as a 'unit' (a neologism used by stamp dealers to cover the increasingly common phenomenon of perforated and imperforate stamps and miniature sheet), cost 55s.

Commenting on these stamps, *The Philatelic Exporter* of May 1967 wrote:

> 'The nature of the issues, and the speed with which St. Lucia acted on achieving Statehood with Great Britain, is yet further testimony to the attractions of the revenue to be derived by an "emergent" nation from a "quickie" stamp issue with an aggregate equivalent face value of some £22,000.
>
> 'Covers bearing sets of the definitive overprinted stamps (including the $2.50 with black overprint) exist, but because of an apparent failure by the sponsors of the issues to appreciate the finer points of public relations techniques, none of these covers was received by any of the very limited number of firms and trade personalities who tend to influence philatelic opinion on the *bona fides* of "surprise" new issues.'

In the preceding chapter I have mentioned the way in which two of the three sultanates of the former Eastern Aden Protectorate, the Kathiri State of Seiyun and the Qu'aiti State in Hadhramaut, had succumbed to the blandishments of an agency. Now, the third sultanate, the Mahra State of Qishn and Socotra, hitherto utterly bereft of a postal service, has begun issuing stamps. The philatelic columnist whose by-line in *The Philatelic Exporter* is 'Strand' prophesied gloomily that, should the Federation of South Arabia split up after the British withdrawal from that area, the twenty-one sultanates which at present comprise the Federation would each issue their own stamps. 'All, so I am given to understand,' he wrote, 'have sold the basic right to issue stamps to a Beirut resident who, in his turn, has sub-contracted it to others currently exploring the thematic field.'

In summing up, it can be seen that ever since stamps have been collected for their own sake there have been governments, postal administrations and philatelic agencies who were ready to exploit this situation by the release of unnecessary stamps. For almost as long, however, collectors have organised themselves to oppose such tactics and boycott these stamps. These retaliatory measures have only been partially successful since philately is essentially a hobby where the individual does as he pleases. Many of yesterday's condemned issues are the sought-after rarities of today and many of today's 'black blot' items may turn out to be not only perfectly acceptable in the long run, but the collectors' pieces of the future. The test of a stamp's worth lies not in its intrinsic value but the value placed on it by a would-be purchaser. Many stamps are universally condemned at the time of their issue, but subsequently rise rapidly in value because future generations of philatelists have adopted a more tolerant attitude (or lower standards, whichever way you look at it) and it is found that an unpopular item, which was boycotted while it was current, eventually appreciates enormously because there are too many collectors chasing too few specimens. As an investment, the examples I have cited in this chapter can hardly be recommended, but who knows in what capricious ways philatelic fashions will alter in the future.

CHAPTER X

PHILATELIC FASHIONS

P HILATELY, like most of the other acquisitive hobbies, has its fashions. Since today's dud may be tomorrow's plum, it would obviously be useful if one could foretell just how these fashions were going to change. Unfortunately fashions in philately are unpredictable. One can only look at what was in vogue in the past and try to determine future trends.

Seventy or eighty years ago the fashion was to collect on a global scale. Not only were the stamps of all countries taken, but collectors showed a general interest in anything connected with the posts—local stamps, vignettes and postal stationery. In addition there was a marked predilection for unused stamps in singles.

A dozen identical stamps mounted on the album page in a pretty pattern were regarded more highly than one block of twelve stamps and it is surprising but true that dealers were in the habit of cutting up blocks which were quite unsaleable as such, but which found a ready market as singles. This way of thinking was dictated by the printed albums which the early collectors favoured.

These provided a printed rectangle (or triangle as the case might be) for all known stamps and collectors often cut up pairs or blocks to fit this Procrustean bed. It was not until the advent of the plain-leaf album at the end of the nineteenth century that collectors were freed from the shackles of the printed album and began to take an interest in blocks and multiples when they could get hold of them. As a consequence of the all-too-liberal use of the scissors, many of the great rarities are not known in multiple form, while many of the

PLATE XII
Long Sets and 'Hardy Annuals'.

(1–2) Netherlands, Child Welfare and Summer stamps, (3) Austria, Costumes, (4) France, Art, (5) Spain, Provincial Arms, (6, 8) Switzerland, 'Pro Juventute' and 'Pro Patria' stamps, (7) New Zealand, Health, (9, 11) West Germany, Youth and Welfare stamps, (10) France, Arms.

early stamps which are still relatively common as singles are often exceedingly scarce in blocks or larger multiples.

Interest in blocks, strips and pairs began to develop as the hobby progressed along scientific lines and the pioneer philatelists began to study the composition of the printing plate in its various states and the layout of the sheet of stamps. For the purpose of plate reconstruction, pairs or larger multiples were necessary since constant varieties and flaws enabled the philatelist to reconstruct the sheet using overlapping stamps in blocks and strips. At a later stage collectors began to take an interest in the various markings found on sheet margins— control numbers, plate numbers, printers' imprints and now, positional arrows, colour dabs and 'traffic lights'—and this impelled them to acquire entire sheets of stamps (providing that these were not too large to house conventionally in an album or folder).

It has long been the practice in the United States for collectors to take a sheet of each new commemorative, not so much in order to study the marginal markings as purely as an investment. But because everybody does it these sheets will always be in plentiful supply. In Britain interest in sheets, or at least part sheets, began when control numbers and letters first appeared in the margins of the Penny Lilac in 1884. Eventually sheets of all stamps up to and including the 1s. denomination bore these markings either on the bottom or the left-hand margin. They were discontinued in 1947, since they no longer served any useful purpose and postal clerks were tired of being continually pestered by collectors who wanted the control blocks. They then went into decline, although the fact that *Gibbons* continues to list them in *Part I* and the *Specialised* catalogues will ensure that they never go completely out of fashion. At the moment many really scarce controls can be picked up for little more than the normal market value of the stamps themselves, but if they come into vogue again prices would undoubtedly stiffen.

Postmarks were originally regarded as dirty blemishes on the face of an otherwise desirable specimen and covers were of little or no interest. Many priceless items, their value greatly enhanced by their unusual postmarks, were unintentionally ruined by their removal from the original envelope or wrapper.

Stamps were divested from their envelopes for the same reason as multiples were frowned on—to fit the spaces in printed albums. At one time collectors would only admit a used specimen if a mint one were not available. Although Overy Taylor advocated a study of postmarks as an adjunct to the study of stamps as early as 1866, many years passed before the majority of philatelists came to realise that it could be possible to authenticate a stamp by examining its postmark. This was found to be especially useful in checking the issues of Heligoland which were extensively reprinted after the island was ceded to Germany in 1890 and ceased to issue its own distinctive stamps. Even then, one had to have a pretty good knowledge of the various postmarks, since an enterprising Hamburg stamp dealer acquired one of the actual date-stamps with which to cancel the reprints in order to pass them off as genuine.

There were always two or three collectors who were ahead of their time, taking an interest in the unfashionable and picking up rarities in their particular field 'for a song'. J. H. Daniels and C. F. Dendy Marshall were two English collectors who, at an early date, appreciated the interest of postmarks for their own sakes, irrespective of the stamps they cancelled. Daniels wrote an excellent little book on the subject, based almost entirely on his remarkable collection and when he died, in 1936, his collection was sold at auction for £1,100. It contained many rarities, such as the Essex Post slogan postmark of 1674 (knocked down for only £11 10s.), which nowadays would fetch a hundred times more than they did thirty years ago. Daniels and another of the early postmark pioneers, George Brumell, were interested mainly in postmarks as such; but Dendy Marshall went a stage further and developed the science of postal history. Whereas Brumell was content with a specimen of a postmark on a small piece, Dendy Marshall preferred his postmarks on complete cover and delighted in reconstructing the story of the route taken by a letter and any other relevant details, from the postal markings, hand-struck or endorsed in manuscript, which were to be found on it.

The study of postal history was born in Britain and given particular impetus by R. C. Alcock of Cheltenham and Robson Lowe, both of whom, by their dealings in and auctions of such material and their numerous publications on the subject, helped to stabilise the market. Postal history is as old as human history itself and the material for study and collection ranges from the earliest cuneiform clay tablets and papyrus scrolls, via the Venetian merchants' letters of the Middle Ages and the campaign covers of the Indian Mutiny, to the latest experiments in the electronic handling and sorting of mail. To the postal historian adhesive stamps are only of incidental importance and postal markings are of paramount significance. There are no convenient catalogues embracing the entire field of postal history (though there are many excellent handbooks and treatises on particular aspects of it which give a guide to market values) so that the collector of this type of material has a greater chance of making his knowledge pay off.

There are even fashions in postal history just as there are in adhesive stamps. Ship letters and paquebot items are currently popular, thanks to the publicity given to them by such books as Alan W. Robertson's monumental *Maritime Postal History of the British Isles* and periodicals like *The Seaposter*; but Travelling Post Office covers, special flight cachets, crash covers and wreck items, campaign letters and censor markings, the pre-adhesive 'entires' of the provincial penny posts and patriotic covers of the American Civil War are also among the 'in' things to collect and study at the moment. A little research into contemporary newspaper files or archives can turn a nondescript cover into a historic relic of great importance and value.

In recent years there has grown up a fashion for 'grangerising'—the decoration of collections (especially of postal history items) with ancillary material such as press cuttings, photographs and ephemera relating to the subject of the collection. This form of collecting is very popular in the United States, Britain and Germany, but is present to some extent everywhere else. Documentary material thus has a market value in itself, as a perusal of postal history sales catalogues will reveal.

Fifty years ago, an article by Derek Ingrams in *Stamp Collecting* entitled 'A Philatelic Navy' was regarded as highly novel, since it attempted to group certain stamps, not according to their country of origin, but according to the ships depicted in their designs. Until about 1930 the majority of postage-stamp designs featured coats of arms or the portraits of rulers, but after that date pictorialism became increasingly popular so that by now symbolic designs and portraits of heads of state are the exception rather than the rule.

There are few things or ideas on this earth which have not been depicted on stamps by now and this has given rise to thematic or topical collecting. These are loose terms used indiscriminately to describe the arrangements and classification of stamps, not according to countries and periods but according to some common factor in their designs. 'Thematics' can be divided into three broad categories: (a) topical or subject collecting, the collecting of stamps depicting fish or flowers or some other subject; (b) purpose of issue collecting, e.g. stamps commemorating the Red Cross Centenary, or the memorial issues for Kennedy and Churchill; and (c) thematic collecting in its strictest sense—the grouping of stamps (often of disparate subjects) in such a way that they illustrate a theme or idea and tell a story, e.g. 'fascism no more' (a very popular theme with collectors in Eastern Europe).

Some dealers cater specifically for the thematic collector, arranging their stocks according to subject. The American Topical Association, already referred to, publishes a great amount of literature about thematics—check lists of various subjects and the magazine, *Topical Time*, which reprints the best articles on this medium from the philatelic periodicals of the world. There are thematic catalogues and magazines and now there are even thematic albums. Schaubek, Lighthouse and Minkus have published special albums for such subjects as Space, Kennedy and the Red Cross while, in England, Philatelic Publishers Ltd. pioneered *Fun With Stamps*, a fixed-leaf album for junior collectors and beginners covering nineteen of the most popular themes; and have now produced a more advanced, loose-leaf thematic album for the medium collector.

The investment potential of a thematic collection is problematical. Purpose of issue collections, especially of such perennial favourites as Roosevelt, Rotary Club, Red Cross, Kennedy
and Churchill issues, have reasonable prospects of financial
increase, since they form a convenient entity in themselves and
will always hold interest for a wide range of collectors. Not so
easy to assess, however, are thematic collections proper, since
the expression of the theme depends largely on the whim of
the individual collector and while a collection tracing the
development of dairy-farming, as depicted on stamps, may be
of absorbing interest to the man who formed it, because he
happens to be a dairy technologist by profession, it might be
difficult to find a purchaser for the collection as it stands. In
the long run the collection may be worth no more than the
market value of its component stamps, and this might be
diminished if only certain denominations of sets are included—
for there is nothing more frustrating to a dealer breaking up a
thematic collection than to find that sets are lacking those
stamps which might have been irrelevant to the theme but
which are necessary to make the sets saleable to another
philatelist. Dealers are reluctant to split up sets in order to let
the thematic collector have the one or two stamps he requires
and conversely are not very happy to purchase broken sets.

Subject collections, provided they are devoted to the more
popular groups such as Sport, Space, Fauna, Flora, Religion
and Art, are a safer bet and it is significant that postal administrations these days (including the conservative British Post
Office) are tending to confine sets of stamps, and even definitive
issues, to one theme. The majority of the 'colonial ensemble'
of the Crown Agents, for example, are currently using definitive
sets devoted to a single theme: ships (Tristan da Cunha,
Gibraltar), birds (Ascension, Gambia, Uganda), flowers
(Malaysia and the forthcoming Falkland Islands series),
historic buildings (Bermuda, Antigua), and so on.

Airmail stamps used to be classed as 'thematics', but aerophilately has now graduated as a distinct branch of the hobby
in its own right. Aerophilately can embrace postal history
(flight covers), thematics (aeroplanes on stamps) or pure philately

(such as a study of the S.C.A.D.T.A. issues of Colombia). Aerophilately reached its zenith before the Second World War when the carriage of mail by air was still a novelty and many countries issued special stamps to frank airmail. Nowadays there is less romance to be associated with the first flight of a new Pan-Am route than there was about the epic flights of Alcock and Brown, Jim Mollison and Amy Johnson, Colonel Lindbergh and Sir Francis Chichester; and now that most mail travels by air anyway there is not the same necessity for issuing special airmail stamps. Nevertheless this is a field which shows no signs of diminishing in popularity (as witness the record prices reached by the sale of the Louise Hoffman Airmail Collection in 1966), and there is growing interest in the collecting and study of aerogrammes or air letter sheets, as well as in the older established flight covers and stamps.

In the good old days when the number of collectable items was fairly small philatelists took a keen interest in local stamps, but this branch of the hobby went into eclipse at the beginning of this century, because the big catalogues ceased to list and price them. They have always had a small following and should they ever come back into fashion they would increase in value enormously. The stamps which come under this heading include the German private posts, the Swiss and Hungarian hotel posts, the Russian *zemstvos* and the issues of various shipping companies which held mail contracts.

Regarding this last group there is some discrepancy in the matter of what should and what should not appear in the stamp catalogues. For example, the 'Lady McLeod' stamp, issued in 1847 to prepay letters carried by the steamer of that name between Port of Spain and San Fernando on the coast of Trinidad, is listed by both *Gibbons* and *Scott* where it rates £750 and $2,250 respectively. Yet the stamps issued by Gauthier Frères and the Imperial Turkish Admiralty Steamship Co. are much rarer, but because they do not figure in any of the main catalogues, they rate a mere fraction of the sum fetched by the 'Lady McLeod'. Some day, perhaps, this situation will change and the Gauthier Frères steamship stamp will come into its own; what now changes hands for a few hundred dollars would then rank with the 'Post Office' Mauritius as a rarity in the $40,000 range.

The same is true of postal stationery, telegraph stamps and fiscals (revenue stamps)—all collected universally at one time, but now largely neglected. Stamped envelopes, wrappers and postcards lost favour with collectors on account of their bulk. There is a tendency, however, for philatelists to include stationery items in their specialised one-country collections, yet the lack of authoritative handbooks and catalogues militates against their widespread popularity at present.

Telegraph stamps are just as worthy of collection as their postage counterparts, but the fact that used examples are usually retained by the telegraph office and eventually destroyed has tended to stifle interest in them.

The unpopularity of fiscal stamps probably springs from the admonition to beginning collectors not to admit fiscally used stamps to their albums. Many high denomination British colonial stamps, inscribed 'Postage and Revenue', could never have been used postally, but were provided for fiscal use. Nevertheless, in unused condition, they are in great demand and include the world records for the most valuable twentieth-century stamps. This has encouraged certain unscrupulous gentry to clean off the cancellation (usually a violet rubber-stamp) on fiscally used copies and, having re-gummed them, to pass them off as genuinely mint examples. This has only served to put collectors off them in the past, but now there is a tendency to admit fiscally used high values to collections whose owners could never afford the mint article. American philatelists have never lost their catholic taste for stationery and revenues as well as postage stamps, so that the market for such material is well-established in the United States. Here again, these classes of philately may become fashionable in Europe eventually.

Other classes of material, at present going cheaply because knowledge of them is scanty and the market nebulous, include poster stamps and exhibition labels, registration labels, parcel stamps, meter franks, permit mailing marks, postal seals and airmail etiquettes. Any or all of these would inevitably prove a sound investment to any shrewd philatelist determined to seek out information and material for himself.

FIRST-DAY COVERS

At one time collectors mailed covers to themselves merely in order to get hold of nicely used examples of new issues as soon as possible. They would go to their post office on the first day of issue, buy a mint pair or a block, plus a few extras to post on self-addressed envelopes. When these duly arrived the stamps would be soaked off and mounted beside the mint copies in the album. No particular significance was attached to the *date* of posting itself.

In the late 1920s, however, American collectors began to keep envelopes bearing stamps cancelled on the first day of issue and, as time passed, these envelopes began to appear for each new commemorative, embellished with some motif relevant to the occasion. In this way the First-Day Cover was evolved and some of these products possess great beauty in themselves (often surpassing the stamps that grace them!). The U.S. Post Office co-operated by providing special First-Day postmarks at selected post offices connected with the event being commemorated, and this has now grown into the often elaborate 'First Day ceremonies' which herald every new issue.

The provision of First-Day Covers (or F.D.C.s as they are usually known) in Europe came after the Second World War and nowadays there are few countries in which they are not part of the business surrounding every new stamp. In Britain the British Philatelic Association and the Philatelic Traders' Society have jointly sponsored attractive F.D.C.s for several years and latterly they have been joined by the excellent productions of several publishers such as Philart, Connoisseur and Lister. Then, in April 1964, the General Post Office joined in by issuing an *official* F.D.C., for the Shakespeare Commemoratives and, at the same time, provided special First-Day handstamps (machine cancellations were introduced for the Paris Postal Conference stamp in May 1963). The cover in this case was designed by David Gentleman, who had also designed four of the stamps, and thus this F.D.C. was of particular interest to the philatelist. Most British commemoratives since then have been provided with official F.D.C.s and though they are ignored by *Gibbons* they are listed and priced by the *Commonwealth* and *Woodstock* catalogues. At one time little interest was shown in F.D.C.s and a collection of American ones could be picked up in Europe for a nominal sum. Now, however, they are fashionable largely because official covers and postmarks (the latter often pictorial in nature) are much more prevalent than they were ten years ago.

'MAXIMUM' CARDS

Dating from the days before the First World War, when postcard collecting was popular, are picture postcards franked by a postage stamp and bearing a postmark both relevant to the view or subject of the card.

Until stamps became predominantly pictorial and commemorative issues were more prolific, this practice could never become very popular. Nowadays there is plenty of scope and some interesting collections have been formed. To qualify as a 'maximum' card, the three criteria must be present: a stamp, a postmark and a picture on the card, all related in some way. For example, in my thematic collection devoted to the Battle of Hastings I have a postcard reproducing a section of the Bayeux Tapestry, bearing one of the 4d. British commemorative stamps depicting the identical scene and cancelled with the special 'Posted at the Battlefield' hand-stamp of Hastings, 19th October 1966.

Ideally, the stamp and postmark must be on the picture side of the card so that all three factors may be apparent simultaneously. Strictly speaking, it is against Post Office regulations in Britain to put stamps on the picture side of postcards so that British 'maximum' cards are not easy to obtain but, should these regulations be relaxed, 'maximum' card-collecting would become more popular. This form of collecting has been fashionable on the Continent for many years now, but only now is it catching on in Britain.

FASHIONS IN COUNTRIES AND PERIODS

In Chapter VIII I have tried to show what countries are

worth collecting now and what the trends might be in the future. It is true to say that fashions in the collecting of countries or certain periods do change and not always for the better.

It became highly fashionable, during the First World War, to collect stamps and covers connected with the hostilities then in progress. In spite of patriotic considerations there was brisk trading in the various issues supplied by Germany for use in the territories occupied by its troops. By contrast, the stamps overprinted for use in the German colonies seized by British Imperial forces were even more popular and some very high prices were obtained by soldiers who happened to be on the spot and got hold of these issues as they appeared. Red Cross and War Charity issues, War Tax surcharges and military occupation stamps boomed so long as the war continued, but no sooner had the Armistice been signed than the bottom suddenly fell out of the market and many a dealer found himself ruined as the value of his stock tumbled. Between the wars these stamps were in the doldrums but now they are steadily climbing back to favour.

When collectors capriciously abandoned the stamps of the Great War they turned their attentions to the issues of 'Neurope' —those countries of the New Europe which emerged from the ruins of the Russian and Austro-Hungarian empires. Suddenly the stamps of Albania, Czechoslovakia, Danzig, Estonia, Finland, Latvia, Lithuania, Poland and Yugoslavia, not to mention the issues of the various 'plebiscite' areas (Saar, Memel, Marienwerder, Slesvig and others) and the League of Nations mandated territories were collected and studied with great avidity. As the novelty wore off, however, these stamps went out of fashion and prices fell. Now they are coming into favour again and the prices are naturally rising again.

OMNIBUS ISSUES VERSUS HARDY ANNUALS

The portmanteau or omnibus series had its inception in 1931 when the International Colonial Exhibition in Paris was marked by 103 stamps in common designs issued by 26 French colonies. Four years later 3 West Indian colonies, Guadeloupe, Guyana and Martinique each issued a set of 6 stamps in similar designs to mark the tercentenary of the Antilles, but 1937 saw the release of the portmanteau series in honour of the Exposition Internationale de Paris and this time 21 colonies issued 6 stamps apiece. In addition they each issued a miniature sheet (3 other territories shared in this), making a grand total of 126 stamps and 24 sheets. Collectors, annoyed by this vast output, were further irritated by the fact that the stamps could only be purchased as a series. One wondered, with some justification, whether the set for Cameroun was equally available in Indo-China. In 1939 no less than 24 French colonies issued a pair of stamps in honour of the New York World's Fair—an ominous portent of the 'mass participation' issues of the present day. In the 25-year period of 1931–56 the French colonial empire saw the release of 21 different omnibus sets and even since that date many countries, both within and outside the French Community, have participated in omnibus issues ranging from the Tenth Anniversary of Human Rights series of 1958 to the Europafrique issues of 1963.

The British Empire was not slow in taking a leaf out of the French notebook. In May 1935 the Silver Jubilee of King George V was celebrated in Britain by 4 stamps and in each of the 42 colonies and protectorates by 4 stamps depicting Windsor Castle. Many of the Dominions also took part in issuing stamps for the occasion and, whether on account of their novelty or due to their handsome appearance, the Silver Jubilee stamps were an immediate success, rapidly rising in price as the late-comers tried to secure complete sets.

Two years later, the Coronation of King George VI was marked by a similar omnibus issue throughout the colonies. This time collectors and dealers were determined not to be caught napping and immediately the stamps were released sales rose to astronomic figures. The Coronation stamp dominated the philatelic scene in 1937, and prices for them were even quoted on the Stock Exchange. Unfortunately this series attracted the unwelcome attentions of the speculators who bought up huge quantities. The result was inevitable. By the spring of 1939 the Coronation series began to plunge in value as the 'investors' unloaded their holdings and at one time a complete set could be had in impeccable mint condition for less than face value. Even today the 1937 Coronation series is a 'dead duck' as far as most collectors are concerned.

Nevertheless, the colonial ensemble were doomed to more and more omnibus sets, some released by all of them, others issued by territories in specific areas only. Up to the present time, for example, Montserrat has issued no fewer than eighteen omnibus series, some of which (such as the sets publicising the World Cup Football Championship and the Inauguration of the World Health Organisation's headquarters in Geneva) must have had little meaning for the average Montserratian.

There is no doubt that collectors resent omnibus issues, with their monotonous designs repeated by all the participating territories. Dealers usually prefer to sell them *en bloc*, thus upsetting philatelists who only want the stamps issued by one or two territories. Interest in and sales of recent omnibus issues had fallen off considerably and now the Crown Agents have decided that no omnibus issues will be made henceforward.

On the other hand, the publication of the sales figures for the International Telecommunications Union series of 1965 shows that the number of complete sets in existence must be relatively small. Though unpopular at the time of issue, these stamps *could* be a bargain for the investor.

The Silver Wedding omnibus set, including a high value for each territory (usually £1 or its equivalent), was a drug on the market for many years and dealers could not get any takers for the complete series at around £45. Recently, however, the complete issue was offered by one dealer at £57 10s. and was immediately snapped up. Perhaps those Coronation sets of 1937 will appreciate in value after all!

Whereas omnibus sets are now being dropped by the Crown Agents and are likely to vanish altogether from the New Issue scene another philatelic phenomenon has appeared to take their place. This is the 'long set' issued in small instalments and is a variation on the hardy annual—the set issued regularly each year such as the Swiss *Pro Juventute* series or the Dutch *Zommerzegels* (summer stamps). The long set is something which evolved gradually so that it is difficult to pinpoint its exact origins.

Perhaps the United States can claim the honour of inaugurating the long set as such, with the Famous Americans series. Seven sets of five stamps, honouring Authors, Poets, Educationalists, Scientists, Composers, Artists and Inventors respectively, were released between January and October 1940.

Then, in 1944, France released four low denominations depicting in full colour the coats of arms of four provinces. At periodic intervals since that date the brightly-coloured, small-format arms stamps have made their appearance and by now there are almost ninety of them. All of them were of ridiculously low face value, never mounting to more than a penny of two, and even today the most expensive one according to *Gibbons* is the 3frs. (arms of Franche Comté), issued in 1951 and now priced at 3s. 6d. Just try to complete a set, both mint and fine used, and you will begin to realise that some of these stamps are very scarce. In order to complete my thematic collection of the Norman Conquest, I required a mint copy of the 20frs. stamp of 1944 depicting the arms of Normandy. I had to trail all over London visiting nearly every stamp shop before I eventually tracked one down in a collection which a dealer happened to be breaking up at that time. Many of the other arms stamps had also disappeared from dealers' stocks.

Austria's post-war definitive series depicted the various female costumes worn in different parts of the country at different periods in history. Increases in postal rates during the period when the series was current necessitated changes of colour in some cases and the introduction of entirely new denominations and designs in others. Eventually there were 37 different stamps in the Costumes set issued between 1948 and 1952. When collectors finally woke up to the financial prospects of this set, it was already too late. One of the scarcest stamps in the set is the 90g., for which there was very little postal requirement. It was only on sale for a few months, from December 1949 to March 1950. Although it had a face value of only 3d. (3½c.) this stamp in unused condition is today rated by *Gibbons* at £5 and by *Scott* at $25—which is a very handsome rate of increase. If only we could have known this would happen. A sheet of a hundred, once obtainable in the Austrian post offices for the equivalent of 25s., would today be worth £500!

The 1960s are the great decade of the long set. Spain issued arms stamps in small instalments between January 1962 and June 1966. They had a face value of 5 pesetas and were available to New Issue subscribers for a shilling each. Now some of them (and not necessarily the earliest ones either) are priced as high as £2 each and will probably go much higher yet. Spain is now in the course of issuing a similar series devoted to Provincial Costumes but, since everyone is forewarned this time, this set may not turn out so well as an investment. The French multicoloured Art series made its début in November 1961 with four stamps totalling 3frs. (less than 6s.) in face value. Today they would cost £2 6s. This series is still in progress and many beautiful stamps have reproduced on them the best of French paintings, stained glass, ceramics and tapestry in the past six years. It is probably not too late to buy the first (and most expensive) stamps, and certainly no time should be lost in getting the present ones as they appear.

PHILATELIC TIPSTERS

So long as there are fashions in stamp collecting there will also be the tipsters. These are the gentlemen who have an ear close to the ground and are quick to detect any change in the popularity of a country or a theme. They also keep a very close watch on the market, observing the rise and fall of prices in the different philatelic centres such as London, New York, Paris and Rome. They are adept at scenting out the bargain, or the stamp which is unconsidered at the moment but which seems to them destined to be in big demand in the future. A good proportion of the success in stamp dealing lies in being able to spot the stamps which show the most promise and being able to take advantage of it before everyone else is on to it. Success comes with being ahead of the fashion, in being able to buy cheaply and sell dearly when the fashion is established.

Collectors instinctively show an acute interest in the market and it is a remarkable (though, in some ways, lamentable) fact that the first page in a philatelic magazine to which they turn is the one carrying the tipsters' column. Most of the general stamp periodicals carry such a column in which the tipster doles out advice on what stamps he prophesies will go up in value, or, occasionally, pats himself on the back and crows 'Told you so!' when the catalogues mark up some of his hot tips of the past.

Tipsters invariably write under a pseudonym, the reason usually given being that, were their identity revealed, all the dealers would besiege them and pester them into 'plugging' items which they were anxious to push. I doubt this myself and would suggest that a tipster prefers to remain anonymous from a natural desire not to stick his neck out, if and when the tips fail to prove sound ones.

Different tipsters have different approaches. At one extreme there is the tipster whose advice is akin to telling someone to lock the stable door after the horse has bolted. His tips are all stamps which are right out of stock everywhere and the collector who blindly follows these tips soon finds that the stamps are not to be obtained from any dealer. It is true to say, however, that many of these stamps are unrealistically priced in the catalogues and the *Gibbons* or *Scott* quotes, for example, are no indication of their real scarcity. Sooner or later the catalogue editors are going to take heed of this anyway and raise the prices—and then the tipster can sit back and congratulate himself for being such a shrewd prophet.

At the other extreme is the tipster who genuinely tries to help the readers of his column, by tipping only those stamps which are still current but likely to go obsolescent in the near future. By pointing out these items, however, he defeats the purpose of the exercise (which is, to point out the 'good' stamps). If everyone acts on such a tip and buys the stamp or stamps in question there is unlikely to be any shortage in future. The more open the secret the less likely the profit. Many stamps which were tipped to the skies while they were freely available have never shown any appreciation since they were taken off sale.

The real value of the tipster is psychological. He acts as a tonic to those who have already acquired the stamps, (preferably those which are obsolete by the time the tip is given) and enables them to pat themselves on the back for having had such foresight themselves. It has been good for my morale, when I have picked up a philatelic magazine and read that a stamp, of which I already have a block-of-four, is being tipped; but I have never acted on a tip. Perhaps some collectors do—I have actually seen advertisements in a magazine where the dealer has listed his wares 'as tipped by ——', naming the market expert of that particular journal.

CHAPTER XI

SELLING STAMPS

Many collectors over-value their stamps. Consequently, when they eventually come to sell their collections they are quickly disillusioned and think that dealers are trying to cheat them. The average schoolboy's collection consists largely of cheap stamps (probably bought in a mixed packet for a few pence from a department store or stationer's shop) together with any which have been culled from his father's business mail or family correspondence.

Unless the latter has had connections with one of the smaller British colonies or one of the more remote countries of the world, business and family correspondence is not usually a lucrative source of material. How often have housewives, during spring cleaning, turned up a collection formed in their childhood days and, with visions of untold riches nurtured by the sensational stories of big philatelic finds which are reported in the lay press, rushed along to a stamp dealer to convert the collection into cash. Dealers are offered collections of this sort every day of the week and seldom are any of them worth a second glance.

Occasionally the proud possessor of one of these jejune accumulations borrows a stamp catalogue from the nearest public library and painstakingly works out the value of every stamp. At one time *Gibbons* actually priced the cheapest stamp at 1d., but now, on account of administrative costs and other overheads, the cheapest stamps are priced at 3d. On this basis the non-philatelist who attempts to assess the value of a collection containing 2,400 stamps, all of the cheapest sort, will place a figure of £30 on it. Yet the dealer may in all honesty offer him £1 for it, or refuse to take it.

The reasons for this are fairly obvious. Although *Gibbons* price individual stamps at a minimum of 3d. each, there are very many stamps which are really worth less than a penny a dozen. *Gibbons* price includes the real worth of the stamp (say ¼d.) plus the labour involved in mounting it in a stock-book or putting it in a packet or the time taken to sell it (say 2¾d.). Cheap stamps often require as much time and labour to handle as expensive items, which is why the cost of handling the former is often out of all proportion to their intrinsic value. Secondly, catalogue prices basically represent a dealer's *selling* price; his *buying* price must evidently be lower in order for him to get a profit. Thirdly, out of 2,400 stamps perhaps 200 may be of some use to a dealer. These he will be able to sell quickly because there is a demand for them; but the remainder will probably gather dust in a cupboard or, with other collection remainders, be tipped into a box for sale as a 'junk lot'.

There *have* been cases of fortunes being made from children's stamp collections. It was in one such album that the last 2d. 'Post Office' Mauritius turned up in in 1903 and was soon afterwards sold for £1,450. But such cases are extremely rare and are usually headline news (in the stamp magazines at least) when they occur. If one has been a general collector, content to draw on such material as could be picked up at little or no cost, then one will have had a lot of recreation, and that in itself should be ample recompense. If the collection should fetch a few pounds when it is ultimately disposed of, this sum should be regarded as a bonus.

For collections to be worth a lot of money, either a lot of money must have been spent on them or the collector must have selected his specimens with discernment and shrewdly profited from his superior knowledge to spot the bargains when they have been going and to realise the significance of material which was of no account to everybody else. Such collections, built up carefully, using only the finest specimens available, tastefully arranged and written up to show the philatelist's knowledge to best advantage, are the ones which make a profit and which find a ready market. Even a collection of stamps from the most unpopular country or group will find a buyer somewhere provided that it is attractively arranged and reasonably complete.

If you have collected wisely and built up a good collection you should not experience much difficulty in disposing of it when the time comes. Of course, it is a good idea to have some idea of its value before trying to sell it and this can be estimated in several ways. Some collectors keep a detailed account of their purchases so that, at any time, they can tell how much money they have spent on the collection. This in itself is a useful basis to work on. Depending on the type and quality of the collection and the length of time which has elapsed since the material was bought, the collector can gauge realistically the worth of his stamps.

For other philatelists a more rough and ready method is the answer. On the supposition that, were the collection to be offered intact to a dealer, the stamps of low value will be discounted, it is a good rule to reckon up the value of the better stamps alone—say those whose catalogue price is 5s. or $1 or more. Even then the total sum would have to be divided by two or three to arrive at a true market value—unless the collection were a particularly fine one, containing stamps at present in great demand, in which case the offering price might be closer to the catalogue figure.

As in buying stamps, there are five main ways of selling them; to a dealer, to another collector, by private treaty, by auction, and by splitting them up and selling them piecemeal in the Club Packet. The best method, for a quick sale yet getting a good price, is to sell it to another collector. In this way there are no dealers' profits or auctioneers' commission to be considered. If, for example, you and Fred Bloggs own the two finest collections of Curtania in existence and you decide to sell yours, it is not unlikely that Bloggs would want to purchase your collection in order to amalgamate it with his own, or at least take the gems of your collection to fill the gaps in his. What he does with the remainder is his problem; he may put it into an auction or break it up for the Club Packet, or sell it in turn to yet another collector with the same interests.

The other quick way of cashing a collection, though not

usually so profitable, is selling it to a dealer. He may well have a customer waiting for just such a collection as yours (particularly if he deals in a fairly specialised type of material) and thus his turnover will be quick. Or he may pick out the gems to sell to his better clients and then break up the remainder, putting the individual sets and odd stamps into his general stock-books.

Selling through an auctioneer is a slower process. It may take several months for a collection to be lotted (i.e. broken up into lots of suitable size) and described, so that the descriptions given in the sale catalogue will be as accurate as possible. Since the auctioneer gets his commission from the vendor it is in his own interest to see that nothing of value or significance is overlooked in the description of lots. Then the sales catalogues have to be printed and mailed to the auctioneer's regular clients (often numbering several thousands) several weeks before the sale so that they will have ample time to study them and, in many cases, have certain lots forwarded to them for viewing.

Payment is usually made within a short time after the sale has taken place. The auctioneer forwards a list of the lot numbers with the sum realised for each one noted against them. From the total figure is deducted the auctioneer's commission plus any other charges incurred. The latter may include photographic fees, particularly if some items are reproduced in the sale catalogue in full colour. This expense is usually worth while since an outstanding item often gains considerably from this publicity and the price realised is correspondingly higher. Since the vendor may need to sell his collection in a hurry in order to raise money quickly the time lag involved in auctioning material may be a deterrent; but most auctioneers are prepared these days to make a cash advance, based on a proportion of their valuation of a collection. Such an advance is, of course, subject to the usual interest but this is normally deducted from the net sum realised (i.e. after deduction of commission).

Another method of sale undertaken by auctioneers is by private treaty. In this way collections are offered intact, through the medium of advertisements, direct to other collectors. The advantages to the purchaser have been discussed in Chapter IV; the chief advantages to the vendor are that this is usually a quicker method than auction and he can salve his conscience at parting with his collection by knowing that it is getting a good home. In order to get a reasonably quick sale, auctioneers and dealers sometimes offer collections by private treaty at a figure below that which it would fetch if it went for auction. This explains why such collections, unsold by private treaty and subsequently sold by auction, often fetch far more than the estimate given in the sale catalogue.

Splitting up a collection and selling it bit by bit through the medium of Club Packets is a slow and arduous process involving remounting the stamps in the Club booklets and pricing each item or set individually. Anything from six months to a year may elapse while the booklets go the rounds of the Packet members on each circuit and in the end much of the material may come back to the vendor—if he has priced it too high! Experience has shown that the better class of material does not sell well in Club Packets; collectors, as a rule, are too intent on getting a bargain to pay for expensive items, even if they are reasonably priced.

One can effect a compromise, by selling or auctioning the better items and liquidating the more humble remainder by means of the Club Packet. In any event it pays to study the prices realised at recent auctions, and it is also useful to peruse the advertisements in philatelic magazines to find out the state of the market. Occasionally dealers advertise the items which they wish to purchase and you may be lucky enough to be disposing of the sort of material that they are particularly looking for.

SOME MARKET MAXIMS

Margot Naylor, one-time financial journalist of the *Observer*, quoted a number of investment maxims, proverbs, adages and old saws in her last article (26th March 1967) and applied them to the does and don'ts of the stock market. Some of these may equally well be applied to investment in stamps.

If you don't speculate you won't accumulate is advice which appeals to the gambler in all of us. In May 1961 a South African friend of mine, playing a hunch at the time the decimal surcharges were appearing in the High Commission Territories, drove 300 miles from Johannesburg to Mbabane in Swaziland with rs. 200 (£100) in his pocket, borrowed from a friend. With this sum he walked into the post office there and bought a sheet of the rs. 2. At that time the rs. 2 (issued in February of that year) was known to exist with two surcharges, with thick and thin type respectively. The thick was already regarded as the rarer of the two and the surcharges on the sheet my friend purchased were of the thin type. But he noticed that the *position* of the surcharge in this particular case was just above the bottom panel, instead of towards the right. Although the postmaster assured him that the surcharge was the same type as the common one he took a chance and purchased the sheet. His premonition that he had stumbled on to something good was subsequently proved right when it was realised by collectors that the 'misplaced' surcharge constituted a third type, of which only 2,000 were printed. He was soon able to sell his sheet of sixty stamps for £10 a stamp—a profit of 900%—and handsomely repaying the original loan. Five years later this stamp was changing hands for twice that sum and now it is listed by *Gibbons* at £25 in mint condition (*Scott* prices it at $70).

Put all your eggs in one basket, but watch the basket is a maxim which might well be applied to the philatelist who specialises in one country or even one period of a country's issues. *Spread your risks*, on the other hand, could be the motto of the general collector who takes all the new issues of the Commonwealth, for example. Some of his purchases will turn out to be good stamps; others will never show much of a profit. On balance, however, his collection should show a steady appreciation over the years.

Nobody ever went broke through taking a profit is sound advice which is backed up by the reflection that the Rothschild millions were based on *always selling too soon*. Many stamp collectors are eternal optimists, however, and believe that if a stamp is booming they can afford to hang on to it a bit longer. They forget another adage, that *the trees don't grow up to the skies*. Everything has a limit and highly tipped items have been known to drop in value. A good example is the first Coin set of Israel which was highly recommended for several years. A collector acquaintance of mine had this set in blocks of four, with marginal 'tabs', and resisted all the offers of a certain dealer to part with them because he thought that, if he waited a while longer, he would get a still better price. Then, suddenly the market for these stamps slumped and in a panic the collector unloaded his blocks to the dealer, who could only give him 70% of the previous offer—a price which the collector was glad to accept. Now the Coin set is making a recovery, so you can never tell where you are in stamp investment. Remember— *no bell rings when the market touches the bottom, or the top.*

I have already demonstrated that *today's goose is often to-morrow's swan*; one of the delights of philately is that a little hard work and diligence can repay the shrewd collector who takes up one of the less fashionable countries which eventually comes into vogue.

Finally, since this chapter is primarily about selling, there is the old adage, *sell in May and go away*. It used to be true that the summer months (in the Northern Hemisphere at any rate) of June, July and August were a slack period in stamp trading —but not any more. As there is now no closed season in philately it matters little when one sells, though the auction season still runs from September to June. Credit Squeezes come and go, but the philatelic market remains remarkably buoyant. In uncertain times, people tend to invest their money in easily portable, easily convertible forms—and what better form is there than stamps?

CHAPTER XII

MAINLY LEGAL: ESTATE DUTY

REPORTING to the Trustees of the British Museum in 1891, on the large whole-world stamp collection bequeathed by Thomas K. Tapling, the Keeper of Printed Books, Dr. Garnett, observed, 'There is probably no object in the world, banknotes and other promissory notes excepted, where value is so curiously out of proportion to the original cost of the material, or to the labour or artistic skill employed in the production, as a rare postage-stamp. Whether this will always be the case is an interesting subject for speculation.'

In the course of this book I have tried to demonstrate that there is money in stamps and that Garnett's observation of more than seventy-five years ago is still true today. Incidentally the valuation set on the Tapling Collection in 1891 was £50,000; today, thirty times that sum would be a conservative estimate. It is true that many of the stamps in the period covered (1840–90) have not gained in value over the years; many others, however, have increased a hundredfold. By and large, a good stamp collection is a valuable asset, on the one hand an easily portable form of wealth (as many refugees from Nazi Europe found to their profit), and on the other an easily convertible form of wealth whose market is universal and regardless of national boundaries and political upheavals.

Like any other form of property, a valuable stamp collection has its legal and tax problems. If you own some property it is in your own best interests to look after it. In recent years there has been an alarming increase in the number of stamp thefts and burglaries in Britain. These have ranged from a £400 collection of Commonwealth stamps stolen from a private house

in Luton recently, to the burglary of the entire £500,000 stock
of the London firm of Bridger and Kay. Stamps have been
stolen from exhibitions. A strip of Penny Blacks, valued at £100,
was stolen from the display of the Queen's stamps at Buckingham Palace in 1966, while in the previous November a determined (but unsuccessful) attempt was made to remove the
unused 2d. 'Post Office' Mauritius from its showcase at the
British Museum. There is no remedy, but museums and exhibitions are tightening up their security, while it behoves the
private collector and the individual stamp dealer to ensure that
he is insured.

Normally, those companies with whom you have your household contents insured will also extend cover to stamp collections,
provided that the value of the latter in proportion to the other
goods and chattels is not above a certain percentage. The
practice in this matter varies from one company to another,
so it is necessary to clear up this point at the outset. Where a
stamp collection is coverable by the normal household policy
there is usually a limit on the value of any single item. If you
have a few stamps which each exceed 10% of the value of the
whole collection it will usually be necessary to get a special
philatelic insurance policy to cover these stamps adequately.
Many of the larger dealers and auctioneers also act as valuers
and insurance brokers so it is worth while to consult them for
precise details in each case.

The insurance company may require an independent valuation set on your stamp collection (particularly if it is a large
and valuable one) and will appoint one of their accredited
experts to carry out the assessment. The cost of these valuations
is calculated either on the time involved or, more usually, as
a percentage of the final value. Valuations and insurance
premiums are not cheap but, with stamp thefts on the increase,
no collector can afford to do without some safeguard against
loss. Money may be small compensation for the loss of a collection which has taken a lifetime to build and which contains
many irreplaceable items, but it is better than nothing at all
and with the insurance collected one can always start all over
again.

If your collection is a more modest one the insurance company may accept your own valuation. In arriving at this figure you should remember that it is the replacement value of the collection which is required. On the one hand a valuation based on Gibbons' full catalogue prices would be regarded as unrealistic; on the other hand some collectors tend to forget that stamp values are rising inevitably as the value of money falls and thus neglect to keep their valuations up to date. It would be rather tedious to revalue a collection every year but the value should be reviewed every five years at least.

For this purpose a little book work is necessary. Some form of inventory should be compiled giving a brief description of the items, sets or covers, with their catalogue numbers and five-yearly valuations. The date and cost of the purchase could also be noted where practicable. This may not be necessary for items of moderate or low value, but, where valuable items are concerned, this is now a vital matter since, under the terms of the 1965 Finance Act, you may be required to disclose to the Commissioners of Inland Revenue the cost of such assets and from whom they were acquired. For this reason, moreover, it is essential to obtain a bill of sale and to keep a file of all receipts where the sum involved is large. Noted in the table opposite are sample entries from a typical philatelic inventory.

Apart from their usefulness to the insurance company, philatelic inventories are of vital importance to executors. In my official capacity at the British Museum I am often approached for advice about stamp collections found in the property of deceased philatelists. Many of them, extremely efficient in their business or profession, have unfortunately been quite unbusinesslike where their hobby was concerned. Wives seldom know how much money their husbands lavish on their stamps. In many cases they have regarded their husband's pastime with amused indulgence, partly condescending and partly tolerant, with little realisation of the value or importance of the asset which is being built up. I remember one extreme case of a man whose wife was so intolerant of his hobby that he used to 'do his stamps' in the questionable comfort of a bus shelter! Yet this

Album 6: Newfoundland 1910–47

Page No.	S.G. No.	Brief Description	1961 £ s. d.	1966 £ s. d.	1971 £ s. d.
1	95–105	Litho. set: mint singles 1c.–15c.	12 0 0	16 0 0	
2–3	—	Set of die proofs in black	50 0 0	100 0 0	
4	95	1c. plate proofs: 2 blocks of four in green and black	25 0 0	30 0 0	
5	95–95a	1c. perf. 12: 2 mint blocks of four, one showing NFW variety. 5 used singles, 1 used pair, mint	5 0 0	5 0 0	
6	106–106a	1c. perf. 12 × 14: mint block of 12 (one NFW)	4 0 0	5 0 0	

woman was agreeably surprised when the collection, sold after
her husband's death, fetched nearly £600.

Fortunately, most wives are not so intolerant, but few ever
take a real interest in their husband's hobby and consequently,
when the collector dies, his widow is often at a loss (a) to
appreciate the value of the collection and (b) to know what to
do with it. If you have spent a lot of money on your stamps,
you owe it to your wife or dependants to make an inventory
(a copy of which should be kept with the albums) and written
instructions regarding the eventual disposal of the collection.
If possible, a philatelic executor should be appointed. In the
'big league' those dealers, who have given a great deal of time
to building up a collection for a client, often act as philatelic
executors; but usually some close friend who shares the hobby
will suffice.

If the collection is to be sold or auctioned off after the death
of the owner written instructions to that effect should be left
with the philatelic executor and, if possible, a dealer or
auctioneer nominated to handle the negotiations. The disposal
of a collection has many advantages, particularly when it is
considered in relation to the rest of the estate.

In the United Kingdom estate duty has to be paid on all
estates totalling more than £5,000—and this sum can easily
be reached by the most modest estate provided the testator
owns a house, car, furniture, etc. The wealthier you are the
greater will be the percentage of duty to which your estate is
liable and a stamp collection can be a useful asset to realise in
order to settle the estate duty without having to disturb commercial investments and other property. A stamp collection is
usually of great *personal* interest only to the collector himself
and it will often be less of a wrench for his widow to dispose
of it than it might be if she were forced to liquidate share
holdings or sell her house to meet the estate duty.

Robson Lowe has prepared a very useful memorandum on
the relationship of a stamp collection to death duties. 'If the
value of the collection represents a reasonable proportion of
the estate, then *the stamps can be sold to pay the estate duty on the
whole estate,* thus allowing the income on the commercial

investments to continue undiminished to the advantage of the beneficiaries.'*

He then gives a table showing what the value of a collection should be, in order to cover estate duty at the rates current in 1967. I reproduce this on page 223.

Looking at these figures, my own feeling is that, at the lower end of the scale these days, the figure for Personal Chattels would be in a higher proportion to Commercial Investments in most cases. How many people owning a £5,000 house for example (an average 'semi-detached' in the Greater London area) would have *any* commercial investments, far less in the £25,000 range? The majority of the collectors personally known to me are in the lower range of the wealth scale and few of them have any commercial investments worth talking about. Such surplus cash as they have, tends to be invested in their stamp collections. In some cases—and these are by no means isolated—there are philatelists who adopt an almost miserly approach to everything, except their stamp collections. Stamp collecting is an addiction with them. A dealer of my acquaintance was once asked to visit a certain town to value a stamp collection which a lady, recently widowed, wished to sell. The dealer was somewhat put off by the mean appearance of the terraced house given as the address and the shabby furniture of the interior. But the collection itself turned out to have been worth the journey and ultimately netted almost £50,000 at auction. Needless to say, the widow was astounded at the value of the collection and highly gratified by the financial return when the collection was sold.

You may not wish to have your collection sold off after your death. You may not agree with the views of Edmond de Goncourt who stated in his will, 'My wish is that my drawings, my prints, my curiosities, my books—those objects of art which have been the joy of my life—shall not be consigned to the cold tomb of a museum, and so laid out to the foolish glancing of the careless passer-by; but I will that all shall be dispersed by the hammer of the auctioneers, so that the pleasure which the acquiring of each one of these has given me shall be given once

* 'Philately and Death Duties', in *A Review of 1965–66* (Robson Lowe, Ltd.).

again, in every case, to someone, the inheritor of my own tastes.'

It is possible that, after a lifetime's investment and study, you have put together an incomparable collection which has won you a reputation among your fellow philatelists and earned you not a few medals and cups in exhibitions. Having shrewdly collected the stamps of your particular country, perhaps when it was unfashionable, you have now assembled a collection which could never be formed again, and were it to be dispersed in the sale-room something which you have created would be lost for ever. How can you ensure that your collection lives on after you, in a way immortalising you? The obvious answer is to present it to some museum, with a deed of donation drawn up to ensure that the collection is to be maintained intact and not broken up, merged with any other collections, sold or otherwise dispersed. Pressure of space and shortage of money prevent museums from being able to put all their collections (philatelic or otherwise) on permanent exhibition—even if this were desirable, which is questionable since such a display often hinders the research student from close and detailed examination of the material.

Bequests to museums or other national institutions may be facilitated by certain concessions in the estate duty law of most countries. Under Section 40 of the Finance Act of 1930 (United Kingdom), for example, objects or collections which are deemed to be of historic, national, artistic or scientific interest may be exempted from death duties. This is a reasonable concession to those who possess a priceless Leonardo, a Caxton incunable or a Fabergé Easter egg, things which are in the nature of heirlooms handed down from generation to generation. No tax is paid on such items, which are considered as worthy of inclusion in the appropriate national collection, provided that they are not sold.

The only instance where you can 'eat your cake and still have it' in this respect is if the object or collection is sold to the British Museum. If circumstances make it necessary for you to part with the family heirlooms this is one way of avoiding the payment of estate duty, an inducement for you not to

PHILATELY AND DEATH DUTIES

Personal Chattels	Commercial Investments	Stamp Collection	Total Estate	Duty
£	£	£	£	£
20,000	100,000	180,000	300,000	180,000
20,000	70,000	110,000	200,000	110,000
20,000	55,000	75,000	150,000	75,000
15,000	40,000	45,000	100,000	45,000
10,000	35,000	30,000	75,000	30,000
5,000	25,000	10,000	40,000	9,600
4,000	20,000	6,000	30,000	5,400
3,000	15,000	3,500	21,500	3,225
2,000	10,000	2,000	14,000	1,120

dispose of priceless treasures to the detriment of the national heritage.

While stamp collections, if they are particularly fine within their scope, can merit exemption from estate duty, I must point out that it has never been the practice of the British Museum to purchase stamps for its collections; so that there is, in Britain at any rate, no way of selling stamps and yet avoiding the payment of duty. On the other hand, the exemption of stamps under Section 40 of the Finance Act, 1930, does not mean that you have to surrender them to the 'appropriate national collection'. Putting it bluntly, investment in stamps of the highest quality, such as to merit exemption, is a shrewd way of passing on to your heirs a form of property without having it whittled away by estate duty. This is an asset which does not earn you or your heirs a regular income, in the way that commercial investments would, but it is an asset which withstands the fall in value of money and should appreciate *per se* as the years go by.

Incidentally, exemption has been applied for, and granted, in respect of collections which were promptly sold at auction. The motive for this appears to be that, as exemption is only granted for the very best collections, the acquisition of an exemption certificate is tantamount to awarding the collection an international gold medal—always a useful selling point in attracting bidders from all over the world.

Application for exemption can only be made after decease; there is no way of arranging this beforehand and you are not permitted to die safe in the knowledge that your heirs and successors will not be forced to sell the collection to pay the death duty on it. You can, however, leave clear instructions to your solicitor and your philatelic executor telling them to apply for exemption. If this were more widely realised a number of fine collections would still be in existence today as potential national assets instead of having been dispersed (often abroad) to pay taxes which could, and ought to, have been avoided.

The situation in the United States is a great deal more liberal. Estate duty, introduced in 1916, has always been more leniently levied and has never had the crippling effect which is sometimes felt in Britain. Moreover, generous tax concessions are given to collectors during their lifetime, enabling them to plough back tax gains into their hobby (whether it be stamps, coins, ceramics or paintings) if they are earmarked for the national collections. In this way, for example, the bequests to the Division of Philately and Postal History at the Smithsonian Institution in Washington have been enormous in scope and value in recent years.

Since the passage of the Finance Act, 1965, British collectors have been faced with capital gains tax. Broadly speaking, this tax is payable on capital gains (profit) made on transactions involving the buying and selling of stocks and shares, land and property. No tax is liable, however, on any profit made on the sale of one's private residence (provided it has been owned for at least twelve months), or on profits on the sale of such things as stamps, jewellery, paintings and *objets d'art* provided that the item in question is under £1,000 in value.

This tax came into operation in the financial year 1965-6 (i.e. from 6th April 1965) and it is from this date that the value and the resulting profit is to be computed. From that date onwards it has become more than ever necessary for collectors to keep exact records of their collections, with an accurate valuation, supported wherever possible by bills of sale and receipts for each new major purchase.

Even at the time of writing, the position regarding capital gains tax is none too clear and I must qualify my statements by adding that the interpretation of the 1965 Finance Act may be subject to change (and, of course, there is always the possibility that further legislation may also alter the situation).

At present it has been held that the £1,000 criterion affecting the payment of tax is to apply not to a collection as a whole but to its components. Thus a collection might fetch £10,000 as a whole, but if it is broken up into a dozen lots of £800 to £900 each, no capital gains tax will be liable. If a lot did fetch more than £1,000, tax would be assessed on the difference between the value of the lot at 6th April 1965 and the sum realised, less the auctioneer's commission and any other incidentals such as valuer's and solicitor's fees.

The standard rate of tax on capital gains is 30% at present but the percentage may be considerably less, depending on the vendor's level of income and the rate at which he pays surtax (if any). Surtax *may* be avoided if the net gains from stamp selling are taxed as income, in cases where the total income is less than £5,000 a year. Taxed separately, surtax might be liable on philatelic earnings if earned income from other sources exceeds £3,000. In problems of this kind it is always advisable to seek the counsel of a good accountant. Furthermore, long-term and short-term gains must be kept separate. Short-term gains are those made on items bought and sold within twelve months, while long-term gains are those made over a longer period.

★   ★   ★   ★   ★

Finally, there is an important aspect of buying and selling stamps which should be discussed. It is important, if possible, to know that the material you are collecting is what it appears to be and not a fake or a forgery. With the more expensive items it is virtually necessary these days to establish their pedigree. It is advisable, when spending a lot of money on a stamp or a cover, to have it authenticated and, conversely, when disposing of such an item it obviously facilitates the sale if it has a certificate of authenticity or at least the signature of an acknowledged expert.

Guarantees of genuineness take two forms. First of all, there is the certificate, usually bearing a photograph of the stamp, which may be regarded as its passport to acceptance into the best collections. Secondly, stamps themselves may be endorsed (usually on the back or on the front of any adjoining marginal paper where possible) with the monogram or signature, either in manuscript or by means of a rubber stamp, of some recognised expert. It pays to be able to recognise the marks applied by such experts as the Dienas (father and son), Pfenninger, Hunziker, Nussbaum, Fulpius, Miro, Behr, Köhler, Oliva, Bolaffi and Balasse. Even this is not foolproof, as cases have been reported of these signatures and marks being forged! At one time endorsement was very much more prevalent in Britain than it is now and the rubber stamps of Stanley Gibbons and Errington & Martin, for example, may be found on the backs of even relatively cheap stamps in old-style collections. Here again, the buyer must beware and one of the tell-tale indications of the faked overprints in the 1916 Salonika 'Levants' is the presence of the Gibbons guarantee mark on the reverse! This was deliberately forged by the perpetrators of the faked overprints to lend an air of authenticity to their doubtful wares.

Many of the experts, particularly in Europe, will attest to the genuineness of stamps for a moderate fee and endorse them. For a larger sum they will also provide stamps with a signed certificate and this should accompany the stamp from then onwards. This happens when a stamp is genuine; but it is amazing how often a 'dud' stamp will turn up, like the proverbial bad penny, presented to an expert for guarantee time and time again by each successive owner. It is easy enough to lose a certificate which exposes a stamp in its true colours!

In the United Kingdom individual experts do not, as a rule, sign stamps or grant certificates. They pool their knowledge and experience which can be drawn on by one or other of the two Expert Committees, formed under the respective auspices of the Royal Philatelic Society and the British Philatelic Association. 'Two heads are better than one' was never truer than when applied to stamp expertisation. Nevertheless, it sometimes happens that one of these committees will grant a certificate of genuineness to a stamp turned down by the other! Each item is given a serial number corresponding with its certificate, to which a photograph is also affixed.

In the United States expertisation is carried out by a committee of the National Philatelic Foundation in New York while, on the Continent, certificates may be given by the Academie de Philatelie in Paris and by the Schweizer Verband de Reuterskjöld in Switzerland. There are so many tricks which the skilled faker and forger can get up to that it pays you to have rare items certified as genuine, even if it appears to you that they are perfectly authentic. Re-gumming 'mint' stamps, perforating an imperforate plate proof (such as the New Brunswick 'Connell'), trimming the perforations off to make an imperforate variety, applying a fraudulent postmark, cleaning off fiscal cancellations and repairing thinned or otherwise damaged stamps are only a few of the ploys to be encountered. As well as forged overprints and postmarks there are faked covers to contend with. In all of the cases I have cited, the basic material—the stamp itself—has been genuine and it was the use of genuine stamps in perpetrating his fakes that enabled Raul de Thuin to hoodwink the philatelists of the world for more than twenty years, until the American Philatelic Society bought him off recently. Collectors are not so likely to be taken in by forgeries of stamps, but even so, master craftsmen like Spiro, Fournier and Sperati have produced some passable imitations which can still deceive the unwary. If in doubt, get it certified.

In this chapter I have tried to deal with the more serious side of philately, the legal and fiscal commitments of the hobby and the problems of authentication. If you are going to spend a lot of money on stamps then these are points which must all be given consideration. There is another side to philately, however, and if I have of necessity been stressing the financial aspects throughout this book and shown that there *is* money in stamps, I hope that as you progress with philately the monetary value of these gaily coloured bits of paper ceases to preoccupy you as your appreciation of stamps for their own sake grows. No other hobby is enjoyed so widely throughout the world, by all levels of society, both rich and poor. It will bring you endless hours of recreation and enjoyment and if, at the end, you decide to part with your collection, you stand a good chance of recouping your original outlay and making a profit. How big a profit will depend on your shrewdness and skill as a philatelist—and I cannot emphasise too much the importance of knowledge and experience—but also, to some extent, on luck.

At any rate philately shows no sign of losing its popularity.

In 1969 the world's premier philatelic society, the Royal
Philatelic Society of London, celebrates its centenary. Philately
has endured for more than a century and we can look forward
confidently to the future, to continue proving that there is
money—and a great deal else besides—in stamps.

INDEX

240 INDEX